JACOB

Being Transformed by Amazing Grace

The Bible Teacher's Guide

Gregory Brown

Publishing

Endorsements

"*The Bible Teacher's Guide* ... will help any teacher study and get a better background for his/her Bible lessons. In addition, it will give direction and scope to teaching of the Word of God. Praise God for this contemporary introduction to the Word of God."

—Dr. Elmer Towns
Co-founder of Liberty University
Former Dean, Liberty Baptist Theological Seminary

"Expositional, theological, and candidly practical! I highly recommend The Bible Teacher's Guide for anyone seeking to better understand or teach God's Word."

—Dr. Young–Gil Kim
Founding President, Handong Global University

"Helpful to both the layman and the serious student, The Bible Teacher's Guide, by Dr. Greg Brown, is outstanding!"

—Dr. Neal Weaver
President, Louisiana Baptist University

"Whether you are preparing a Bible study, a sermon, or simply wanting to dive deeper into a personal study of God's Word, these will be very helpful tools."

—Eddie Byun
Missions and Teaching Pastor, Venture Christian Church, Los Gatos, California
Author of Justice Awakening

"I am happy that Greg is making his insights into God's truth available to a wider audience through these books. They bear the hallmarks of good Bible teaching: the result of rigorous Bible study and thoroughgoing application to the lives of people."

—Ajith Fernando
Teaching Director, Youth for Christ
Author of A Call to Joy and Pain

"The content of the series is rich. My prayer is that God will use it to help the body of Christ grow strong."

—Dr. Min Chung
Senior Pastor, Covenant Fellowship Church, Urbana, Illinois
Adjunct Professor, Urbana Theological Seminary

"Knowing the right questions to ask and how to go about answering them is fundamental to learning in any subject matter. Greg demonstrates this convincingly."

—Dr. William Moulder
Professor of Biblical Studies, Trinity International University

"Pastor Greg is passionate about the Word of God, rigorous and thorough in his approach to the study of it... I am pleased to recommend The Bible Teacher's Guide to anyone who hungers for the living Word."

—Dr. JunMo Cho
Professor of Linguistics, Handong Global University
Contemporary Christian Music Recording Artist

"I can't imagine any student of Scripture not benefiting by this work."

—Steven J. Cole
Pastor, Flagstaff Christian Fellowship, Flagstaff, Arizona
Author of the Riches from the Word series

Contents

Preface

And entrust what you heard me say in the presence of many others as witnesses to faithful people who will be competent to teach others as well.
2 Timothy 2:2 (NET)

Paul's words to Timothy still apply to us today. The church needs teachers who clearly and fearlessly teach the Word of God. With this in mind, The Bible Teacher's Guide (BTG) series was created. This series includes both expositional and topical studies, with resources to help teachers lead small groups, pastors prepare sermons, and individuals increase their knowledge of God's Word.

Each lesson is based around the hermeneutical principle that the original authors wrote in a similar manner as we do today—with the intention of being understood. Each paragraph and chapter of Scripture centers around one main thought, often called the Big Idea. After finding the Big Idea for each passage studied, students will discuss the Big Question, which will lead the small group (if applicable) through the entire text. Alongside the Big Question, note the added Observation, Interpretation, and Application Questions. The Observation Questions point out pivotal aspects of the text. The Interpretation Questions facilitate understanding through use of the context and other Scripture. The Application Questions lead to life principles coming out of the text. Not all questions will be used, but they have been given to help guide the teacher in preparing the lesson.

As the purpose of this guide is to make preparation easier for the teacher and study easier for the individual, many commentaries and sermons have been accessed in the development of each lesson. After meditating on the Scripture text and the lesson, the small group leader may wish to follow the suggested teaching outline:

1. Introduce the text and present the Big Question.
2. Allow several minutes for the members to discuss the question, search for the answers within the text, and listen to God speak to them through His Word.

3. Discuss the initial findings, then lead the group through the Observation, Interpretation, and Application Questions.

On the other hand, the leader may prefer to teach the lesson in part or in whole, and then give the Application Questions. He may also choose to use a "study group" method, where each member prepares beforehand and shares teaching responsibility (see Appendices 1 and 2). Some leaders may find it most effective to first read the main section of the lesson corporately, then to follow with a brief discussion of the topic and an Application Question.

Again, The Bible Teacher's Guide can be used as a manual to follow in teaching, a resource to use in preparation for teaching or preaching, or simply as an expositional devotional to enrich your own study. I pray that the Lord may bless your study, preparation, and teaching, and that in all of it you will find the fruit of the Holy Spirit abounding in your own life and in the lives of those you instruct.

Introduction

Among all the biblical heroes, Jacob's story is peculiar. In many ways, he is more like a villain. He manipulates his brother, deceives his father and father-in-law, and raises up ruthless children who murder the men of a village and sell their own brother into slavery. However, with Jacob, we learn that God can redeem and change the worst of sinners—people like us. We are all part of God's redemption story, in which he transforms people from Jacobs to Israels—from sinners to saints. As God layers grace upon us and our failures, he transforms us into people he can use greatly to bless the world. Let's study God's gracious work in Jacob, so we can better recognize and respond to God's amazing grace and help others do the same. Thank you, Lord! Amen!

Experiencing God's Promises

This is the account of Isaac, the son of Abraham. Abraham became the father of Isaac. When Isaac was forty years old, he married Rebekah, the daughter of Bethuel the Aramean from Paddan Aram and sister of Laban the Aramean. Isaac prayed to the LORD on behalf of his wife because she was childless. The LORD answered his prayer, and his wife Rebekah became pregnant. But the children struggled inside her, and she said, "If it is going to be like this, I'm not so sure I want to be pregnant!" So she asked the LORD, and the LORD said to her, "Two nations are in your womb, and two peoples will be separated from within you. One people will be stronger than the other, and the older will serve the younger." When the time came for Rebekah to give birth, there were twins in her womb. The first came out reddish all over, like a hairy garment, so they named him Esau. When his brother came out with his hand clutching Esau's heel, they named him Jacob. Isaac was sixty years old when they were born. When the boys grew up, Esau became a skilled hunter, a man of the open fields, but Jacob was an even-tempered man, living in tents. Isaac loved Esau because he had a taste for fresh game, but Rebekah loved Jacob.
Genesis 25:19-28 (NET)

In Genesis 12, God called Abraham out from the pagans of this world to begin a work of reconciliation. Through Abraham, God planned to bring forth a people named Israel—who would be the stewards of God's temple and God's Word. They were to be lights to the world who had rejected God. From this nation was to come the messiah—Jesus—who would die for the sins of the world, so that they might be saved and have a relationship with God. This promise passed from Abraham to his son, Isaac, and eventually to Isaac's son, Jacob.

Jacob's story is peculiar among the stories of biblical heroes. Though all of the biblical heroes had clay feet, as they failed and made mistakes, it seems that none failed as much as Jacob. He doesn't seem like the right choice for God to begin a missionary nation through. It was not Abraham or Isaac who was the direct father of Israel, it was Jacob. He had twelve sons, from whom the twelve tribes of Israel originated. The climax of Jacob's story is when he wrestles with God and God calls him Israel (Gen 32)—one who God commands or who prevails with God.

Throughout his narrative, he seems nothing like a hero, and in many ways, he appears to be a villain. He manipulates his brother, deceives his father and his father-in-law, and raises up ruthless children who murder the men of a village and sell their own brother into slavery. However, it's with Jacob where we learn that God can redeem and change the worst of sinners—people like us. We are all part of God's redemption story, where he is taking people from sinners to saints, from Jacobs to Israels. It is not a fast work but a calculated and slow one, as God is patient with our failures. As we study Jacob, we see ourselves—maybe even more so than with other biblical heroes.

F.B. Meyer said this about Jacob:

> His failings speak to us. He takes advantage of his brother when hard pressed with hunger. He deceives his father. He meets Laban's guile with guile. He thinks to buy himself out of his trouble with Esau. He mixes, in a terrible mingle-mangle, religion and worldly policy. His children grow up to hatred, violence, and murder. He cringes before the distant Egyptian governor, and sends him a present. Mean, crafty and weak, are the least terms we can apply to him. But, alas! Who is there that does not feel the germs of this harvest to be within...[1]

Unlike many biblical heroes, we will learn more from Jacob's failures than his successes. In addition, we learn a great deal about God and his redemptive grace, as we consider the depths of Jacob's failures.

Here specifically in Jacob's birth narrative, we see how God fulfills his promise to Isaac. God gives children to Isaac after years of waiting—continuing his original promise to Abraham to make him a great nation. From this, we learn principles about experiencing God's promises.

We all have promises from God; many of them are made clear to us in the Scripture—some conditional and others unconditional. Second Peter 1:3-4 says:

> I can pray this because his divine power has bestowed on us everything necessary for life and godliness through the rich knowledge of the one who called us by his own glory and excellence. Through these things he has bestowed on us his precious and most magnificent promises, so that by means of what was promised you may become partakers of the divine nature, after escaping the worldly corruption that is produced by evil desire.

It's been calculated that there are some 3,000 promises in Scripture—all given to us so that we can take part in the divine nature (become righteous) and escape the corruption of the world (separate from sin). In addition, God has given us many personal promises, which he reveals during our intimacy with him and confirms through our hearts and the validation of others. These personal promises may be for a career, a ministry, a family, a revival, or even for healing from some pain. Ephesians 2:10 says, "For we are his workmanship, having been created in Christ Jesus for good works that God prepared beforehand so we may do them." God prepared works for each one of us to accomplish, even before we were born. As we walk in him, he develops desires in our hearts and works in us to complete them (cf. Psalm 37:4).

How can we experience God's promises as Abraham, Isaac, and Jacob did?

Big Question: What principles about experiencing God's promises can we learn from Jacob's birth narrative?

To Experience God's Promises, We Must Be Willing to Wait

This is the account of Isaac, the son of Abraham. Abraham became the father of Isaac. When Isaac was forty years old, he married Rebekah, the daughter of Bethuel the Aramean from Paddan Aram and sister of Laban the Aramean. Isaac prayed to the LORD on behalf of his wife because she was childless. The LORD answered his prayer, and his wife Rebekah became pregnant.
Genesis 25:19-21

Since the narrative says Isaac was married at forty (v. 19) and had a child at sixty (v. 26), it is clear that Isaac and Rebekah waited twenty years to have children. Rebekah was barren, which would have been very hard on them for many reasons: (1) It was probably hard because of lofty expectations. Isaac, no doubt, had told Rebekah, God was going to make a great nation out of their seed and that their seed would be like the stars of the sky and the sands on the seashore. In fact, before Rebekah left her home to marry Isaac, her parents prayed that she would be the mother of thousands (Gen 24:60). So they probably had lofty expectations, which made the barrenness more difficult. They probably thought, "If we are going to fulfill God's plan of forming a great nation, we have to start popping out kids!" (2) In addition, this waiting would have been hard simply because of cultural expectations. Women were expected to birth children in that culture—it was how the family name was carried on, how a work-force was developed, and how elderly parents were provided for in retirement. To not be able to have multiple children would have been very discouraging. A woman without children would have considered herself a failure. We saw this with Hannah, the mother of Samuel. Her infertility was a constant source of tension in her marriage (1 Sam 1). Thus, this waiting season would have been especially difficult for Isaac and Rebekah.

It must be known that waiting seasons are common when God is preparing somebody to experience his call and promises. With Joseph, he had a vision of his family bowing down before him, but soon after, he was sold into slavery and later went to prison. After all that, God exalted him to second in command in Egypt, where his family did eventually bow down before him. We also saw this with Moses. In the beginning, he killed an Egyptian, thinking that the people would be ready to follow him; however, it wasn't God's timing yet. Therefore, he escaped into the desert for forty years (cf. Stephen's speech in Acts 7:23-29). There God humbled him, as he served as a shepherd. After those forty years, God called him to set Israel free. With Israel, after Moses delivered them from Egypt, God made them wait in the wilderness for over a year before allowing them to attempt to enter the promised land. Even Christ waited to fulfill God's call. For thirty years, Scripture, for the most part, is silent about him. We don't know much about his childhood and early manhood. However, at thirty years old, he approaches John the Baptist, is baptized, and the Holy Spirit comes upon him. Then, he waits for one more season in the wilderness, as he fasts for forty days and was tempted by the devil. It was then that the Holy Spirit came upon him in power, and he began his ministry. Even the Son of Man had to wait to fulfill God's promise. God often sends his people into a waiting season before he fulfills his promises to them—the promise of a spouse, children, a ministry, or some great work.

Application Question: Why does God make his people wait before they experience many of his promises?

1. In the waiting season, God teaches us how weak we are.

    With Abraham, his wife's womb was dead. Only God could bring life to it. All of Abraham's striving by marrying another woman only brought pain. Often young people who are waiting for God to bring them a mate, get tired and therefore go find "Mr. or Miss. Right Now" instead of "Mr. or Miss. Right." In that season, they bring themselves heartache and pain. Sometimes, they create life-time consequences like Abraham. In the waiting season, God humbles his people to show them how weak they are. In the flesh, we cannot bring about his promises.

2. In the waiting season, God teaches us to trust and depend on him more.

As we are weaned off our flesh, we learn to trust God more. God's power is made perfect in those who recognize their weakness and rely totally on him. Our weakness and dependency are fertile ground for God's power. So much so, God often allows storms or trials to create the fertile ground in us, so he can use us more. When Paul understood this about his "thorn in the flesh," he began to boast in his weaknesses, for when he was weak, then he was strong (2 Cor 12:9-10). He had learned to trust and depend on God more.

3. In the waiting season, God teaches us contentment.

Often what happens when God gives us a specific promise by placing desires in our hearts and confirming them through circumstances and others, the promise can become our focus and even our idol, as we think on it and pursue it more than God himself. Therefore, in the waiting season, we learn to be content with God alone—whether we ever experience the promise or not. In the waiting season, God cleanses us from idolatry and teaches us to be content with the Giver, even if we never experience the gift. Some promises that God gives us will be taken up by later generations, as we see with Abraham's posterity. God may put the seed of revival in our hearts for a person, a church, or a city and we may only see it through eyes of faith. Though we participate in the labors for it, the fulfillment may await another generation. Sometimes, we sow, and others reap. Sometimes we get to do both.

The waiting season can be a blessed time, if we are faithful in it. When it seems like God isn't working, he is working in us and those around us to eventually fulfill his promise. Are you willing to wait?

Application Question: In what ways has God made you wait for his promises in the past? What are some promises that God is calling you to wait on currently? What are some negative tendencies of people in God's waiting seasons?

To Experience God's Promises, We Must Persevere in Prayer

> Isaac prayed to the LORD on behalf of his wife because she was childless. The LORD answered his prayer, and his wife Rebekah became pregnant.
> Genesis 25:21

We don't know how long Isaac and Rebekah tried to have children; it could have been five years, ten years, or for the whole twenty. Either way, Isaac is to be commended for his response of praying. Many years earlier in Abraham's waiting season, instead of praying and waiting, he married another woman—

Hagar. His sin created two competing seeds—Isaac and Ishmael. The conflict between their people still exists today between the Jews and the Arabs.

As we consider this, it must be noted that we do not have to continue in the sins of our parents. Sadly, this is often exactly what happens. God declared that the sins of those who hate him will follow the children to the fourth generation (Ex 20:5). Frequently sins follow family lines—neglect of family for career, domestic abuse, addictions, marital unfaithfulness, divorce, witchcraft, etc. Sins tend to follow generations. However, it does not need to be this way. Isaac broke that trend. Instead of sinning against God in his waiting season, he instead committed himself to prayer.

This probably wasn't a one-time prayer, but a fervent persevering prayer. Many of God's promises don't come without persevering prayer. In order for Isaac to receive the promise, he had to faithfully pray. Similarly, before Christ began his ministry, he spent forty days in fervent prayer and fasting. We need prayer to receive God's promises.

Is God going to mightily use one's church, heal one's family, or bring revival to a city? It must come through persevering prayer. Christ taught us to ask and keep asking, seek and keep seeking, knock and keep knocking and God would answer our prayers (Matt 7:7-8 in the original Greek). In Luke 18, Christ gave his disciples a parable of a widow that continually came before a judge, seeking justice. Though her request was originally denied, she continued to petition the judge, and finally, he granted her request. Christ taught that in the same way, his disciples must pray and not faint (v. 1).

Are you praying or fainting? Without faithful prayer, we'll often get discouraged or give up in waiting seasons and various trials. God's promises come through prayer, but we must persevere in those prayers to experience them.

Application Question: Why is it hard to persevere in prayer? In what ways is God calling you to practice persevering prayer? What blessings have you already received through persevering prayer?

To Experience God's Promises, We Must Expect Difficulties and Seek God's Wisdom During Them

> But the children struggled inside her, and she said, "If it is going to be like this, I'm not so sure I want to be pregnant!" So she asked the LORD, and the LORD said to her, "Two nations are in your womb, and two peoples will be separated from within you. One people will be stronger than the other, and the older will serve the younger."
> Genesis 25:22-23

Often the mistake of God's people when pursuing God's promises is that they believe the answers or blessings will come without problems. That seems to be the situation with Rebekah. After she gets pregnant, she finds that her pregnancy is difficult. Verse 22 says, "the children struggled inside her." The Hebrew word for "struggled" means "to crush or oppress."[2] It was clear to Rebekah that something was wrong. She declared, "If it is going to be like this, I'm not sure I want to be pregnant!" The promise didn't come in the way she expected.

As with Rebekah's situation, God's promises often come with pain—leading to disillusionment. We see this in his dealings with many others in the biblical narrative. After Abraham finally obeyed God and left his home for the promised land, he arrived, to find a famine there (Gen 12). In Abraham's disillusionment, he left the promised land for Egypt, where he almost lost his wife to Pharaoh. Similarly, Joseph boasted about God's promise of his family bowing down before him. However, soon after, he was sold into slavery and, later, became a prisoner. Scripture doesn't tell us about Joseph's thought process, but most likely it was disillusionment: "God, I thought you were about to exalt me! God, I thought you were going to use me! Why am I going through this?" To prepare Abraham and Joseph for their promises, they had to go through struggles and so did Rebekah.

Unlike Abraham, Rebekah didn't rebel against God in the season of difficulty and disillusionment; instead, she drew near God. It says, "So she asked the Lord" (v. 23). We don't know how she approached the Lord. Maybe, she sought a priest. Though Abraham was unique in that he worshiped the one true God in a time when the majority worshiped many gods, he wasn't the only God follower. In Genesis 14, Abraham gave tithes to Melchizedek who was the king of "Salem," which would later become known as Jerusalem. Melchizedek was also a priest of God. Maybe, she sought the word of the Lord through a priest. Or, maybe, she simply built an altar and sacrificed to the Lord, as she sought his counsel. Either way, God spoke to her—revealing that there were twins inside her that would become two warring nations. Esau, the oldest, would become the nation of Edom, and Jacob would become Israel. Esau, and Edom, would ultimately submit to Jacob, and Israel (cf. 2 Chronicles 21:8).

Interestingly, Jewish legend says that Jacob and Esau were trying to kill each other in the womb—which obviously would play out in real life, both individually and nationally. Legend also said that every time Rebekah got near an idol, Esau got excited—representing his profane nature. Also, every time Rebekah got near an altar of God, Jacob got excited—representing his tendency towards God.[3]

Either way, if we are going to receive God's promises, we must expect difficulties, and in the midst of them, we must seek the Lord and his wisdom like Rebekah did. Psalm 25:14 says, "The Lord's loyal followers receive his guidance, and he reveals his covenantal demands to them." God still speaks and reveals his will to his people today.

Application Question: How should we seek the Lord's wisdom in the midst of our difficulties?

1. God's wisdom comes through prayer.

In the context of believers going through trials, James said, "But if anyone is deficient in wisdom, he should ask God, who gives to all generously and without reprimand, and it will be given to him" (1:5). In the midst of our trials, we must cry out to God for wisdom—for he gives it liberally to his children, just like any parent.

2. God's wisdom comes through abiding in his Word.

Psalm 119:105 says, "Your word is a lamp to walk by, and a light to illumine my path." Rebekah didn't have the benefit of God's written Word, as there was none at that time. Therefore, God commonly spoke to people in more charismatic ways. God can still do that today, if he wants, but God's primary way of speaking to us is through his completed Word, found in the Bible. His Word either tells us what to do (especially in moral situations) or gives us principles to apply. When we are in the Word, it's like the lights are on. When we are not in God's Word, it's like trying to navigate life in darkness.
Are you living in God's Word? Are you walking in the light?

3. God's wisdom comes through the counsel of godly saints.

Proverbs 24:6 says, "for with guidance you wage your war, and with numerous advisers there is victory." God has chosen to do his work on the earth through his body—the church. Often, he will guide us and speak to us through the counsel of godly saints. Therefore, when encountering family, health, or career issues, we should share with others in order to receive both prayer and counsel. Often God's wisdom will be given through them. Therefore, we should listen intently for God's voice when we seek their counsel.

Application Question: In what ways have you experienced difficulties while waiting on God's promises? In what ways has God spoken to you in the midst of difficulties through times in prayer, God's Word, and/or through the counsel of others?

To Experience God's Promises, We Must Accept God's Choice of Operating through Weakness

and the LORD said to her, "Two nations are in your womb, and two peoples will be separated from within you. One people will be stronger than the other, and the older will serve the younger."
Genesis 25:23

Interpretation Question: Why did God choose Jacob, the youngest, to receive the promise over Esau, the eldest?

Again, when Rebekah sought the Lord, he gave her a prophecy about the children's futures. Two nations would come from them—Edom and Israel. In the same way that Edom would eventually serve Israel, Esau would serve Isaac. This did not fit cultural norms. Typically, the oldest son in the family would become the patriarch or chief, when the father died or no longer could lead the family. However, God said it would be different with them. This would be hard for a family to accept in that day, and this was true in the case of Isaac. As the story unfolds, regardless of the prophecy, Isaac decided that the blessing would still go to Esau, which caused conflict with Rebekah (cf. Gen 27).

In Romans 9, Paul spoke of God's choosing Jacob over Esau, when describing God's sovereignty in the election of those who will be saved. Consider what he said:

Not only that, but when Rebekah had conceived children by one man, our ancestor Isaac—even before they were born or had done anything good or bad (so that God's purpose in election would stand, not by works but by his calling)—it was said to her, "The older will serve the younger," just as it is written: "Jacob I loved, but Esau I hated." What shall we say then? Is there injustice with God? Absolutely not! For he says to Moses: "I will have mercy on whom I have mercy, and I will have compassion on whom I have compassion." So then, it does not depend on human desire or exertion, but on God who shows mercy.
Romans 9:10-16

Paul quotes Malachi 1:2-3 where it says, "Jacob I have loved, but Esau I have hated." Paul makes the argument that God chose Jacob not because of works or future works but so that God's purpose in election might stand— meaning to demonstrate God's sovereignty, his right to choose. Now, when God talks about loving Jacob and hating Esau, this did not mean that God literally hated Esau. This was a common Hebraism. Christ used it in Luke 14:26, when he said that anybody that comes after him must hate his father, mother, wife,

21

children, brothers, and sisters. Are Christians supposed to hate their families? No! Christ simply meant that our affection for our families must pale in comparison to our affection for Christ. In the same way, the extent that God favored Jacob over Esau could be compared to hate. It must be noted that God was not condemning Esau to damnation or hell. His selection of Jacob had to do with receiving Abraham's blessing, which included the messianic line— Christ would come through Jacob and not Esau.

Why did God choose Jacob over Esau? Again, it had nothing to do with merit or future merits, as they weren't even born yet. It was based solely on God's choice. However, his choice represents how God commonly operates with people. He commonly chooses the weak over the strong. We see this throughout Scripture. If we were going to choose somebody to become a great nation, why choose Abraham and Sarah who were barren or Isaac and Rebekah who had the same struggle? Wouldn't we, at the minimum, pick a fertile couple to create a great nation? When God found somebody to lead Israel in conquering the Midianites, he found the guy who was hiding and threshing grain, Gideon. He didn't find a great warrior or somebody who others would recognize as such. God commonly chooses the weak to fulfill his purposes. First Corinthians 1:26-29 says:

> Think about the circumstances of your call, brothers and sisters. Not many were wise by human standards, not many were powerful, not many were born to a privileged position. But God chose what the world thinks foolish to shame the wise, and God chose what the world thinks weak to shame the strong. God chose what is low and despised in the world, what is regarded as nothing, to set aside what is regarded as something, so that no one can boast in his presence.

God chooses the weak in order to glorify his name. He works through them in such a way that everyone knows that the work could have only been done through God. The strong are not weak enough to be used by him—they would boast in their family-background, finances, education, competency, etc.

Isaac showed great faith earlier in his narrative when it seems that he was willing to give his life on Abraham's altar. In Genesis 22, we see no fight. He seems to be a Christ-like figure. In obedience to his father and in trust to God, he believed that the Lord would resurrect him (cf. Heb 11:17-19). Also, Isaac showed great faith in the beginning of this narrative, as he prayed, and God opened Rebekah's womb. However, after the birth, as seen in the unfolding of the rest of the story, Isaac was unwilling to accept God's sovereign right to choose Jacob over Esau (cf. Gen 27). Why? Esau was the obvious choice! He was the firstborn! He was strong and a hunter! Everybody would choose Esau! Isaac was a momma's boy who liked to cook soup and stay at home. He probably had no hair on his chest and couldn't grow a beard! He was the "weakling." Even in the womb, though he fought to come out first, he lost—he was left grabbing his brother's heal, eating his proverbial dust.

However, this is how God often works, and if we are going to see his promises fulfilled, we must accept it. Often when God decides to use us, he calls us to serve in areas of weakness where we don't feel equipped. Like Moses, we cry, "Lord, I can't speak! I can't lead! You've got the wrong person!" However, when God calls, he typically calls the weak—asking them to step out in faith in their weakness. Moses could have missed God's best if he had not accepted God's sovereign right to call him to serve in his weakness. Sadly, in Jacob's narrative, Isaac worked against God's promise, as he later tried to select Esau for the blessing. Often, we do the same by not accepting God's sovereignty.

Are you willing to accept God's call, even though you feel too weak and incompetent? Are you willing to see others as God sees them and not the way the world classifies them based on their beauty, athletic ability, education, or socio-economic status? If not, we may fight against and potentially hinder the fulfillment of God's promises.

Application Question: How should we apply this reality of our need to accept God's sovereign right to choose the weak over the strong?

1. We must accept the fact that God may allow us to become weak or call us to work in an area of weakness in order to reveal his power in us.

With Paul, he had a thorn in the flesh—possibly some sickness. When he asked God to take it away, the Lord responded, "My grace is enough for you, for my power is made perfect in weakness" (2 Cor 12:8). God decided to not take away his thorn but instead to manifest power through Paul's weakness. God may do the same with us—he may allow a trial, a sickness, or call us to serve in an area where we are weak. He does this, so he can empower us. He works more powerfully through weak vessels. We must be willing to accept this, if we are going to allow God to fulfill his promises and plans in us.

2. We must be careful to not misjudge others.

Again, God chose the youngest—not the oldest. He similarly chose David over his older brothers. His selections are not the obvious choices. Elijah was a mountain man who wore animal clothing and ate bugs. He lacked the high-level education of somebody who went to school in the capital, Jerusalem. He was not the obvious choice. Christ came from the ghetto (John 1:46), and Scripture seems to indicate that there was nothing attractive about him (Is 53:2)—nothing that would draw people to himself. Many of the disciples lacked formal education, as they were fishermen (Acts 4:13). Be careful to not misjudge others. In God's economy, the first will be last and the last will be first (Matt 20:16)—the servant will be the greatest of all (Matt 23:11).

3. We must learn to humble ourselves so that God may lift us up.

He passes over the proud and self-confident and finds the humble—those who have a proper view of themselves in comparison to God. They see themselves as sinful, unwise, and weak. They are not like the Pharisees who saw themselves as righteous, wise, and strong. God opposes the proud and exalts the humble (James 4:6).

Are you willing to humble yourself—confessing your pride and weakness—so that God can use you?

Application Question: Why does God choose the weak instead of the strong? How have you experienced God using you or others in their weakness? What are your thoughts in regard to God's sovereignty in the election of those who will be saved—apart from anything they have done, before the creation of the earth (cf. Rom 9:10-24, Eph 1:4-5, 1 Peter 1:1-2)?

To Experience God's Promises, We Must Foster Healthy Relationships

> When the time came for Rebekah to give birth, there were twins in her womb. The first came out reddish all over, like a hairy garment, so they named him Esau. When his brother came out with his hand clutching Esau's heel, they named him Jacob. Isaac was sixty years old when they were born. When the boys grew up, Esau became a skilled hunter, a man of the open fields, but Jacob was an even-tempered man, living in tents. Isaac loved Esau because he had a taste for fresh game, but Rebekah loved Jacob.
> Genesis 25:24-28

At birth, the first child was red and hairy. Therefore, they called him Esau, which meant hairy. This probably symbolized the vitality he would be known for. He would become a man's man—a hunter. The youngest came out with smooth skin. Unlike Esau, the youngest would be a man of the home who did not prefer the outdoors. He came out holding Esau's heel and was therefore called Jacob. The name originally meant "may God protect" but later developed the negative connotation of heal grabber or deceiver[4]—like a wrestler grabbing the heel of an opponent to trip him. Both aspects of this name were seen in Jacob; throughout his life God protected and blessed him, and yet Jacob also tried to work apart from God—deceiving others to gain his desires. Like an immature believer, he had strong swings between the spiritual and the carnal, the heavenly and the earthly.

Esau and Jacob's time in the womb and birth was a prophetic picture of their lives and the people that would come from them. In fact, the foreboding picture continued in verse 28 when it says: "Isaac loved Esau because he had a taste for fresh game, but Rebekah loved Jacob." When the narrator, Moses, shared this, he was setting the stage for future conflict. Not only did these children battle in the womb, but their enmity was enhanced through their parents' unwise displays of affections. Since the father enjoyed wild gamey food, he gravitated towards Esau—the hunter—and the mom gravitated towards Isaac, since he was a man of the house. It's normal for people to gravitate towards those with similar interests; however, when this happens with parents and their children, it causes great conflict. Jacob would later commit the same sins of his parents, as he would love Joseph more than his other sons and therefore gave him a jacket of many colors. This created an animosity among the older brothers towards Joseph, and eventually, they sold him into slavery.

As mentioned, when Jacob and Rebekah played favorites, it not only provoked the sinful natures in their children but also threatened God's promise. God's promise was that through Jacob a great nation would come. However, the enmity and trickery between the brothers, incited by the parents, would later cause Esau to seek to kill Jacob (Gen 27:41). How Isaac and Rebekah related to their children threatened God's promise of a great nation coming through Jacob. Similarly, how Jacob related to Joseph also threatened the promise over Joseph's life. In both situations, God took the evil instigated through unwise parenting and used it for good.

It is no different for us. God's plan for our lives will be fulfilled or hindered, in part, through our relationships with others. We are not a body unto ourselves, but only part of God's body with which he fulfills his plans on the earth. An eye can't say to the hand I don't need you (1 Cor 12:21). We need each other. Therefore, we must foster healthy relationships with others.

Our relationships will either help us fulfill God's promises or hinder us from fulfilling them. Solomon's marriages to pagan women led him to worship idols and come under God's discipline. Rehoboam's ungodly friendships and their counsel led to the split of the Jewish kingdom. In contrast, the prophets Samuel and Nathan helped David fulfill God's promise on his life. Elijah discipled and mentored Elisha. Christ mentored and developed the disciples. Consider the following verses:

> The one who associates with the wise grows wise, but a companion of fools suffers harm.
> Proverbs 13:20

Do not be deceived: "Bad company corrupts good morals."
1 Corinthians 15:33

Are your relationships with others helping you fulfill God's promises or hindering them? Are there any relationships you need to change or let go of in order to fulfill God's promises to you?

Isaac and Rebekah, though they loved their children, only caused discord between them and were a hindrance to God's plans. Sadly, many delay or miss God's best because of unhealthy relationships as well. Is God pleased with the relationships you are cultivating?

Application Question: Why are relationships so important in helping us fulfill God's promises? How can they affect us both negatively and positively? In what ways is God calling you to pursue relationships with those experiencing God's promises, so they can help you experience yours (cf. Prov 13:20, Eph 2:10)?

Conclusion

How can we experience God's promises and not miss God's best for our lives, families, churches, and communities?

1. To Experience God's Promises, We Must Be Willing to Wait
2. To Experience God's Promises, We Must Persevere in Prayer
3. To Experience God's Promises, We Must Expect Difficulties and Seek God's Wisdom During Them
4. To Experience God's Promises, We Must Accept God's Choice of Operating through Weakness
5. To Experience God's Promises, We Must Foster Healthy Relationships

Missing God's Best

Now Jacob cooked some stew, and when Esau came in from the open fields, he was famished. So Esau said to Jacob, "Feed me some of the red stuff—yes, this red stuff—because I'm starving!" (That is why he was also called Edom.) But Jacob replied, "First sell me your birthright." "Look," said Esau, "I'm about to die! What use is the birthright to me?" But Jacob said, "Swear an oath to me now." So Esau swore an oath to him and sold his birthright to Jacob. Then Jacob gave Esau some bread and lentil stew; Esau ate and drank, then got up and went out. So Esau despised his birthright.
Genesis 25:29-34 (NET)

Why do so many Christians miss God's best—God's plans for their lives?

Scripture is full of stories of those who, for whatever reason, missed God's calling on their lives. God's plan for Israel was for them to enter the promised land; however, the majority died in the wilderness. It was also God's plan for Moses to lead them into the promised land; however, he was only allowed to look into it before he died. Ephesians 2:10 says, "We are God's workmanship, created in Christ Jesus for good works, which he prepared beforehand that we should walk in" (paraphrase). God prepared a spiritual blueprint for each of our lives—people we were called to minister to and works we were called to accomplish; however, many, if not most, miss God's best.

In Genesis 11, at the tower of Babel, the people rebelled against God by deciding to no longer spread throughout the earth, and to instead stay in one place and make a monument to themselves. In God's anger, he confused their languages, so they would spread to the corners of the globe. After this rebellion, God called a man named Abraham to begin a work of reconciliation—to draw people back to himself. Most worshiped many gods instead of worshiping the true God. God promised to bless Abraham and use him to be a blessing to many. Through Abraham's descendants a messiah would come who would save the world. That blessing passed from Abraham to Isaac and then to Isaac's seed.

In the previous narrative, Isaac had twins. Esau was the oldest and therefore would receive the birthright. The birthright included a double-portion of Isaac's goods, becoming the chief of the family, and becoming the family's priest or spiritual leader. The spiritual leader would also carry on the blessing of

Abraham. Before the children were born, Rebekah, Isaac's wife, received a prophecy that the oldest would serve the youngest (Gen 25:23). The blessing would instead go to Jacob.

Though God sovereignly chose Jacob, Scripture puts the blame for losing the birthright on Esau. Consider Hebrews 12:16-17:

> And see to it that no one becomes an immoral or godless person like Esau, who sold his own birthright for a single meal. For you know that later when he wanted to inherit the blessing, he was rejected, for he found no opportunity for repentance, although he sought the blessing with tears.

Though God is sovereign over all things, including salvation, his sovereignty does not remove human responsibility. Jacob did receive the blessing, but Esau rejected it, though he later wished he had received it.

Therefore, as we look at this narrative, we learn principles about missing God's best. We learn them not only from Esau but also from Jacob, who likewise misses God's best when he manipulated Esau to receive the birthright. As we consider this story, we must ask ourselves, "What is holding us back from receiving God's best—our heavenly birthright?"

Big Question: What principles can be discerned from this narrative about why people often miss God's best?

Lack of Faith Can Lead to Missing God's Best

> Now Jacob cooked some stew, and when Esau came in from the open fields, he was famished. So Esau said to Jacob, "Feed me some of the red stuff—yes, this red stuff—because I'm starving!" (That is why he was also called Edom.) But Jacob replied, "First sell me your birthright." Genesis 25:29-31

Hebrews 11:6 says, "Now without faith it is impossible to please him, for the one who approaches God must believe that he exists and that he rewards those who seek him." Faith is the doorway to all of God's promises. It is the way that we receive salvation (cf. Eph 2:8-9, Rom 10:9-10). It is the way that we have peace in the midst of chaos (cf. Phil 4:6-7). It is the way we access God's power for service (cf. Eph 1:19). Jacob is to be commended for wanting the blessing, as it showed that he cared for spiritual things. The birthright was more than Isaac's inheritance; more importantly, it was to take part in God's promise to Abraham of being a blessing to the world. However, Jacob's problem was that though he had faith, it was little faith. God had promised him the blessing, even

28

before he was born. But Jacob believed he needed to manipulate others in order to receive it. Kent Hughes said it this way:

> At the very heart of Esau's demise is the sad reality that he did not believe the word of God. God's promise was, to him, intangible and unreal. In contrast, Jacob believed the promise and cherished it with all his being. Ironically, the stumbling in Jacob's life came because though he believed in the promise, he did not believe that God's promise could be his apart from his own sinful manipulation of Esau. Nevertheless, despite his faults and ungodly manipulation, Jacob stands as a man of faith.[5]

Many today also miss God's best or delay it because of a lack of faith. Israel didn't believe God, and therefore, the promise of entering Canaan was delayed for forty years. Faith is necessary to receive God's promises. We must remember that Christ said, "all things are possible for one who believes" (Mk 9:23) and "If you have faith as a mustard seed, you can move mountains" (Matt 17:20 paraphrase).

Are you trusting God or doubting him in your situation? He has given you many promises, even as he did, Jacob. He promises that he will save you eternally if you put your trust in his son (Rom 10:9-10), meet your needs, guide you in the paths of righteousness, and protect you (Ps 23). Doubting God can lead to missing God's best, but believing him, despite our circumstances or negative thoughts, opens the door to his blessings.

Application Question: How can we increase our faith?

1. *Our faith in God increases as we study and believe his Word.* Romans 10:17 says faith comes by hearing and hearing by the Word of God. When we are in his Word, our faith grows. When we are not, it decreases. Are you abiding in God's Word and thus growing in faith?

2. *Our faith in God increases as we develop a history with God.* As we walk with God and he delivers us, heals us, and guides us, it gives us confidence that he will continue to do so. Are you allowing yourself to develop a history with God? Are you remembering his acts of faithfulness to you or are you forgetting them?

3. *Our faith in God increases as we walk with those who have great faith in God.* Their trust inspires our trust. Like iron sharpening iron, they sharpen us (Prov 27:17). In the same way, when we walk with those

who don't trust God, our trust decreases (Prov 13:20). Who are you walking with? Are they strengthening your faith or helping it decrease?

Application Question: How would you rate your current level of trust or faith in God on a scale of 1-10? Why would you give it this rating? How can we discern when we should be active in pursuing God's promises and blessings and when we should wait in faith? How have you struggled at times with the tension between faith and activity?

Selfish Ambition Can Lead to Missing God's Best

> Now Jacob cooked some stew, and when Esau came in from the open fields, he was famished. So Esau said to Jacob, "Feed me some of the red stuff—yes, this red stuff—because I'm starving!" (That is why he was also called Edom.) But Jacob replied, "First sell me your birthright."
> Genesis 25:29-31

As mentioned, the fact that Jacob desired the birthright was a good thing. However, it is possible to pursue the right thing in a wrong way. Abraham desired a seed to fulfill God's promise, so he married another woman, Hagar, causing discord in his family and future generations. Jacob desired God's blessing, and the Lord had already told him he would have it. But instead of waiting on God, he manipulated his brother to secure the blessing.

There was nothing inherently wrong with Jacob's bargaining. Most likely, they had talked about the birthright previously, and it was clear Esau cared nothing for it. Ancient evidence shows us that birthrights were transferable. In one ancient contract, a brother paid three sheep for part of the inheritance.[6] The fact that Esau swore made this bargain official—most likely there was a witness watching.

What was wrong with Jacob's bargain? As mentioned, it not only demonstrated a lack of faith, but also the motivation was purely selfish. He took advantage of his brother. Though it was God's will for Jacob to receive the promise, it would not ultimately be given to him through selfish means. James said that when jealousy and selfish ambition are in our hearts, those desires are earthly, natural, and demonic in origin (cf. Jam 3:14-15). The future fruit of Jacob's manipulations was that Esau eventually planned to kill him. Thus, Jacob had to run away from his family for some twenty years. Jacob's selfish ambition almost cost him God's blessing and ultimately delayed it.

People often miss God's best when they try to secure it through selfish ways. Philippians 2:3 says, "Instead of being motivated by selfish ambition or vanity, each of you should, in humility, be moved to treat one another as more important than yourself." The world seeks greatness through selfish-ambition, but in the kingdom, greatness comes through humbling ourselves. In Matthew

23:11-12, Jesus said, "The greatest among you will be your servant. And whoever exalts himself will be humbled, and whoever humbles himself will be exalted."

A great example of God exalting the humble and not the prideful is seen in Christ. Over two thousand years after Jacob, Christ, instead of holding onto his rights as deity, gave them up to become human. He further humbled himself by becoming a servant and dying for humanity. Philippians 2:6-11 describes this:

> who though he existed in the form of God did not regard equality with God as something to be grasped, but emptied himself by taking on the form of a slave, by looking like other men, and by sharing in human nature. He humbled himself, by becoming obedient to the point of death—even death on a cross! As a result God exalted him and gave him the name that is above every name, so that at the name of Jesus every knee will bow—in heaven and on earth and under the earth—and every tongue confess that Jesus Christ is Lord to the glory of God the Father.

Because Christ humbled himself, God exalted him by giving him a name above all names. In the same way, those who humble themselves like Christ will be exalted—they will receive God's best. However, those who, like the world, selfishly exalt themselves, shall be humbled. Christ said this in Matthew 5:5, "Blessed are the meek for they will inherit the earth." Those who fight, cheat, and manipulate others to gain the world, shall lose it, but those who willingly give up the world and its esteem, will be blessed by the Lord.

Application Question: How can we practice selflessness instead of selfishness?

1. To practice selflessness, we must put others and their desires before our own.

Hebrews 10:24 says, "And let us take thought of how to spur one another on to love and good works." Are we taking thought of others and putting them first or primarily thinking about our needs and wants? We must ask ourselves questions like: "How can we bless others? What might help them grow in Christ? What might make their life easier and more comfortable?"

2. To practice selflessness, we must remember that God blesses humble servants and judges the prideful.

Again, in God's economy the first will be last and the last will be first (Matt 20:16). If you want to become the greatest, you must become the servant

31

of all. It is the meek who will inherit the earth. Those who give shall receive (Lk 6:38). Those who refresh others shall themselves be refreshed (Prov 11:25). Those who humble themselves shall be exalted (Matt 23:12). Remembering this kingdom reality will keep us from worldly selfishness that misses God's best.

Are you missing God's best because of selfishness? Jacob seems to delay God's best, as his selfish and manipulative actions eventually lead to his running away from home for twenty years.

Application Question: Why is it so hard to practice humility and selflessness? In what ways is God calling you to humble yourself and seek what's best for others?

Being Undisciplined Can Lead to Missing God's Best

> Now Jacob cooked some stew, and when Esau came in from the open fields, he was famished. So Esau said to Jacob, "Feed me some of the red stuff—yes, this red stuff—because I'm starving!" (That is why he was also called Edom.) But Jacob replied, "First sell me your birthright." "Look," said Esau, "I'm about to die! What use is the birthright to me?"
> Genesis 25:29-32

It seems that Esau was an athlete. He enjoyed the sport of hunting, and his father gave him freedom apart from any real responsibilities. Esau therefore became an undisciplined man driven by his desires. Like a spoiled child, when he wanted something, he had to have it then and couldn't wait. The fact that he was without discipline led to his desires controlling him. Hebrews 12:16-17 says this about him:

> And see to it that no one becomes an immoral or godless person like Esau, who sold his own birthright for a single meal. For you know that later when he wanted to inherit the blessing, he was rejected, for he found no opportunity for repentance, although he sought the blessing with tears.

The writer of Hebrews said that he was not only godless—not caring about spiritual things—but also immoral, which can be translated sexually immoral (ESV). His lust dominated, controlled, and eventually destroyed him. This led him to miss God's best, including salvation.

It is good to remember that how we train our children can either help them know God or reject him. Being spoiled by his father, Isaac, helped Esau choose a life full of pride and self, instead of a life of humility and discipline in serving God.

It must be noted that there was nothing wrong with Esau having a bowl of soup—food is good. It's a gift from God. However, when our desire for food, sleep, or any other pleasure, keeps us from doing God's will, it has become an idol. Work, family, entertainment—all gifts from God in their own right—can become evil when we pursue them over God. First Corinthians 6:12 says, "'All things are lawful for me'—but not everything is beneficial. 'All things are lawful for me'—but I will not be controlled by anything." When something starts to control us—other than God—it is sin. Esau was an addict. He was dominated by his desires, which caused him to lose his birthright. Uncontrolled passions, whether sinful ones or not, often do the same for believers—causing them to miss God's best.

How many miss God's best because they are addicted to TV, social media, video games, food, career, money, sleep, or some drug? The church is full of people that sell their heavenly birth right for some passing pleasure.

Therefore, in order to receive God's best, we must be disciplined with our desires. In 1 Corinthians 9:24-27, Paul said it this way:

> Do you not know that all the runners in a stadium compete, but only one receives the prize? So run to win. Each competitor must exercise self-control in everything. They do it to receive a perishable crown, but we an imperishable one. So I do not run uncertainly or box like one who hits only air. Instead I subdue my body and make it my slave, so that after preaching to others I myself will not be disqualified.

Because of a lack of discipline with his desires, Esau was disqualified from God's blessing.

Application Question: How can we protect ourselves from being controlled by our passions?

When talking about the war between our sinful desires and the Spirit, Paul simply said, "Live in the Spirit and you will not gratify the desires of the flesh" (Gal 5:16). When we are living in God's Word, prayer, fellowship, and service, we will find our fleshly desires weaker or non-existent. Because Esau was a godless man, who had no real time for spiritual things, his flesh ruled him, and if we do the same, our flesh will rule us as well. If we neglect spiritual disciplines, we will find ourselves controlled by pride, anger, discord, unforgiveness, lust, etc., as our flesh becomes stronger than our Spirit. Live in the Spirit and the flesh will not control us and keep us from God's best.

Application Question: What are the areas you struggle with having discipline over? How do you try to discipline yourself in those areas? How is God calling you to practice discipline, so you won't miss God's best?

33

Undervaluing God's Blessings Can Lead to Missing God's Best

"Look," said Esau, "I'm about to die! What use is the birthright to me?"
Genesis 25:32

One of the reasons that Esau missed God's best was because he undervalued it. He thought to himself, "Living is more important than God!" Now of course, Esau was not about to die, but he was so hungry he might have felt that way. The problem was food and life were more valuable to him than God and his blessing.

It's very interesting to consider that Christ faced a similar temptation. In the wilderness, Satan tempted Christ to turn a rock into bread. In Matthew 4:4, Christ replied, "Man shall not live by bread alone but by every word that comes from the mouth of God." Christ essentially said, "Obeying God is more important than eating!" If it was God's will for him to fast and not use his power to eat, then he would fast. Life did not matter; obeying God did. This was the attitude of the apostles who sacrificed their lives instead of denying Christ. To them obedience to God was more important than living. In Luke 14:26-27, Christ said that anyone who followed him must be willing to hate his own life and take up his cross—be willing to die.

Esau's problem was he undervalued God and his blessing. He undervalued the fact that he was raised in a family that believed in and worshiped the Lord. He undervalued the calling to be a blessing to the world. Ultimately, this means he overvalued the temporary—like a bowl of soup.

Be careful of undervaluing God's blessing: Don't undervalue the privilege of reading and listening to God's Word. Don't undervalue the privilege of church and Christian fellowship. Don't undervalue the privilege of serving God. When you undervalue God's blessings, you will overvalue something lesser and miss God's best.

Application Question: How can we properly appreciate the blessings of God?

1. To appreciate God's blessings, we must take advantage of them often.

God has given us many blessings: worship, his Word, prayer, fellowship, the ability to serve, etc. The more we take advantage of them, the more we will typically enjoy and appreciate them. When we neglect them, we will appreciate them less.

2. To appreciate God's blessings, practice giving thanks for them.

34

Thank God for your salvation often. Thank him for the opportunity to worship him. Thank him for your church—though it is imperfect. Thank him for your job—though it at times causes you pain. Give thanks in all situations for this is God's will for your life (1 Thess 5:17). This will help you appreciate his blessings.

3. To appreciate God's blessings, practice remembering them.

When God provided Israel with manna in the wilderness, he had them place some manna in the Ark of the Covenant, so they would always remember. When God split the Jordan River, so Israel could walk across dry land, they were called to take twelve stones, so they, and their children would always remember. Often the Patriarchs would build altars as memorials of God's blessings. We are forgetful, and so we need to do the same. We're prone to forget how God delivered us from a trial, how he provided for us in a dry season, how he healed us, and because of that, we often complain instead of giving thanks. We fear instead of living in faith.

Practice remembering your blessing. Do this by not only giving thanks, but also by writing them down in journals, so you can rejoice over them in times of difficulty. Sometimes, it might also be beneficial to take a keep-sake or build a memorial to help you remember what God has done.

Application Question: Why are we so prone to forget the blessings and victories God has given us? How have you benefited from disciplines like journaling or taking memorials? What blessings from God are you most thankful for? How is God calling you to grow in appreciation of his blessings?

Conclusion

Though God, in his sovereignty, had promised Jacob the blessing, Scripture says Esau despised and rejected it (Heb 12:16-17). He gave up his birthright, and the spiritual blessing that came with it, for a bowl of soup. Sadly, many choose the temporary over the eternal, the flesh over the Spirit, the earthly over the heavenly. Why do so many miss God's best—their heavenly birthright as children of God?

1. Lack of Faith Can Lead to Missing God's Best
2. Selfish Ambition Can Lead to Missing God's Best
3. Being Undisciplined Can Lead to Missing God's Best
4. Undervaluing God's Blessings Can Lead to Missing God's Best

Application Question: What are some other reasons people miss God's best? In what ways have you missed God's best in the past or are currently missing

God's best? How is God calling you to begin to redeem what was lost (cf. Joel 2:25)?

Signs of Not Trusting God

...Now Rebekah had been listening while Isaac spoke to his son Esau. When Esau went out to the open fields to hunt down some wild game and bring it back, Rebekah said to her son Jacob, "Look, I overheard your father tell your brother Esau, 'Bring me some wild game and prepare for me some tasty food. Then I will eat it and bless you in the presence of the Lord before I die.' Now then, my son, do exactly what I tell you! Go to the flock and get me two of the best young goats. I'll prepare them in a tasty way for your father, just the way he loves them. Then you will take it to your father. Thus he will eat it and bless you before he dies." "But Esau my brother is a hairy man," Jacob protested to his mother Rebekah, "and I have smooth skin! My father may touch me! Then he'll think I'm mocking him and I'll bring a curse on myself instead of a blessing." So his mother told him, "Any curse against you will fall on me, my son! Just obey me! Go and get them for me!" So he went and got the goats and brought them to his mother. She prepared some tasty food, just the way his father loved it. Then Rebekah took her older son Esau's best clothes, which she had with her in the house, and put them on her younger son Jacob. She put the skins of the young goats on his hands and the smooth part of his neck. Then she handed the tasty food and the bread she had made to her son Jacob. He went to his father and said, "My father!" Isaac replied, "Here I am. Which are you, my son?" Jacob said to his father, "I am Esau, your firstborn. I've done as you told me. Now sit up and eat some of my wild game so that you can bless me." But Isaac asked his son, "How in the world did you find it so quickly, my son?" "Because the Lord your God brought it to me," he replied. Then Isaac said to Jacob, "Come closer so I can touch you, my son, and know for certain if you really are my son Esau." So Jacob went over to his father Isaac, who felt him and said, "The voice is Jacob's, but the hands are Esau's." He did not recognize him because his hands were hairy, like his brother Esau's hands. So Isaac blessed Jacob. Then he asked, "Are you really my son Esau?" "I am," Jacob replied. Isaac said, "Bring some of the wild game for me to eat, my son. Then I will bless you." So Jacob brought it to him, and he ate it. He also brought him wine, and Isaac drank. Then his father Isaac said to him, "Come here and kiss me, my son." So Jacob went over

and kissed him. When Isaac caught the scent of his clothing, he blessed him...
Genesis 27 (NET)

What are signs of not trusting God? In one sense, not trusting God is the root of all sin. When Satan tempted Eve, he told her that God's Word wasn't trustworthy and that God was holding back the best from her. Consequently, when she doubted God, she ate of the tree.

In the same way, when we don't trust God's Word, his character, or his plan, we'll be prone to sin and its various consequences. That's what happens in the Genesis 27 narrative. We see Isaac, who doesn't trust God's plan to bless Jacob, choose to, instead, bless the oldest son, Esau. Rebekah and Isaac don't trust God, who prophetically told them that Esau would serve Jacob, so they came up with a deceptive plan to secure the birthright. Esau, who seems like a victim, Scripture calls a godless man who despised his birthright (Heb 12:16)—he didn't trust that God's plan to bless Jacob was best. Nobody in this family trusted God, and therefore they hurt one another and themselves. Not trusting God always leads to harmful consequences.

However, trusting God always leads to blessings. Isaiah 40:30-31 (NIV) says:

Even youths grow tired and weary, and young men stumble and fall; but those who hope in the LORD will renew their strength. They will soar on wings like eagles; they will run and not grow weary, they will walk and not be faint.

Jeremiah 17:7-8 says,

My blessing is on those people who trust in me, who put their confidence in me. They will be like a tree planted near a stream whose roots spread out toward the water. It has nothing to fear when the heat comes. Its leaves are always green. It has no need to be concerned in a year of drought. It does not stop bearing fruit.

God blesses those who trust him and disciplines those who don't. In this narrative, we see God's discipline, as the family experiences the terrible consequences of not trusting in God. In the end, we see Esau planning to kill Jacob and Jacob being estranged from his family for some twenty years (Gen 27:42-44). Not trusting God only leads to consequences both individually and corporately.

In this narrative, we'll study signs of not trusting God—to discern if we don't trust him, to inspire us to trust him more, and also to protect us from the harmful consequences of mistrust.

Big Question: In the Genesis 27 narrative, what are some signs (or consequences) of not trusting God, as displayed in Isaac's family?

When We're Not Trusting God, We're Prone to Idolatry

> When Isaac was old and his eyes were so weak that he was almost blind, he called his older son Esau and said to him, "My son!" "Here I am!" Esau replied. Isaac said, "Since I am so old, I could die at any time. Therefore, take your weapons—your quiver and your bow—and go out into the open fields and hunt down some wild game for me. Then prepare for me some tasty food, the kind I love, and bring it to me. Then I will eat it so that I may bless you before I die…
> Genesis 27:1-4

At this time, Isaac is about 137 years old.[7] He is bedridden, almost blind, and seems to have hearing loss (cf. Gen 27:22). Since Isaac believed that he would die soon, he decided to bless Esau, even though God had clearly chosen Jacob and made it clear through a prophecy. Though he thinks he is about to die, Isaac lives for another forty-three years (Gen 35:28).

As Isaac aged, his spirituality declined, as he developed idols in his heart that came before his relationship with God. His two idols were his firstborn, Esau, and comforts, like tasty food. Therefore, when Isaac was about to die, he asks Esau to prepare him a delicious dish.

What one thinks about or does before death often shows his or her priority. It's interesting to consider that when David was about to die, he makes preparations to build God's temple (1 Chr 22). When Paul was about to die, he asks for Timothy and Mark to come see him and bring scrolls so he can read God's Word and write (2 Tim 4). However, when Isaac is about to die, he asks his son to bring him delicious food. This shows how consuming his love for food and comfort was.

However, Isaac is not the only one in this family with idols. Esau developed the same idolatry as Isaac; he loved creature-comforts, like food, more than God. Previously, he sold his birthright to gain a bowl of soup (Gen 25). In addition, Rebekah's idol was her son, Jacob. In this narrative, she was willing to deceive her husband, estrange her oldest son, and even bare any potential curse on Jacob, in order that he would receive Isaac's blessing. Finally, Jacob's idol was the blessing, which he was willing to repeatedly deceive his father for.

39

This is common when we are not trusting God—our hearts will become idol factories. Many things, including good things, will take God's place in our lives and the devotion that belongs to him—career, academics, family, sports, video games, coffee, etc. Many choose these over God, and therefore, God is neglected and often disobeyed.

Finishing Well

In addition, as we consider Isaac specifically, we must recognize how hard it is to finish our spiritual lives well. When Isaac was a boy, as much as we can discern, he was willing to die on Abraham's altar because he believed God would raise him from the dead (cf. Gen 22, Heb 11:19). When his wife, Rebekah, couldn't bear children, he prayed and she became pregnant (Gen 25). He was a man of great faith! But here at the end of his life, Isaac disregards God because of his love for his firstborn and creature-comforts. Sadly, this is common throughout biblical history. Many don't finish well. The last we see of Noah, a great man of faith, is him being drunk, naked, and cursing his grandson, Canaan (Gen 9). Moses, who led Israel out of Egypt, dies outside the promised land (Deut 34). Demas, a missionary associate of Paul, left him and possibly Christ because he loved this present world (2 Tim 4:10). Many begin well but don't finish well. Certainly, this must challenge us to be careful of anything that might slowly erode our faith—like the love of idols.

When we are not trusting and worshiping God, we will develop idols that pull us away from him and also hurt our relationships with others. What are your idols—what is keeping you away from giving time and devotion to God and loved ones?

Application Question: How can we tell when something is an idol in our life? What are your idols, which vie for your focus and affection? How is God calling you to deal with them, so that he might be first and everything else in its proper order?

When We're Not Trusting God, We're Prone to Anxiety and Haste

Now Rebekah had been listening while Isaac spoke to his son Esau. When Esau went out to the open fields to hunt down some wild game and bring it back, Rebekah said to her son Jacob, "Look, I overheard your father tell your brother Esau, 'Bring me some wild game and prepare for me some tasty food. Then I will eat it and bless you in the presence of the LORD before I die.' Now then, my son, do exactly what I tell you! Go to the flock and get me two of the best young goats. I'll prepare them in a tasty way for your father, just the way he loves them. Then you will take it to your father. Thus he will eat it and bless you before he dies." "But Esau my brother is a hairy man," Jacob protested to his mother Rebekah, "and I have smooth skin! My father may touch me! Then he'll think I'm mocking him and I'll bring a curse on myself instead of a blessing." So his mother told him, "Any curse against you will fall on me, my son! Just obey me! Go and get them for me!" Genesis 27:5-13

When Rebekah overhears Isaac's plan to bless Esau, she creates a counter-plan. The fact that she comes up with this plan so fast, means she probably had already been contemplating it. Rebekah tells Jacob to go and get goats, so she can prepare tasty food and also for him to put on Esau's best clothes. In addition, she clothes Jacob with goat hair in order to deceive Isaac. This section of the narrative is full of haste. In verse 9, she says, "Go to the flock." In verse 13, she says "Go and get them for me!" Also, in verse 43, after finding out that Esau was planning to kill Jacob, Rebekah said, "Run away immediately to my brother Laban in Haran." When Rebekah and Jacob were not trusting God, anxiety and haste manifested in their lives.

This is true for us, as well, when we're not trusting God and instead operating in our own wisdom and strength. We'll typically feel anxious and rushed. Our minds will keep us up late at night—playing various scenarios over and over. We will rush to graduate, rush to get a job, rush to get married, rush to make a decision, rush for this and rush for that. When our hearts are anxious, it typically leads to haste and bad decisions. Be careful of making decisions with an anxious heart—anxiety and haste are often signs of not being right with God. Also, when our desires are unfulfilled, anxiety leads to discouragement. Proverbs 12:25 says, "Anxiety in a person's heart weighs him down."

This is not God's plan for his people. Scripture commonly tells us to not be afraid and to be anxious for nothing (Is 41:10, 2 Tim 1:7, Phil 4:6). When we're trusting God, typically, we will have his peace and not anxiety. Colossians 3:15 says, "Let the peace of Christ be in control in your heart." The phrase "be in control" can also be translated "decide." It was used of an umpire in an athletic game. Christ's peace or lack of peace should help us make decisions. Instead, many are ruled and guided by their anxieties and fears instead.

Application Question: How can we overcome our anxiety and sense of hurry?

Philippians 4:6-7 says,

Do not be anxious about anything. Instead, in every situation, through prayer and petition with thanksgiving, tell your requests to God. And

41

the peace of God that surpasses all understanding will guard your hearts and minds in Christ Jesus.

1. *If we are going to overcome anxiety, we must recognize it as a sin.* God has not given us a Spirit of fear but of power, love, and self-control (2 Tim 1:7). When we lack self-control and a sound mind, we must recognize that it's not from God. We must discern its root and remove it.

2. *If we are going to overcome anxiety, we must pray about every situation.* We typically don't do this. We sometimes pray when things are bad, but often not when things are good. We have to learn to live in an atmosphere of prayer. As a part of praying in everything, we must give thanks in everything and also present our requests to God in everything. To give thanks in everything is a step of faith. It means saying, "God, I trust you with this difficulty, even though it hurts, and I don't understand." Like Job, we must learn to say, "The Lord gives, and the Lord takes away. May the name of the Lord be blessed!" (Job 1:21).

When we do this, God promises to give us his peace. These are all things that Rebekah should have done. Instead of seeking to deceive her husband, she should have prayed to the Lord and sought his face. This is what she did when she was having a war in her belly with the two twins. She sought the Lord and he gave her a prophecy (Gen 25:22-23). Similarly, she should have prayed and then talked with her husband, and, if that didn't work, she should have trusted that God would fulfill his plans, with or without Isaac's blessing.

When we are not trusting God and instead trusting in ourselves, others, our job, or the economy, we will find ourselves often anxious and in a hurry. We must remember that God is our Shepherd and we will not be in want. Our Lord will guide us beside still waters, lead us into the right paths, protect us in the valley, anoint us with oil when we're hurt, and allow our cups to overflow with things that bring joy (Ps 23). We don't need a map when we have a guide. We don't need to fight for ourselves, when vengeance is the Lord's. He will take care of us and therefore we should accept his peace.

Are you living in peace or anxiety? When we're not trusting him, we'll lack peace and be full of anxiety and haste—leading to bad decision-making and discouragement.

Application Question: In what ways have you experienced anxiety and haste when not fully trusting God? How has that anxiety produced negative fruits, like bad decision-making and discouragement, in your life? In what ways is God calling you to seek his peace and allow it to rule in your life?

When We're Not Trusting God, We're Prone to Deception

Now Rebekah had been listening while Isaac spoke to his son Esau. When Esau went out to the open fields to hunt down some wild game and bring it back, Rebekah said to her son Jacob, "Look, I overheard your father tell your brother Esau, 'Bring me some wild game and prepare for me some tasty food. Then I will eat it and bless you in the presence of the LORD before I die.' Now then, my son, do exactly what I tell you! Go to the flock and get me two of the best young goats. I'll prepare them in a tasty way for your father, just the way he loves them. Then you will take it to your father. Thus he will eat it and bless you before he dies." "But Esau my brother is a hairy man," Jacob protested to his mother Rebekah, "and I have smooth skin! My father may touch me! Then he'll think I'm mocking him and I'll bring a curse on myself instead of a blessing." So his mother told him, "Any curse against you will fall on me, my son! Just obey me! Go and get them for me!" So he went and got the goats and brought them to his mother. She prepared some tasty food, just the way his father loved it. Then Rebekah took her older son Esau's best clothes, which she had with her in the house, and put them on her younger son Jacob. She put the skins of the young goats on his hands and the smooth part of his neck. Then she handed the tasty food and the bread she had made to her son Jacob. He went to his father and said, "My father!" Isaac replied, "Here I am. Which are you, my son?" Jacob said to his father, "I am Esau, your firstborn. I've done as you told me. Now sit up and eat some of my wild game so that you can bless me." But Isaac asked his son, "How in the world did you find it so quickly, my son?" "Because the LORD your God brought it to me," he replied. Then Isaac said to Jacob, "Come closer so I can touch you, my son, and know for certain if you really are my son Esau." So Jacob went over to his father Isaac, who felt him and said, "The voice is Jacob's, but the hands are Esau's." He did not recognize him because his hands were hairy, like his brother Esau's hands. So Isaac blessed Jacob. Then he asked, "Are you really my son Esau?" "I am," Jacob replied. Isaac said, "Bring some of the wild game for me to eat, my son. Then I will bless you." So Jacob brought it to him, and he ate it. He also brought him wine, and Isaac drank. Then his father Isaac said to him, "Come here and kiss me, my son."
Genesis 27:5-26

Deception runs throughout this narrative. When Isaac tells Esau to go hunt and prepare some tasty food, so he could bless him, this was a form of deception. In those days, the passing on of the blessing and birthright was a big deal. It was typically a public affair where all the household would come, watch, and celebrate (see Gen 49). However, Isaac does it in secret because he knows Rebekah and Jacob will disapprove. The fact that this was done in secret shows that Isaac's intentions were not fully honorable.

Also, there is deception when Rebekah hatches the plan to deceive her husband, and Jacob goes along with it. Jacob is dressed with Esau's best clothes and the hair of goats, and given a goat meal to deceive Isaac. Jacob lies to his father three times: when he says that he is Esau (v. 19), when he says that he secured the game early because God blessed his hunt (v. 20), and when the father doubted because of his voice, Jacob again claimed to be Esau (v. 24). Finally, he sealed his lies with a kiss (v. 27). Often one lie leads to another and then another. In addition to Isaac's, Rebekah's, and Jacob's deceptions, Esau was also being deceptive. He was breaking his deal with Jacob, who he had already promised the birthright.

When we are not trusting God and instead trusting in our own strength and wisdom, we are prone to bend the truth. When Abraham went to Egypt, he lied about his wife because he didn't believe God would protect them (Gen 12). He did the same when he encountered Abimelech (Gen 20). In both circumstances, he lost his wife and then God delivers her. God cursed Pharaoh and Abimelech, who took Sarah as their own. Each time God showed Abraham, "You can trust me. I will bless those who bless you and curse those who curse you. I will be your shield and great reward!"

Like our spiritual patriarchs and matriarchs before us, we also tend to scheme and deceive others when we're not trusting God. When we feel like we're going to get in trouble, we lie or shade the truth to protect ourselves. Why? We do this because we don't believe God will use our earned consequences for our best. When we feel like we're going to fail a test, we're tempted to cheat. Why? Because we don't believe God will help us pass or redeem our failure for the good. With taxes or illegal downloads, we're tempted to break the law. Why? We believe that the extra saved money is better than God's pleasure and favor. When we don't trust God, we'll be tempted to deceive.

In addition, not only are we tempted to deceive others when we're not trusting God, but we're also prone to being deceived. Isaac's family had developed some mystical understanding of Isaac's blessing. Yes, technically, Isaac could pass on the leadership of his home to whomever he wanted. However, his prayer of blessing was only effective if it lined up with God's Word. His prayer meant nothing unless it was in accord with God's will (cf. 1 John 5:14-15). Isaac was deceived about this and so was Rebekah, Jacob, and Esau. Throughout this narrative, it is clear that only God's will, will stand, not the deception and striving of people.

In the same way, when we're not trusting in God, we're prone to deception as well. When we don't accept what God says about us, we'll accept what Satan says, the world says, or ourselves—to our own demise. As we do so, we'll find ourselves either prideful or discouraged. Often pride or insecurity come because we've rejected God's Word and accepted the lies of the enemy.

In what ways are you deceiving others or being deceived instead of trusting God?

Application Question: In what ways is deception often rooted in not trusting God and his will for our lives? In what ways is telling the truth rooted in our trust for God? In what ways is God calling you to accept/practice truth and reject any form of deception?

When We're Not Trusting God, God Will Discipline Us to Increase Our Trust of Him

> Isaac had just finished blessing Jacob, and Jacob had scarcely left his father's presence, when his brother Esau returned from the hunt. He also prepared some tasty food and brought it to his father. Esau said to him, "My father, get up and eat some of your son's wild game. Then you can bless me." His father Isaac asked, "Who are you?" "I am your firstborn son," he replied, "Esau!" Isaac began to shake violently and asked, "Then who else hunted game and brought it to me? I ate all of it just before you arrived, and I blessed him. He will indeed be blessed!"...
> Genesis 27:30-46

After Isaac finishes blessing Jacob, Esau comes into the house seeking the blessing. Isaac starts violently shaking, and they both realize that Jacob had stolen the blessing. However, instead of reversing the blessing, Isaac strongly asserts that Jacob will be blessed (v. 33). He then gives Esau a blessing, which is really a nonblessing. When Jacob would receive the dew of the sky and the richness of the earth (v. 28), Esau's blessing would be "away" from the dew of the sky and the richness of the earth (v. 39). History tells us Esau's people, the Edomites, became desert-dwellers [8], who lived by the sword—meaning violence.[9] Many people would serve Jacob including his brother (v. 29). This was fulfilled in the Davidic kingdom, as Israel ruled over many people groups including the Edomites. However, Isaac did prophesy that Esau would become restless and break Jacob's yoke off of his neck. This eventually happened under Joram's reign, where the Edomites won their freedom (2 Kings 8:20–22).[10]

Interestingly, regarding Isaac's blessing on Jacob, we learn in the book of Hebrews that Isaac blessed Jacob by faith. Hebrews 11:20 says, "By faith also Isaac blessed Jacob and Esau concerning the future." How was this by faith if he was deceived? It seems to be that after Isaac had his shaking and realized that he was deceived, he came to a spiritual revelation. He couldn't contend with God. God's will would be done—no matter what he did. Therefore, when Isaac said that Jacob would indeed receive all those blessings—that was spoken in faith (v. 33). And when he blessed Esau, he also spoke in faith (v. 39-40). God's will would be done. Isaac couldn't outwit God, and neither can we.

After all Isaac's rebelling, God still won. God crushed Isaac's idols. His oldest son would not rule—his youngest would. And, instead of receiving wild game, he got seasoned goat. Similarly, God destroyed the idols of Rebekah, Jacob, and Esau. Rebekah's idol was her youngest, Jacob. After she hears that Esau wants to kill him, she sends him off to her family where he stays for twenty years (v. 42-46). Most likely, she never saw him again. God removed the rival in her heart to his glory. With Jacob, though he wanted to rule Esau, he spent twenty years serving his father-in-law, Laban, who deceived and mistreated him many times. Then when Jacob flees Laban, he is scared Esau will kill him. He offers him gifts, calls him Lord, and bows down to him (Gen 33). He didn't rule his brother, in the way he hoped. God destroyed his idol. With Esau, he wanted the blessing, but God gave it to Jacob. This is what God will do to us when there are rivals in our hearts. Every son he loves, he disciplines (Heb 12:6). He does this to help us trust in him alone.

Psalm 39:11 (ESV) says: "When you discipline a man with rebukes for sin, you consume like a moth what is dear to him; surely all mankind is a mere breath! Selah." God will have no rivals before him. With Abraham, when Isaac became the focus of his heart, God asked Abraham to sacrifice him (Gen 22). In the same way, when comfort becomes our idol, God will remove it. When career becomes an idol, he will shake it. He consumes like a moth what is dear to us, until he is our all in all. As with Isaac, he will shake us until we are willing to submit to his will again. With the prodigal son, all his wealth and worldly joys were eventually taken away from him, so that he came to his senses and returned to the father's house (Lk 15). God will allow the same to happen to us.

What are your idols? What are you trusting in other than God?

Application Question: Why does God allow us to go through trials/discipline (Heb 12:6-7)? In what ways have you experienced the discipline of God removing idols?

Conclusion

How can we know when we're not trusting God? When we look at the story of Isaac's family fighting over the birthright, we see the consequences and signs of not trusting God.

46

1. When We're Not Trusting God, We're Prone to Idolatry
2. When We're Not Trusting God, We're Prone to Anxiety and Haste
3. When We're Not Trusting God, We're Prone to Deception
4. When We're Not Trusting God, God Will Discipline Us to Increase Our Trust of Him

Application Question: What sign of not trusting God spoke to you most and why? How is God calling you to grow in your trust for him?

Experiencing Intimacy with God

So Isaac called for Jacob and blessed him. Then he commanded him, "You must not marry a Canaanite woman! Leave immediately for Paddan Aram! Go to the house of Bethuel, your mother's father, and find yourself a wife there, among the daughters of Laban, your mother's brother. May the sovereign God bless you! May he make you fruitful and give you a multitude of descendants! Then you will become a large nation. May he give you and your descendants the blessing he gave to Abraham so that you may possess the land God gave to Abraham, the land where you have been living as a temporary resident." So Isaac sent Jacob on his way, and he went to Paddan Aram, to Laban son of Bethuel the Aramean and brother of Rebekah, the mother of Jacob and Esau. Esau saw that Isaac had blessed Jacob and sent him off to Paddan Aram to find a wife there. As he blessed him, Isaac commanded him, "You must not marry a Canaanite woman." Jacob obeyed his father and mother and left for Paddan Aram. Then Esau realized that the Canaanite women were displeasing to his father Isaac. So Esau went to Ishmael and married Mahalath, the sister of Nebaioth and daughter of Abraham's son Ishmael, along with the wives he already had. Meanwhile Jacob left Beer Sheba and set out for Haran. He reached a certain place where he decided to camp because the sun had gone down. He took one of the stones and placed it near his head. Then he fell asleep in that place and had a dream. He saw a stairway erected on the earth with its top reaching to the heavens. The angels of God were going up and coming down it and the LORD stood at its top. He said, "I am the LORD, the God of your grandfather Abraham and the God of your father Isaac. I will give you and your descendants the ground you are lying on. Your descendants will be like the dust of the earth, and you will spread out to the west, east, north, and south. All the families of the earth will pronounce blessings on one another using your name and that of your descendants. I am with you! I will protect you wherever you go and will bring you back to this land. I will not leave you until I have done what I promised you!" Then Jacob woke up and thought, "Surely the LORD is in this place, but I did not realize it!" He was afraid and said, "What an awesome place this is! This is nothing else than the house of God!

This is the gate of heaven!" Early in the morning Jacob took the stone he had placed near his head and set it up as a sacred stone. Then he poured oil on top of it. He called that place Bethel, although the former name of the town was Luz. Then Jacob made a vow, saying, "If God is with me and protects me on this journey I am taking and gives me food to eat and clothing to wear, and I return safely to my father's home, then the LORD will become my God. Then this stone that I have set up as a sacred stone will be the house of God, and I will surely give you back a tenth of everything you give me."
Genesis 28 (NET)

How can we experience intimacy with God?

In this part of Jacob's narrative, he leaves home because his brother, Esau, desires to kill him. Rebekah hears of his plan and convinces Isaac to send Jacob to Haran to marry one of her brother's daughters. Jacob, who is about seventy-seven years old, leaves for Haran to find a wife.[11] While camped at a place later called Bethel, God reveals himself to Jacob. In Jacob's dream there was a stairway between heaven and earth, with angels ascending and descending, and God at the top of the stairway.

There at Bethel, Jacob experiences a greater intimacy with God—leading to a greater commitment. It's not that Jacob didn't know God, he did. He had been raised in a God-fearing family—one that believed in God's promises to Abraham. However, Jacob had never really allowed God to take a hold of his life. Jacob was still living for himself and not trusting God. This is often true for those raised in Christian homes. At a young age, they develop head-knowledge but still live on the faith of their parents; however, at some point, their faith has to become their own. God has to become their God and not just their parents' God.

Each of us needs an experience with God. Some still need an experience that leads to salvation. Others, because of apathy or even luke-warmness, need a fresh experience—leading them to greater intimacy and greater commitment. This would be Jacob's first-time meeting with God, but he would have many other fresh experiences—including another dream (Gen 31), a time where he wrestles with God and God renames him (Gen 32), and a time where, it seems, God physically appeared to him (Gen 35). We need to continually experience intimacy with God as well.

As we study this narrative, we learn principles about experiencing intimacy with God, so we can experience him in fresh new ways.

Big Question: What principles can we discern from Genesis 28 about experiencing intimacy with God?

To Experience Intimacy with God, We Must Practice Obedience

So Isaac called for Jacob and blessed him. Then he commanded him, "You must not marry a Canaanite woman! Leave immediately for Paddan Aram! Go to the house of Bethuel, your mother's father, and find yourself a wife there, among the daughters of Laban, your mother's brother. May the sovereign God bless you! May he make you fruitful and give you a multitude of descendants! Then you will become a large nation. May he give you and your descendants the blessing he gave to Abraham so that you may possess the land God gave to Abraham, the land where you have been living as a temporary resident." So Isaac sent Jacob on his way, and he went to Paddan Aram, to Laban son of Bethuel the Aramean and brother of Rebekah, the mother of Jacob and Esau. Esau saw that Isaac had blessed Jacob and sent him off to Paddan Aram to find a wife there. As he blessed him, Isaac commanded him, "You must not marry a Canaanite woman." Jacob obeyed his father and mother and left for Paddan Aram. Then Esau realized that the Canaanite women were displeasing to his father Isaac. So Esau went to Ishmael and married Mahalath, the sister of Nebaioth and daughter of Abraham's son Ishmael, along with the wives he already had.
Genesis 28:1-9

Previously, when seeking a wife for Isaac, Abraham made his servant promise to not take a wife from Canaan; the people of Canaan were ungodly and their character would have threatened the promise (Gen 24). However, Esau, who did not care about God's promises, married two women from Canaan, which caused great distress in Isaac's household. Therefore, twice Isaac commands Jacob to not marry a Canaanite, in verse 1 and verse 6, and in obedience, Jacob left for Haran to marry from Rebekah's family (v. 7).

When Esau discovers that his ungodly marriages displeased his parents, he marries one of Ishmael's daughters, which no doubt, only exasperated the problem (v. 8-9). Though Scripture does not hide the fact that some of Scripture's heroes had multiple wives, it always shows these marriages in a negative light. There was conflict between Sara and Hagar, Abraham's wives. There will later be conflict between Jacob's wives. There was also jealousy and conflict between Elkanah's wives, of which one of them was Hannah, the mother of Samuel. Solomon's many wives led him away from God. Scripture clearly teaches that it is God's ideal for one man to marry one woman. In Genesis 2:24, we see that man is supposed to leave his family and cleave to his wife, and they become one flesh. The kings were commanded to not multiply wives, which none of them seems to have obeyed (Deut 17:17). In the NT, the requirements for an elder is that he should be the husband of but one wife (1 Tim 3:2). Esau's marriage was a failed attempt to please his father, that really showed that he was unrepentant and only wanted Isaac's favor and not God's.

However, the main application, we should take from this is that obedience leads to experiencing God's presence. Jacob's obedience to his parents, and ultimately God, in not marrying one of the pagan women preceded the manifestation of God's presence. Obedience commonly is the pathway to intimacy with God and ultimately his blessing. We see this in many Scriptures:

John 15:10 says: "If you obey my commandments, you will remain in my love, just as I have obeyed my Father's commandments and remain in his love." To remain in Christ's love means to constantly experience it and be aware of it. It includes having our prayers answered and experiencing God's presence. Therefore, to not obey God means to not experience God's love as we should.

Philippians 4:8-9 says it this way:

Finally, brothers and sisters, whatever is true, whatever is worthy of respect, whatever is just, whatever is pure, whatever is lovely, whatever is commendable, if something is excellent or praiseworthy, think about these things. And what you learned and received and heard and saw in me, do these things. And the God of peace will be with you.

The promise for thinking on godly things and practicing them is that the "God of peace" will be with us. Those who practice godliness in their meditations and actions experience God. They experience him in the work place, in their families, in worship, and in leisure. These people live anointed lives, as God's favor showers over them. The opposite of this is true when our thinking and living are ungodly. This leads to missing God's presence and opens the door for all types of evil. It was when Saul was in rebellion that the Spirit of God left him, and a demon spirit was allowed to torment him (1 Sam 16:14).

If we are going to experience the God of peace, we must walk in obedience. It is no surprise that Jacob's obedience led to an intimate experience with God.

Are you living in obedience and therefore growing in the knowledge of God? Or living in disobedience and growing farther away from the Lord? If we cherish iniquity in our hearts, David said the Lord will not hear us—we will miss his presence and blessing (Ps 66:18).

Application Question: How have you experienced God's presence when being obedient to God and how have you lacked it in seasons of rebellion?

To Experience Intimacy with God, We Must Practice Solitude

> Meanwhile Jacob left Beer Sheba and set out for Haran. He reached a certain place where he decided to camp because the sun had gone down. He took one of the stones and placed it near his head. Then he fell asleep in that place and had a dream. He saw a stairway erected on the earth with its top reaching to the heavens. The angels of God were going up and coming down it...
> Genesis 28:10-12

As mentioned, in obedience to Isaac, Jacob left his home and started a 500-mile journey to Haran. There are two things that are interesting about Jacob's journey and stop in Luz, which is later called Bethel. (1) First, Jacob seems to be alone. When Abraham's servant went to Haran to find a wife for Isaac, he left with a large caravan that included servants and camels in order to prove to the family that his servant, Isaac, would be able to provide for a young maiden (Gen 24). However, Jacob was totally alone. This was probably because Isaac was disciplining him for his deception. (2) Also, typically when traveling, one would stop at an inn for housing or be welcomed into someone's home. However, Jacob intentionally decided to avoid the city and camp outside by himself.

This may seem insignificant, but this is actually a very important step to experiencing intimacy with God. We must practice the discipline of solitude—intentionally getting away from people and work to focus on God. Jacob's family was very wealthy. In Genesis 14, Abraham defeated several armies with 318 servants. Isaac inherited all of Abraham's wealth and also increased it. He became so wealthy that the Philistines envied him (Gen 26:13–14). Because of this, Jacob was accustomed to being around a booming estate with many servants and business activities to take part in. Now, however, he was all alone.

We must, at times, put ourselves in the same environment to experience intimacy with God. Moses met God by himself on a mountain, as God appeared in a fiery bush. Gideon met God while by himself threshing grain. Elijah met God in a cave. It was while Christ was in the wilderness fasting that angels came and ministered to him after his temptation (Matt 4:11).

Sadly, many of us never intentionally get alone with God, so we can experience him in deeper ways. Our lives are filled with rushing. We rush to work, rush from work, rush through eating, rush to bed, rush through our devotions. We often don't take time to just sit, listen, and speak with God. Psalm 46:10 (NIV) says, "Be still and know that I am God." "Be still" can also be translated "stop striving." We need to practice intentional solitude to experience God.

Application Question: How can we practice the discipline of solitude?

1. *Be intentional.* Set a time and a place to meet with God daily and even multiple times a day. Daniel prayed to God, in his room with his window open towards Jerusalem, three times a day (Dan 6). Christ got up early in the morning and went to the mountain to meet with God (Mark 1). Consider practicing not only daily disciplines but seasons of concentrated time with God. Go to a retreat or a discipleship school. Choose to fast for a week by neglecting a meal or more daily for extra time with God. Christ fasted for forty days and experienced special grace (Matt 4). Moses fasted for forty days and experienced God in a special way as well (Ex 34). We must be intentional about our times of solitude with God. How are you being intentional about your time with God?

2. *Be zealous in guarding your solitude.* (a) To do this, be careful of timewasters. Too much of good things like Internet, playing video games, hobbies, etc., can actually hinder our relationships with others and God. (b) Also, be careful of busyness. Sometimes we think of busyness as spiritual. However, Christ rebuked Martha for her busyness, even though she was serving God and others, and praised Mary for sitting at his feet (Luke 10). Don't let busyness crowd God out of your life—including the busyness of serving.

Application Question: What types of spiritual disciplines have you found most helpful in experiencing intimacy with God? What are your time-wasters that you have to be careful of? In what ways have you seen busyness crowd God out of your life? How is God calling you to intentionally practice solitude?

To Experience Intimacy with God, We Must Recognize Our Brokenness

Meanwhile Jacob left Beer Sheba and set out for Haran. He reached a certain place where he decided to camp because the sun had gone down. He took one of the stones and placed it near his head. Then he fell asleep in that place and had a dream. He saw a stairway erected on the earth with its top reaching to the heavens. The angels of God were going up and coming down it...
Genesis 28:10-12

54

While Jacob was on this journey, we can assume that he was hurting in various ways. Certainly, he was experiencing some fear, as he ran for his life and was potentially on his own for the first time. In addition, he was probably experiencing some shame. Not only had he manipulated his brother but also deceived his blind father. No doubt, this was a difficult time for Jacob. He was probably afraid and ashamed. Maybe, that's why he wanted to be alone, instead of going to the gate of Luz and finding lodging.

However, Jacob's brokenness was the perfect place for him to experience God. And this is often true for us. It is when we are broken, weak, lost, and lonely that God can move miraculously in our lives. Psalm 34:18 says, "The LORD is near the brokenhearted; he delivers those who are discouraged." Steve Cole said it this way:

> In problem solving, the first step is to recognize and define the problem. Often our problem is that we don't clearly see the problem. We aren't aware of our great need, so we aren't open for God to move into our lives to begin working on the problems. Many times it takes a crisis, where we are brought to the end of our own abilities and schemes, for us to be able to see our need and be open to God's breaking into our lives.[12]

Matthew 5:3 says: "Blessed are the poor in spirit for theirs is the kingdom of heaven." It is when we are in a state of poverty of spirit—when we recognize our sin and weakness before God—that we experience his kingdom both in salvation and in sanctification.

Since this is necessary to experience God, in his grace, he often allows us to experience trial and weakness. That is why Scripture says, "Consider it pure joy when you encounter various trials and tribulations because it is the testing of your faith" (James 1:2). We can consider our trials pure joy because we know what God is doing in our lives—he is revealing himself to us and transforming us into his image.

Application Question: How should we respond to the fact that God often meets with people in special ways during times of brokenness?

1.   We should thank God when he allows us to be weak, lonely, or broken.

James 1:9-10 says, "Now the believer of humble means should take pride in his high position. But the rich person's pride should be in his humiliation, because he will pass away like a wildflower in the meadow." The humble person, meaning the poor, should thank God for his state in life. His poverty creates weakness and helps him trust in God more. However, the rich should take pride when God humbles him, because it teaches him the brevity of life. Trials are a blessing from God because they show us our weakness and brokenness, which prepares us to experience a harvest with God—one of intimacy and spiritual growth.

2. We should recognize times of trial or brokenness as opportunities to minister to others.

Often when we are trying to share the gospel with an unbeliever or help an immature believer grow, they many times don't want to hear God's Word. They don't want to hear it because they are comfortable with their lives as they are. In those situations, we should wisely love them and wait for opportunities to minister to them. Typically, their ears and hearts open in times of trial. Trials make their hearts good ground for the precious seed of God's Word. It is then that we should prayerfully share God's message and wait for God to bear fruit. Trials are a strategic time to minister to others.

Colossians 4:5 (ESV) says, "Walk in wisdom toward outsiders, making the best use of the time." The Greek word for "time" used here is not "chronos" for chronological time, but "kairos" for seasons. There are certain seasons in people's lives when they are more open to God's Word, and those seasons are often times of trial or brokenness. We must patiently wait for those seasons and then strategically plant God's Word, while hoping for a spiritual harvest.

Application Question: How have you experienced special times of brokenness or trials when God met with you in a special way? How have you experienced openness in others to the things of God in times of trial or difficulty?

To Experience Intimacy with God, We Must Have a Revelation of God's Word

… He saw a stairway erected on the earth with its top reaching to the heavens. The angels of God were going up and coming down it and the Lord stood at its top. He said, "I am the Lord, the God of your grandfather Abraham and the God of your father Isaac. I will give you and your descendants the ground you are lying on. Your descendants will be like the dust of the earth, and you will spread out to the west, east, north, and south. All the families of the earth will pronounce blessings on one another using your name and that of your descendants. I am with you! I will protect you wherever you go and will bring you back to this land. I will not leave you until I have done what I promised you!"
Genesis 28:12-15

The prophetic words God spoke over Jacob of a land, seed, and blessing were the same things, Isaac prayed over Jacob before he started his journey (v. 3-4). It was the blessing that Jacob had initially tricked his father into giving him (Gen 27). But now, Isaac willingly spoke it over Jacob's life. Jacob, no doubt, had heard about the promises of Abraham his whole life. But, when God spoke these over him while at Bethel, he finally had a revelation of them. God was truly going to make a great multitude through Jacob and give the land to his descendants. Now, those words weren't just words that he had heard his parents speak or that his father prayed over him, now they were God's Words. As Jacob met with God, he had a revelation of God's Word and promises.

Similarly, we cannot have a true revelation of God apart from his Word. It is through God's Word that he reveals himself to us. In Jacob's time, they didn't have the written revelation of Scripture, as we do; therefore, God would speak to them in more charismatic ways. However, God has given us his written Word, by which we test everything and know God more. For those who love God's Word, meditate on it daily, and obey it, God promises many blessings. Psalm 1:1-3 describes some of these blessings. It says:

> How blessed is the one who does not follow the advice of the wicked … Instead he finds pleasure in obeying the Lord's commands; he meditates on his commands day and night. He is like a tree planted by flowing streams; it yields its fruit at the proper time, and its leaves never fall off. He succeeds in everything he attempts.

God blesses those who delight, meditate on, and obey his Word—everything that they do will prosper. They'll experience God in the mundane, their work, their family, their ministry, and especially in their trials.

Application Question: How can we have a revelation of God's Word, in order to experience God's presence?

1. *To have a revelation of God's Word, we must depend on God.* Consider David's prayer in Psalm 119:18-19: "Open my eyes so I can truly see the marvelous things in your law! I am like a foreigner in this land. Do not hide your commands from me!" David understood that apart from God's revelation, he couldn't understand God's Word. Therefore, his posture was humble prayer. Pride hinders our reception of God's Word, while humble prayer opens the door for understanding. We should pray before we study God's Word, while studying it, and after studying it. As we do this, God will meet with us and give us revelation.

2. *To have a revelation of God's Word, we must depend on others.* In Ephesians 4:13, Paul taught that God gave us pastors and teachers to help us "attain to the unity of the faith and of the knowledge of the Son of God—a mature person, attaining to the measure of Christ's full stature." Through the teaching of others, God helps us understand the faith, know Christ more, and grow in maturity. We need godly believers speaking and explaining God's Word to us. Therefore, we should saturate our life with attending church and small groups, reading godly literature, etc., in order to have a revelation of God's Word.

3. *To have a revelation of God's Word, we must turn away from sin.* James 1:21 says, "So put away all filth and evil excess and humbly welcome the message implanted within you, which is able to save your souls." In order to welcome God's Word and allow it to change us, we must put away filth and evil. It has been said that either God's Word will keep us from sin or sin will keep us from God's Word. When we're walking in sin, we don't want to read our Bible or go to church. Our hearts aren't good ground for God's seed, and therefore, the Word can't change us. Are you getting rid of sin, so you can have a revelation of God through his Word? Or is sin helping you get rid of God's Word?

Application Question: In what ways have you experienced how God's Word keeps us out of sin or sin keeps us out of God's Word? In what ways is God calling you to get rid of sin, in order to prepare your heart for a greater revelation of God through his Word?

To Experience Intimacy with God, We Must Accept God's Grace

and had a dream. He saw a stairway erected on the earth with its top reaching to the heavens. The angels of God were going up and coming down it and the Lord stood at its top. He said, "I am the Lord, the God of your grandfather Abraham and the God of your father Isaac. I will give you and your descendants the ground you are lying on. Your descendants will be like the dust of the earth, and you will spread out to the west, east, north, and south. All the families of the earth will pronounce blessings on one another using your name and that of your descendants. I am with you! I will protect you wherever you go and will bring you back to this land. I will not leave you until I have done what I promised you!"

Another aspect of Jacob's experience with God that must stand out to us is the fact that it was full of grace. God speaks to him, "I will give you and your descendants the ground you are lying on... I am with you... I will protect you... and will bring you back to this land. I will not leave until I have done what I promised you!" God's Words don't make sense. God doesn't condemn him for stealing the birthright/blessing. God just declares that all the promises would be completed through God's power. Jacob would have the land and descendants, and his family would be a blessing to the nations. God would protect him and bring him back to the land. Jacob could not secure the promise on his own—his deception made him a fugitive. But, God was going to accomplish it by grace—Jacob just needed to believe and accept that reality.

This is true with us as well. If we are going to experience God, we must accept his grace. This is true in salvation. We can't work for it or earn it, we must simply believe and accept it. Many miss salvation by trying to gain it through works—church attendance, baptism, giving to the poor, etc. By seeking to gain it through self-effort, as Jacob did with the birthright, they miss it. But those who humbly accept Christ's finished work on the cross will gain salvation. John 3:16 says whoever believes shall be saved. And this is true with many of God's promises. They are offered, not because we are righteous, but because he is faithful. Philippians 1:6 says that the work God began in us, he will complete until the day of Christ (paraphrase). Until Christ comes, God will work in us to complete his works. Grace doesn't mean that we don't have a role in knowing God or fulfilling his promises; it just means that even our role doesn't happen apart from grace. Ephesians 2:8-9 says, "For by grace are you saved through faith and that not of yourselves. It is the gift of God, not of works lest anyone should boast" (paraphrase). Even our faith is a gift of God. Philippians 2:12-13 says God works in us to will and do of his good pleasure (paraphrase). The desire to accomplish his works and the empowerment to do it all come from God and his grace.

In fact, in this narrative, the grace of God was changing Jacob's heart not only through the experience of God's spoken promises but also Jacob's vision in general. In the vision, he sees a stairway that went from the ground to heaven. At the top of this stairway was God and going up and down the ladder were angels. This would have reminded Jacob that God was sovereign over the affairs of the world. He was the king. His angels reminded Jacob that he was not alone and had no reason to fear. God was managing his affairs on the earth through angels. Angels are specifically sent to minister to those who will inherit salvation, according to Hebrews 1:14. Angels would protect Jacob, provide for him, and help guide him, all according to God's will. This would give him tremendous peace and it should do the same for us. Christ told the disciples to not despise one of God's little ones, as their angels always see the face of God

(Matt 18:10). They are waiting for a word from God to defend, strengthen, or encourage.

Specifically, with the stairway, this was an Old Testament shadow of Christ. In John 1, Christ used Jacob's stairway to explain to Nathaniel that he was the only way to heaven. Many believe that Nathaniel was meditating on Jacob's stairway under a tree—maybe marveling at God's grace to a deceptive man. When Christ meets with Nathaniel, he says, "Look, a true Israelite, in whom there is no deceit" (John 1:47). Maybe, Christ was saying, "You are not like Jacob—a deceiver!" After Nathaniel recognizes that Jesus was in fact the messiah, Christ said: "I tell all of you the solemn truth—you will see heaven opened and the angels of God ascending and descending on the Son of Man" (v. 51). Christ was essentially saying, "You are not a deceiver like Jacob, but you need the same grace. I'm the stairway to heaven!"

Interpretation Question: As a picture of Christ, what did the stairway, or ladder, symbolize?

1. *The stairway symbolizes that there is a gulf between heaven and earth—God and man.* Since the gulf is so large, nobody can reach heaven apart from a supernatural work of God.[13]

2. *The stairway symbolizes that a way has been provided for man to reach heaven.* Again, the stairway is a shadow, which fully became realized in Christ.[14] Christ said, "I am the way, the truth, and the life. No one comes to the father but by me" (John 14:6). In John 10:9, Christ also said: "I am the door. If anyone enters through me, he will be saved, and will come in and go out, and find pasture."

The Old Testament is full of pictures and shadows that represent Christ. He was the sacrificial lamb that covered the sins of the people. He was the Sabbath day on which people found rest. He was the temple in which God's presence dwelled. He was the priest who interceded on behalf of the people. He was the righteous king, who would one day have an eternal kingdom. He was Israel who spent years in Egypt. In all these shadows, Christ is pictured. In John 5:39-40, Christ said this to the Pharisees, "You study the scriptures thoroughly because you think in them you possess eternal life, and it is these same scriptures that testify about me, but you are not willing to come to me so that you may have life." The OT is not only full of prophecies about Christ but also pictures to help prepare people for the messiah.

As Jacob experiences God, he experiences grace—unmerited favor on his sinful life. He must give up his striving and deception, as the promise would come through God's grace. And it's the same for us. This is true in

60

salvation—to work for salvation is to never experience it. It comes by grace through faith alone (Eph 2:8-9). But it is also true in sanctification, anything good in and through us comes from God's grace, so no one can boast (Phil 2:12-13).

Application Question: How can we experience more of God's grace in order to grow in intimacy with God?

1. We must humble ourselves to experience more of God's grace.

James 4:6 says, "God opposes the proud, but he gives grace to the humble." The prideful reject God and don't depend on him. They are independent instead of dependent. Instead of depending on God's Word, prayer, his body, etc., they depend on themselves and miss God's grace. However, those who humble themselves before God and depend on his grace like a child (cf. Matt 18:1-4), experience much grace and intimacy with God. It was said of Moses that God spoke to him face to face, unlike with other prophets, and he was the humblest man on the earth (Num 12:3).

Are we prideful and independent or humble and dependent? We can tell by how much time we pray, study God's Word, and rely upon God's people. The prideful are too blind to know their great need for these things; therefore, they neglect them.

2. We must respond with faith and commitment to experience more of God's grace.

In response to God's revelation, Jacob anoints a stone, which was a symbol of worship and devotion to the Lord.[15] Then he made a vow to God saying:

> "If God is with me and protects me on this journey I am taking and gives me food to eat and clothing to wear, and I return safely to my father's home, then the Lord will become my God. Then this stone that I have set up as a sacred stone will be the house of God, and I will surely give you back a tenth of everything you give me."
> Genesis 28:20-22

Commentators are divided on exactly what Jacob was saying. "If" can be translated "since."[16] If "if" is the correct translation, Jacob is bargaining with God. If God would protect him and bring him back to the land, Isaac's God would be his God. That is quite possible since Jacob's character is a bargainer. However, if "since" is correct, which many believe, Jacob is saying "Because God will do all these things, I will remain faithful to him, name the place the house of God, and give a tenth of my earnings."

Either way, Jacob responded to God's grace in faith, even if it was imperfect. We must do the same. To continue to experience God, we must respond in faith. True faith is not simply belief. It always has the corresponding fruits like commitment and devotion. Similarly, if we're going to experience intimacy with God, we must respond to God's grace with faith.

Christ said this, "So listen carefully, for whoever has will be given more, but whoever does not have, even what he thinks he has will be taken from him'" (Lk 8:18). If we respond to God's grace, he will continue to give us more of it, including himself. If not, he will take away.

How are you responding to God's grace? Are you committed or uncommitted? Hot or lukewarm? Zealous or apathetic? To experience God, we must respond to his unmerited favor. He has given us Christ, his Word, communion, the saints, opportunities to serve, and even the grace of trials so that we might seek him and know him more. Are you responding to God's grace? Those who do receive more. By his faithful response, Jacob was preparing the way for a greater revelation of God, and we must do the same.

Application Question: Share your salvation story. How did you come to accept God's grace in salvation? Share a time when you experienced a deeper intimacy with God after salvation and therefore a greater commitment. How would you rate your current commitment and zeal for God on a scale of 1-10 and why?

Conclusion

Jacob was raised knowing who God was. He was raised in a believing family. However, in Genesis 28, he experienced the God of his parents and his faith became his own. We need to experience God in salvation and then have constant fresh experiences of him. Like Moses, we should constantly cry out, "Show me your glory!" (Ex 33:18). How can we experience intimacy with God?

1. To Experience Intimacy with God, We Must Practice Obedience
2. To Experience Intimacy with God, We Must Practice Solitude
3. To Experience Intimacy with God, We Must Recognize Our Brokenness
4. To Experience Intimacy with God, We Must Have a Revelation of God's Word
5. To Experience Intimacy with God, We Must Accept God's Grace

Application Question: How is God calling you to pursue intimacy with God?

Equipped in God's Boot Camp

...Then Laban said to Jacob, "Should you work for me for nothing because you are my relative? Tell me what your wages should be." (Now Laban had two daughters; the older one was named Leah, and the younger one Rachel. Leah's eyes were tender, but Rachel had a lovely figure and beautiful appearance.) Since Jacob had fallen in love with Rachel, he said, "I'll serve you seven years in exchange for your younger daughter Rachel." Laban replied, "I'd rather give her to you than to another man. Stay with me." So Jacob worked for seven years to acquire Rachel. But they seemed like only a few days to him because his love for her was so great. Finally Jacob said to Laban, "Give me my wife, for my time of service is up. I want to have marital relations with her." So Laban invited all the people of that place and prepared a feast. In the evening he brought his daughter Leah to Jacob, and Jacob had marital relations with her. (Laban gave his female servant Zilpah to his daughter Leah to be her servant.) In the morning Jacob discovered it was Leah! So Jacob said to Laban, "What in the world have you done to me! Didn't I work for you in exchange for Rachel? Why have you tricked me?" "It is not our custom here," Laban replied, "to give the younger daughter in marriage before the firstborn. Complete my older daughter's bridal week. Then we will give you the younger one too, in exchange for seven more years of work." Jacob did as Laban said. When Jacob completed Leah's bridal week, Laban gave him his daughter Rachel to be his wife. (Laban gave his female servant Bilhah to his daughter Rachel to be her servant.) Jacob had marital relations with Rachel as well. He loved Rachel more than Leah, so he worked for Laban for seven more years.
Genesis 29:1-30 (NET)

When entering the military, soldiers have to go through basic training to orient them to military life. Sometimes it's called boot camp. It's often been said that when boys go through boot camp, they become men. In boot camp, the military aims to deliver one from being an individual to being part of a team, from being out of shape to being in shape, from being a civilian to becoming a war-fighter.

It is an intense training where one is broken down physically and mentally, so one can be built up.

In the same way, when God prepares his warriors, he sends them through an intense training—a Divine boot camp. AW Tozer said it this way: "It is doubtful whether God can bless a man greatly until He has hurt him deeply." Christ said, "Every branch that bears fruit, God prunes so that it can bear more fruit" (John 15:2 paraphrase). When God is preparing somebody for a great task, he cuts them. He gets rid of things in their lives that would keep them from maximum fruitfulness. With Jacob, God had a lot of work to do. He was a manipulator; he trusted in himself and had low character. In this narrative, Jacob has been running for his life, as his older brother, Esau, is trying to kill him for taking his birthright. His father, Isaac, seems to have sent Jacob away alone and without money for his deceptive practices. He still received his father's blessing and birthright, but that didn't come without discipline. Isaac's discipline was just part of how God was working to change Jacob's character, so he could use him greatly.

The boot camp Jacob went through lasted some twenty years. Others may have longer boot camps or shorter ones. After God called Joseph, he spent around thirteen years as a servant and prisoner before God exalted him to second-in-command in Egypt. Moses spent forty years in the desert. Christ didn't begin his ministry until he was thirty years old, after forty days of fasting and temptation. In God's boot camp, there is no rush. He chisels and shapes a person until he or she is ready to be used—not beforehand.

In Genesis 29, Jacob arrives in Haran to seek a wife from Rebekah's relative; however, while there he encounters hardship and difficulty—all meant, from God's perspective, to develop his character. God was delivering him from being Jacob, the deceiver, to being Israel, the overcomer—the one who wrestles with God and prevails.

As we study this narrative, we will learn about how God equips those he will greatly use. In the military, typically, a person only goes through one boot camp, but in God's economy, as we are fruitful, he often sends us back for further training—to further prune us to bear fruit (John 15:2). By understanding how God equips us in his boot camp, we will learn to identify training seasons, be more faithful in them, and better encourage others going through them.

Big Question: As discerned from Genesis 29, how does God equip his people through times of intense training—through a Divine boot camp?

In God's Boot Camp, He Equips Believers Through His Word and His Promises

So Jacob moved on and came to the land of the eastern people.

64

When Genesis 29:1 says, "Jacob moved on," it can literally be translated "Jacob lifted up his feet."[17] One Jewish commentator remarked, "His heart lifted up his feet."[18] After receiving the promises of God and seeing the vision of the ladder with angels ascending and descending (Gen 28), Jacob was energized for his journey. He knew that wherever he went, the ladder went. God would never leave him nor forsake him. Before when he was running for his life, he was struggling with loneliness, shame, and fear; now, he was motivated by God's promises.

It should be the same for us. In God's boot camp, he teaches us to rely on God's Word and his promises. Sometimes, it may even feel as though, God's Word is all we have. Second Peter 1:4 says,

> Through these things he has bestowed on us his precious and most magnificent promises, so that by means of what was promised you may become partakers of the divine nature, after escaping the worldly corruption that is produced by evil desire.

These promises include such things as his empowerment, peace, guidance, and presence. Like Jacob, God will never leave us or forsake us. Arthur Pink said this:

> And, reader, do not we need to be reminded that our Lord has promised, "Lo, I am with you always, even unto the end"? If our hearts drew from this cheering and inspiring promise the comfort and incentive, it is designed to convey, should not we "lift up" our feet as we journey through this world? Oh! It is unbelief, failure to rest upon the "exceeding great and precious promises" of our God, and forgetfulness that He is ever by our side, that makes our feet leaden and causes us to drag along so wearily.[19]

God's Word and promises encourage us during desert seasons— times of intense training. They enable us to persevere and have joy in the storm. Joseph's vision of his parents bowing down before him, no doubt, helped encourage him in the times of slavery and imprisonment. God was not done with him yet. Similarly, Jacob was about to enter a season where he reaped what he sowed. He was about to be deceived by his uncle, Laban, and become his servant for twenty years. However, it was God's promises that would carry him through. Paul said something similar to Timothy: "I put this charge before you, Timothy my child, in keeping with the prophecies once spoken about you, in order that with such encouragement you may fight the good fight" (1 Tim

1:18). Through God's promises and words over us, we also must fight the good fight.

Are you being motivated by God's promises? Typically, in God's boot camp, in order to stay faithful, we must live in Scripture; we must listen to it, memorize it, and quote it. Like Christ in the desert, we must fight off Satan and his lies with it. Before entering God's boot camp, we may have neglected or taken God's Word for granted. However, in God's boot camp, we are trained to make it our life-line. Like Job in his trials, we learn to say, "I have treasured the words of his mouth more than my daily bread" (Job 23:12 NIV).

Have you learned to treasure God's Word and his promises? Are they your daily bread or your occasional snack? Are they your life or your hobby?

Application Question: In what ways has Scripture encouraged and strengthened you during certain seasons of your walk with God? Was there a certain event or events that helped you begin to love and treasure God's Word more? If so, what happened? If you eventually lost your passion for God's Word, what made you lose it?

In God's Boot Camp, He Equips Believers Through Providential Circumstances

He saw in the field a well with three flocks of sheep lying beside it, because the flocks were watered from that well. Now a large stone covered the mouth of the well. When all the flocks were gathered there, the shepherds would roll the stone off the mouth of the well and water the sheep. Then they would put the stone back in its place over the well's mouth. Jacob asked them, "My brothers, where are you from?" They replied, "We're from Haran." So he said to them, "Do you know Laban, the grandson of Nahor?" "We know him," they said. "Is he well?" Jacob asked. They replied, "He is well. Now look, here comes his daughter Rachel with the sheep." Then Jacob said, "Since it is still the middle of the day, it is not time for the flocks to be gathered. You should water the sheep and then go and let them graze some more." "We can't," they said, "until all the flocks are gathered and the stone is rolled off the mouth of the well. Then we water the sheep." While he was still speaking with them, Rachel arrived with her father's sheep, for she was tending them. When Jacob saw Rachel, the daughter of his uncle Laban, and the sheep of his uncle Laban, he went over and rolled the stone off the mouth of the well and watered the sheep of his uncle Laban. Then Jacob kissed Rachel and began to weep loudly. When Jacob explained to Rachel that he was a relative of her father and the son of Rebekah, she ran and told her father. When Laban

heard this news about Jacob, his sister's son, he rushed out to meet him. He embraced him and kissed him and brought him to his house. Jacob told Laban how he was related to him. Then Laban said to him, "You are indeed my own flesh and blood." So Jacob stayed with him for a month.
Genesis 29:2-14

When Jacob first arrives in Haran, he encounters and questions shepherds, who were waiting at a well while supervising three flocks. Since there were no sign posts in those days, Jacob asked the shepherds where they were from and they said, "Haran." Then, he asked them if they knew Laban, and they replied, "Yes." He then asked if Laban was well. They replied, "He is" and then told him that Laban's daughter Rachel was approaching the well with her sheep.

As Jacob went through this seemingly chance circumstance, his mind might have wondered back to how Isaac's servant found Rebekah (Gen 24). Isaac's servant came to Haran and also stopped at a well. There he prayed for God to lead him to the one Isaac would marry, and sure enough, God did. The first woman Isaac's servant encountered at the well was Rebekah. Similarly, Jacob encounters a beautiful woman at the well, who just happens to come from the same family.

After Jacob sees Rachel on her way, he seemingly tries to get rid of the shepherds, so he could be alone with her. He essentially says to the shepherds, who were probably shepherd boys, "It's not time to rest, water the sheep, and then go and graze." However, they replied with the fact they had to wait until all the flocks were gathered. This was probably some type of community agreement in order to have an even distribution of water.[20]

When Rachel comes, Jacob moves the stone from the well, a herculean task, and waters her flock. He ignores the three flocks that were there first. After watering Rachel's flock, he immediately kisses Rachel, weeps uncontrollably, and then introduces himself. It was normal for family members to greet one another with a kiss, but what made this strange was the fact that Jacob didn't introduce himself first. [21] He kissed her and then wept uncontrollably. Maybe, this was why he was trying to get rid of the shepherds. He knew that his emotions were about to spill out. He had been running for his life, encountered God on the way, and the Lord guided him right to his family and a woman he might potentially marry. It was too much for Jacob. He was experiencing God's sovereign leading. God would surely be with him wherever he went and complete the promises made to him.

Now certainly, God is never mentioned in this passage. Unlike with Isaac's servant, Jacob doesn't stop at the well and pray for God's guidance. However, God was clearly there—guiding his circumstances. He just "happened" to arrive at the same well that Laban's flocks drank from. Rachel, the woman he would soon marry, just "happened" to be guiding the flock to the well, at the same time he was there. This was all part of God's sovereignty, and it's the same way in our lives. It is part of how God molds our character and helps us trust him more.

Ephesians 1:11 says God "accomplishes all things according to the counsel of his will." Certainly, we see this throughout Scripture. When Moses' mother put him in the river, Pharaoh's daughter just "happened" to be at the river that day, and she felt pity for Moses and took him as her child (Ex 2). Moses just "happened" to be saved from the slaughter Pharaoh ordered by becoming part of Pharaoh's family. Obviously, there was no safer place in all of Egypt. Then Pharaoh's daughter just "happened" to hire Moses' real mother to breast feed him. Similarly, when the king of Persia had set a decree for the genocide of the Jews, it just so "happened" that the woman he married was a Jew named Esther. She eventually helps save the Jews and empower them to take vengeance on their enemies. In addition, when Ruth, the Moabitess, left her home and family to come to Israel, she just "happened" to pick grain in a relative's field, who eventually marries her and cares for both Ruth and her mother-in-law.

God sovereignly guides the circumstances of his people for his glory and their character development. As part of Jacob's training process, he was experiencing this. It is very easy to see why Jacob burst into tears—he was overwhelmed with the sovereignty of God. The one who controls all things was guiding his life and working all things for his good.

Again, God does the same with us. As imperfect as they may seem, the city we live in, the family we were born into, the school that we attended, and the job that we work at, are all part of God's beautiful tapestry for our lives. In Psalm 139:16, David said: "Your eyes saw me when I was inside the womb. All the days ordained for me were recorded in your scroll before one of them came into existence." There are no chance happenings for God's people.

God uses the good, the bad, the mundane, the great, and the supernatural to shape his people. All are meant to draw us to himself and help us trust him more. Don't miss God's sovereign hand over your circumstances! Let them teach, shape, and encourage you!

Application Question: Share a time when you experienced God's providence over your circumstances in a special way. In what ways did God's providence affect you? How is God currently molding you through your circumstances?

In God's Boot Camp, He Equips Believers Through Serving

When Jacob explained to Rachel that he was a relative of her father and the son of Rebekah, she ran and told her father. When Laban

heard this news about Jacob, his sister's son, he rushed out to meet him. He embraced him and kissed him and brought him to his house. Jacob told Laban how he was related to him. Then Laban said to him, "You are indeed my own flesh and blood." So Jacob stayed with him for a month. Then Laban said to Jacob, "Should you work for me for nothing because you are my relative? Tell me what your wages should be." (Now Laban had two daughters; the older one was named Leah, and the younger one Rachel. Leah's eyes were tender, but Rachel had a lovely figure and beautiful appearance.) Since Jacob had fallen in love with Rachel, he said, "I'll serve you seven years in exchange for your younger daughter Rachel." Laban replied, "I'd rather give her to you than to another man. Stay with me." So Jacob worked for seven years to acquire Rachel. But they seemed like only a few days to him because his love for her was so great.
Genesis 29:12-20

After Jacob shares with Rachel about God's favor, she runs to tell her father, Laban. Laban comes, kisses Jacob, and then brings him to his house. There Jacobs shares his story.

How much did Jacob share? Did he share about his deception of Isaac or how he met with God at Bethel? It's very possible that Jacob told him everything. Since Jacob was wealthy, it would be very strange for him to come alone and without money, especially if he was looking for a wife. So most likely, Jacob shared the whole story with Laban, and Laban became convinced that he was family. Laban replies, "You are indeed my own flesh and blood" (v. 14).

After Jacob had stayed a month, Laban said, "Should you work for me for nothing because you are my relative? Tell me what your wages should be" (v. 15). It is not clear if Jacob had been working already or not. It was customary for people to show hospitality for a few days, but a month was a long time.[22] If Jacob was not working, Laban was saying, "Sorry, you are not going to free-load forever! You must work!" If Jacob had been working, Laban, being a shrewd businessman, was trying to guarantee that Jacob continued working by making a contract with him. Jacob, also a shrewd business man, asked to marry Rachel in exchange for seven years of work. The going dowry price was three to four years, so Jacob essentially offers a double dowry, and Laban agrees.[23] Little did Jacob know that he would work for not only seven years, but fourteen years, during which he would earn two wives, plus room and board. He would work another six years after that, earning a regular wage—twenty years in total.

At this stage of God's boot camp, Jacob was learning how to serve, and not just serve, but work hard at serving. Before this time, Jacob had probably never worked hard. He was the son of a large estate owner. Surely, he had worked before, but he typically had people work for him. Jacob knew how to be served but didn't really know how to serve others—his life was about himself. This is what God was going to change in boot camp.

Servanthood is an important lesson that God instills in his trainees. It must be remembered that Moses served sheep for forty years. Joseph was a servant and prisoner for thirteen years. David cared for a tiny flock. In fact, Scripture says that when Christ came to the earth, he took the form of a slave (Phil 2:7)—not a master nor a king. Christ did not come to be served but to serve others (Matt 20:28). Therefore, those who will be like him must learn to serve as well. It is a natural work of the flesh to desire to be served and exalted. It is a work of the Spirit to humble oneself and desire for others to be exalted. John the Baptist said that he must decrease while Christ increased (John 3:30). John was simply a servant seeking for his master to be glorified.

In the same way, God prepares those he uses greatly by teaching them how to humbly serve others. Their service, at least initially, is often humble. It may be stacking chairs, doing paperwork, serving children, or doing some behind the scenes work. Sometimes, his people struggle with shock at the humble positions God places them in, but those positions contain great lessons for preparing his people for more. For it is only when we are faithful with little that God makes us faithful over much (cf. Lk 16:10, Matt 25:23).

Application Question: Why is serving others such an important lesson in God's boot camp?

1.   Through serving, we develop the heart and ethic of a servant.

Serving God is often a thankless job. It often doesn't come with praise, adoration, or a high salary; in fact, it often comes with criticism and low wages, if any. The very congregation that Paul founded in Corinth doubted his apostleship. He wrote a whole letter to correct the Corinthians and defend himself in 2 Corinthians. Similarly, while Paul was imprisoned in Rome, people were preaching the gospel out of spite towards him—trying to make his situation worse (Phil 1:17).

This will be true for us as well. Unless, we learn to be servants, we will find ourselves disillusioned in the service of Christ. Consider that the disciples Christ served intimately for three years, eventually denied and betrayed him. The Jews, who Christ sacrificed for and preached to, eventually killed him. Being a servant is a hard job. Everybody likes the concept of serving, but nobody really likes being treated like a servant. It is easy to serve others when thanked, appreciated, and even compensated. But in this stage of God's kingdom, it isn't always like that. In fact, it's often the opposite.

A real servant serves to obey his authorities and bless others. No praise is needed; faithfulness to the Master is enough. If God is going to use us greatly, he must develop the heart and ethic of a servant in us.

70

2. Through serving, we are prepared and promoted to leading others.

The greatest leaders were typically the greatest followers. Only through faithfully following others, do we learn how to treat and motivate those who will eventually follow us. As mentioned, as we're faithful with little, God will make us faithful over much. Elisha washed the hands of Elijah, as his servant, before eventually taking his place (2 Kings 3:11). Nehemiah was a cup bearer to the king of Persia before he was the governor of Israel. Christ was a carpenter before he began his ministry. Now God has given him a name above all names, at which every knee will bow (Phil 2:6-11). God develops great leaders in the classroom of service.

Are you willing to serve others?

Application Question: What are some characteristics of good servants? Why is it important to learn how to serve before being placed into areas of leadership? What makes serving others difficult? In what ways is God calling you to humbly serve your church or community?

In God's Boot Camp, He Equips Believers Through Difficult Relationships

Finally Jacob said to Laban, "Give me my wife, for my time of service is up. I want to have marital relations with her." So Laban invited all the people of that place and prepared a feast. In the evening he brought his daughter Leah to Jacob, and Jacob had marital relations with her. (Laban gave his female servant Zilpah to his daughter Leah to be her servant.) In the morning Jacob discovered it was Leah! So Jacob said to Laban, "What in the world have you done to me! Didn't I work for you in exchange for Rachel? Why have you tricked me?" "It is not our custom here," Laban replied, "to give the younger daughter in marriage before the firstborn. Complete my older daughter's bridal week. Then we will give you the younger one too, in exchange for seven more years of work." Jacob did as Laban said. When Jacob completed Leah's bridal week, Laban gave him his daughter Rachel to be his wife. (Laban gave his female servant Bilhah to his daughter Rachel to be her servant.) Jacob had marital relations with Rachel as well. He loved Rachel more than Leah, so he worked for Laban for seven more years. Genesis 29:21-30

Jacob worked for seven years for Rachel, but to him it only felt like a few days, because he loved her so much. Then, when it was time to marry, he approached

71

Laban and said, "Give me my wife for my time of service is up" (v. 21). The fact that there was no "please," or other pleasantries, implies that Laban was in no hurry to hand Rachel over—maybe he was even trying to delay it. However, Laban agrees and prepares a marriage feast. In the evening, though, Laban brought Leah to Jacob instead of Rachel. In the morning, after having relations with her, Jacob was shocked. He had been deceived by Laban and Leah.

How could Jacob not know it was Rachel? Well, similar to Jacob's deception of Isaac, Leah probably wore Rachel's clothes and perfume. It was dark, which made it difficult to see, and maybe Jacob had too much to drink at the celebration. Either way, Jacob had been hoodwinked. When Jacob approached Laban about this, Laban replied that it was not part of their custom to wed the youngest before the oldest. He told Jacob after fulfilling the marital week, he could then marry Rachel. In those days, the marital celebration lasted seven days. The first day was the banquet and the consummation of the marriage, and then the following six days, the married couple was treated as a king and queen. After that week, Jacob received Rachel but then had to work another seven years. Later the narrative tells us that after finishing those seven years, Jacob worked another six years, and throughout it, Laban changed Jacob's wages several times. Eventually, both Jacob and his wives got so tired of Laban, they ran away in the middle of the night (Gen 31).

It must be noted that this is not uncommon in God's boot camp. He often trains us through difficult relationships. When God called David to be king, he spent years in the service of King Saul, who was jealous of him and constantly tried to kill him. Eventually, David ran away. However, even while on the run, David always honored the king—calling him God's anointed. He even executed the man that confessed to murdering Saul. God used Saul as sand paper on David's life—smoothing out the rough edges. God will occasionally bring these people into our lives, as well. They might be a mom, a dad, a spouse, a sibling, a boss, a co-worker, a friend, etc. Our job is to love, honor, and serve them even as Jacob did with Laban, and as David did with Saul. We must love and honor them, even when they don't love and honor us.

It must be remembered that God even placed Judas among Christ's disciples. Though Judas was a devil and a thief, Christ still loved him and gave him chances to repent. Even amongst the church, God allows weeds to be planted and grow among the wheat. They will stay until the time of harvest, when the angels will throw them into the fire and take the wheat into the kingdom (Matt 13:36-43). The weeds have a purpose in God's kingdom. God uses them to cultivate the character of the wheat. He develops in his saints, not only humility, but also all the fruits of the Spirit—patience, love, perseverance, self-control, joy, etc. One can't learn patience without having difficult people in one's life. We must make sure we respond the right way to these people. If we respond the right way, God will bless us—we will grow and become more useful to him. If we treat them the wrong way, God will discipline us, and we will repeat the test.

Steve Cole said this about our response to difficult people:

Don't run from the difficult people in your life until God gives you the okay. If you're married to the difficult person, God isn't giving the okay! But with Jacob, the day came when God told him to leave Laban and return to Canaan. Then it was okay. Before then, Jacob would have been wrong to run. We all tend to run from the difficult people God puts in our lives to shape us. A teenager gets married to escape her difficult parents. Guess what? She marries a difficult husband! Or a teenager is fed up with his parents' rules, so he joins the army. I've never been able to figure out that one! If you've got a difficult person in your life, rather than complaining about him and running from him, ask yourself what God is trying to teach you about yourself through this person.[24]

There may be a time to separate from them; however, we should seek the Lord's guidance to discern when to do so. Until then, we must learn the lessons God wants to teach us through them—even if it is only perseverance. Perseverance leads to character and character leads to hope in God (Rom 5:3-4). Even the difficult person is part of God's perfect work in our lives.

Application Question: In what ways has God used difficult relationships to help you grow and trust in God more? How should we respond in these difficult relationships, so that we may grow and that God may be pleased? How do we discern when it's time to cut off a relationship or step away from it?

In God's Boot Camp, He Equips Believers Through Experiencing Sin's Consequences

Finally Jacob said to Laban, "Give me my wife, for my time of service is up. I want to have marital relations with her." So Laban invited all the people of that place and prepared a feast. In the evening he brought his daughter Leah to Jacob, and Jacob had marital relations with her. (Laban gave his female servant Zilpah to his daughter Leah to be her servant.) In the morning Jacob discovered it was Leah! So Jacob said to Laban, "What in the world have you done to me! Didn't I work for you in exchange for Rachel? Why have you tricked me?" "It is not our custom here," Laban replied, "to give the younger daughter in marriage before the firstborn. Complete my older daughter's bridal week. Then we will give you the younger one too, in exchange for seven more years of work." Jacob did as Laban said. When Jacob completed Leah's bridal week, Laban gave him his daughter Rachel to be his wife. (Laban gave his female servant Bilhah to his daughter Rachel to be her servant.) Jacob had marital relations with Rachel as well. He loved Rachel more than Leah, so he worked for Laban for seven more years. Genesis 29:21-30

As mentioned, after Jacob works for seven years for Rachel, Laban initially only gives him Leah and therefore tricks Jacob into working another seven years for Rachel. The parallels to Jacob's deception of Isaac are hard to miss: Jacob was encouraged to deceive his father by his mother, Rebekah; Leah was encouraged to deceive Jacob by her father, Laban. Jacob tricked his father, Isaac; Jacob was tricked by his father-in-law, Laban. Jacob tricked his blind father; Jacob was tricked by Leah in the dark. Jacob swindled the firstborn's birthright; Jacob was prohibited from marrying Rachel because of the firstborn's rights. Jacob was reaping the consequences of his sin.

Scripture clearly teaches this as a universal principle. Galatians 6:7-8 says:

Do not be deceived. God will not be made a fool. For a person will reap what he sows, because the person who sows to his own flesh will reap corruption from the flesh, but the one who sows to the Spirit will reap eternal life from the Spirit.

What a person sows, he will reap. Now this doesn't mean that God doesn't forgive us. He does. He forgave us judicially at the cross in Christ (Rom 5:1), and he forgives us from a familial stand point when we confess our sins (1 John 1:9). However, most times, though God forgives us, he doesn't remove the consequences of our sin. They remain as a warning to remind us to never compromise again. When David committed adultery with Bathsheba and murdered her husband, God said that David was forgiven and that he would not die, which was the civil consequence both for murder and adultery. But, because of David's evil acts, the sword would never depart from his household. (1) First, his baby through Bathsheba would die. (2) His son Absalom would kill his brother, who previously raped Absalom's sister. (3) Later, Absalom tried to kill his father, David. There were many consequences to David's private sin—most of them were public. Every time David experienced the consequences of his sin, it reminded him that a person will reap what he sows. It was a constant reminder to guard himself because compromise ultimately leads to destruction.

God does the same with us. Yes, he forgives us; but sometimes, he allows us to experience the consequences of our cheating, lying, gossiping, lust, etc. The consequences ultimately remind us to never go down that path again, and they draw us near God, so we will not succumb to temptation again.

In Psalm 119:67, David said: "Before I was afflicted I used to stray off, but now I keep your instructions." Proverbs 13:15 (KJV) says, "Good understanding giveth favor: but the way of transgressors is hard." Jacob's way was hard—it was the consequence of his sin. When Israel didn't believe God and failed to enter the promised land, their way was hard. They spent forty years in the wilderness, where most of them died. Certainly, God can redeem our hard paths and even shorten them, but we must be faithful in them to experience his grace.

When Jacob met Laban, the deceiver met his match. Jacob experienced what he had done to his father, and the consequences ultimately lasted a lifetime. Often God allows us to experience the consequences of our sin to train us as well. The seeds we sow will bear fruit—either to life or death.

Application Question: In what ways have you experienced the negative aspects of reaping what you sowed? How did the consequences change you? In what ways have you experienced God's grace, by not experiencing the full consequences of what you deserved?

In God's Boot Camp, He Equips Believers Through Experiencing God's Grace

Throughout this whole ugly process, God's grace shines through, even though we never see Jacob seeking the Lord. When Isaac's servant went looking for a wife for his master, he began with prayer and then God confirmed who Isaac should marry (Gen 24). We don't see Jacob praying about marrying Rachel. We don't see him pray about whether he should accept a polygamous marriage with Leah. Later, Jacob also marries Rachel's handmaid to produce more children, and then Leah's handmaid to do the same. Ultimately, Jacob had thirteen children, including a daughter Dinah, and four wives. Though his marriages were built on deception instead of truth, polygamy instead of monogamy, prayerlessness instead of prayerfulness, God blessed them. From Jacob's twelve sons came the twelve tribes of Israel. While working for Laban after the fourteen years, God prospered him financially; in fact, he became wealthier than Laban (31:1). God's beautiful grace runs throughout this ugly narrative.

Even with Leah specifically, we see God's unmerited favor. Verse 17 says her eyes were tender, either meaning that she had bad eyesight[25] or that her eyes just weren't attractive. In the ancient east, eyes with a sparkle or glow were prized.[26] Obviously, Rachel's eyes were beautiful while Leah's weren't. The text also says that Jacob loved Rachel more than Leah (v. 30). Jacob may have loved Leah; however, his love for her was far less than for Rachel. Despite the fact that Rachel was more beautiful and loved more, God chose to especially favor Leah. Through Leah came both Judah and Levi—the kingly

75

tribe and the priestly tribe. From Judah, the messiah would ultimately come. Because of this, many commentators believe that Leah was the only one Jacob should have married.

Throughout this text, we see God's grace on the undeserving. He blesses the deceiver by using Jacob's unfortunate and ungodly circumstances for good. He also blesses the unloved by making Leah the grandmother of the messiah.

In God's boot camp, we experience grace, often over our failures and that of others. Romans 2:4 says God's kindness draws men to repentance. His mercy over our sin and light over our darkness transforms us and makes us more into his image. God vowed to fulfill his promises to Jacob (Gen 28), and therefore, God's finger-prints are seen throughout Jacob's boot camp story. They can be seen over our story as well—starting with our salvation (Eph 2:8-9) and continuing throughout our sanctification (Phil 2:12-13).

Our lives may experience times of intense darkness, but even amongst the darkness, there will be great light. Our Shepherd goes with us through the valley of shadows. His rod and staff comfort us. God's grace will never leave us because God will never leave us. Thank you, Lord, for your amazing grace! Complete the work you began in us till the day of Christ (Phil 1:6)!

Application Question: In what ways does God's kindness and grace often draw people to repentance? In what ways do people commonly take advantage of or despise God's grace? How have you experienced special times of God's grace (possibly through a person or over a circumstance), which especially helped shape your character and the direction of your life?

Conclusion

When God chooses to use somebody, like the military, he equips them in a boot camp. He aims to deliver them from selfishness to selflessness, from being unloving to being loving, from being impatient to being patient. He humbles them, so he can eventually exalt them. How does God equip his saints through his Divine boot camp?

1. In God's Boot Camp, He Equips Believers Through His Word and His Promises
2. In God's Boot Camp, He Equips Believers Through Providential Circumstances
3. In God's Boot Camp, He Equips Believers Through Serving
4. In God's Boot Camp, He Equips Believers Through Difficult Relationships

5. In God's Boot Camp, He Equips Believers Through Experiencing Sin's Consequences
6. In God's Boot Camp, He Equips Believers Through Experiencing God's Grace

Protecting Our Families from Sin and Dysfunctionality

When the LORD saw that Leah was unloved, he enabled her to become pregnant while Rachel remained childless. So Leah became pregnant and gave birth to a son. She named him Reuben, for she said, "The LORD has looked with pity on my oppressed condition. Surely my husband will love me now." She became pregnant again and had another son. She said, "Because the LORD heard that I was unloved, he gave me this one too." So she named him Simeon. She became pregnant again and had another son. She said, "Now this time my husband will show me affection, because I have given birth to three sons for him." That is why he was named Levi. She became pregnant again and had another son. She said, "This time I will praise the LORD." That is why she named him Judah. Then she stopped having children. When Rachel saw that she could not give Jacob children, she became jealous of her sister. She said to Jacob, "Give me children or I'll die!" Jacob became furious with Rachel and exclaimed, "Am I in the place of God, who has kept you from having children?" She replied, "Here is my servant Bilhah! Have sexual relations with her so that she can bear children for me and I can have a family through her." So Rachel gave him her servant Bilhah as a wife, and Jacob had marital relations with her. Bilhah became pregnant and gave Jacob a son. Then Rachel said, "God has vindicated me. He has responded to my prayer and given me a son." That is why she named him Dan. Bilhah, Rachel's servant, became pregnant again and gave Jacob another son. Then Rachel said, "I have fought a desperate struggle with my sister, but I have won." So she named him Naphtali. When Leah saw that she had stopped having children, she gave her servant Zilpah to Jacob as a wife. Soon Leah's servant Zilpah gave Jacob a son. Leah said, "How fortunate!" So she named him Gad. Then Leah's servant Zilpah gave Jacob another son. Leah said, "How happy I am, for women will call me happy!" So she named him Asher. At the time of the wheat harvest Reuben went out and found some mandrake plants in a field and brought them to his mother Leah. Rachel said to Leah, "Give me some of your son's mandrakes." But Leah replied, "Wasn't it enough that you've taken away my husband? Would you take away my son's mandrakes too?" "All right," Rachel said, "he may sleep with you tonight in exchange for your son's mandrakes." When Jacob came in from the fields that evening, Leah went out to meet him and said, "You must sleep with me because I have paid for your services with my son's mandrakes." So he had marital relations with her that night. God paid attention to Leah; she became pregnant and gave Jacob a son for the fifth time. Then Leah said, "God has granted me a reward because I gave my servant to my husband as a wife." So she named him Issachar. Leah became pregnant again and gave Jacob a son for the sixth time. Then Leah said, "God has given me a good gift. Now my husband will honor me because I have given him six sons." So she named him Zebulun. After that she gave birth to a daughter and named her Dinah. Then God took note of Rachel. He paid attention to her and enabled her to become pregnant. She became pregnant and gave birth to a son. Then she said, "God has taken away my shame." She named him Joseph, saying, "May the LORD give me yet another son." Genesis 29:31- 30:24 (NET)

How can we protect our families from sin and dysfunctionality?

In this part of Jacob's narrative, he had recently married two sisters. Jacob worked seven years to marry his uncle Laban's youngest daughter, Rachel; however, on the wedding night, Laban sent his oldest daughter, Leah, to Jacob's tent without Jacob knowing. In the morning, Jacob realized that he had been deceived. After questioning Laban, Jacob struck a deal to also marry Rachel, but he would owe another seven years of work.

Therefore, after finishing Leah's bridal festivities, Jacob was also given Rachel in exchange for the labor. Unfortunately, the deal led to Leah being unloved throughout the marriage. Leah longed for Jacob to love her and believed that she could win his heart by bearing children. God saw her sorrow and gave her many children. She initially bore four boys. With the names she gave them, she showed her desperation to be loved by her husband. Out of jealousy over Leah's children, Rachel gave Jacob her handmaid, Bilhah, for him to marry and bear children through. She had two boys through Bilhah. In response, Leah did the same and had two boys through Zilpah. Then God blessed Leah with two more boys and one girl—seven overall. Eventually, God heard Rachel's prayer and gave her a son, Joseph, who would eventually save his family from a future famine, when he became second-in-command over Egypt. In Genesis 35, one more son would be born to Rachel resulting in her death. His name was Benjamin. From these twelve boys came the twelve tribes of Israel.

This story is messy. It's full of sin and discord. If these were people in covenant with God, one can only imagine how bad the pagan families were.

Sadly, this is not uncommon amongst believing families today. Though they should be full of peace and love for one another, they are often dysfunctional.

As with all the narratives in Scripture, this story is descriptive—not prescriptive. It tells us what happened—not necessarily what should have happened. Often, we are called to learn from the negative examples of Scripture's heroes. They serve as warnings that challenge us to not miss God's best for our lives. In talking about how God disciplined Israel in the wilderness, Paul said: "These things happened as examples for us, so that we will not crave evil things as they did" (1 Cor 10:6). In the same way, by studying the story of Jacob's dysfunctional family, we learn how to avoid sin and dysfunctionality in our families or future families.

Big Question: What principles can we learn about protecting our families from sin and dysfunctionality, as we consider the tragic story of Jacob's family?

To Protect Our Families, We Must Not Imitate Our Parents' Sins

> When the Lord saw that Leah was unloved, he enabled her to become pregnant while Rachel remained childless. So Leah became pregnant and gave birth to a son. She named him Reuben, for she said, "The Lord has looked with pity on my oppressed condition. Surely my husband will love me now." She became pregnant again and had another son. She said, "Because the Lord heard that I was unloved, he gave me this one too." So she named him Simeon. She became pregnant again and had another son. She said, "Now this time my husband will show me affection, because I have given birth to three sons for him." That is why he was named Levi. She became pregnant again and had another son. She said, "This time I will praise the Lord." That is why she named him Judah. Then she stopped having children. When Rachel saw that she could not give Jacob children, she became jealous of her sister. She said to Jacob, "Give me children or I'll die!" Jacob became furious with Rachel and exclaimed, "Am I in the place of God, who has kept you from having children?" She replied, "Here is my servant Bilhah! Have sexual relations with her so that she can bear children for me and I can have a family through her."
> Genesis 29:31-30:3

Since Rachel was favored, Leah felt alone and unloved. Therefore, Leah was jealous of Rachel. When Leah started having children, Rachel became jealous in response. Similar to a national arms race, these sisters had a child-race—

each child was a missile—birthed in hopes of having a competitive advantage in securing Jacob's love. It was an unhealthy and toxic home.

Unsurprisingly, this is exactly the home environment that Jacob grew up in (Gen 25, 27). His father, Isaac, favored Esau. Jacob's mother, Rebekah, favored him. When it came to who would receive the birthright, the family was divided. Isaac and Esau were on one team, and Rebekah and Jacob were on the other. Rebekah and Jacob ultimately deceived Isaac into giving Jacob the birthright. Jacob's parents showed favoritism which ultimately divided the kids. Similarly, Jacob showed favoritism which divided his wives. Eventually, he will show favoritism to his kids—favoring Rachel's oldest son, Joseph, causing the other brothers to hate him and sell him into slavery (Gen 37).

Not only does Jacob practice the sins of his parents by showing favoritism—leading to a competitive home—but he also marries multiple wives—just like his grandfather, Abraham, and his brother, Esau. In both of those situations, the polygamous marriages only led to discord in the home. Sadly, Jacob repeated the sins of his family.

These sins would ultimately cause havoc in the children's lives. As mentioned, the children would sell Joseph into slavery and lie to Jacob—saying that Joseph had died. A few of the children would also murder an entire village of people (Gen 34). Consider what F.B. Meyer said about this:

> What wonder, then, that the children grew up wild and bad? Reuben, unstable as water, excitable and passionate: Simeon, quick to obey, but quick to desperate cruelty; and Levi, a willing accomplice in his crime. When children turn out badly, and the beautiful gate of childhood does not lead to the fair temple of mature life, it is generally the fault of the home-training; and it is more often the result of what they see than of what they are taught. Whatever Jacob may have been—and I fear that his example was none of the best,—yet the impressions received in the women's tents, of high words and evil passion, would be enough to ruin any child. Beware how you act at home. Remember what keen little eyes are watching you; and with what absolute mimicry they will repeat what they see.[27]

Sadly, this is often true for us as well. None of us have perfect parents or families, and we tend to adopt the sins they practiced. In Exodus 20:5-6, God said:

> You shall not bow down to them or serve them, for I, the LORD, your God, am a jealous God, responding to the transgression of fathers by dealing with children to the third and fourth generations of those who reject me, and showing covenant faithfulness to a thousand generations of those who love me and keep my commandments.

God does not punish us for our family's sins; however, the sins of the parents tend to show up for three to four generations. This shows how difficult it is to break family sins. When there is drunkenness, divorce, neglect of the children or the spouse, abuse, materialism, witchcraft, etc., these tend to be passed from generation to generation. Positively, family faithfulness is even harder to break, as it lasts for thousands of generations.

Often when going through pre-marital counseling, couples are called to evaluate their parents' marriages and parenting to identify both the good and the bad. This is done so they can decide what they will continue and what they will not. Many people never critically evaluate their family's short-comings and therefore simply repeat them.

What family sins have been passed down to us? What sins are we practicing, which we must stop so they don't hinder the blessings of future generations?

Application Question: What are your family's short-comings/generational sins? How have you seen these show up in your life? How are you trying to break them? In what ways have you experienced family blessings, which have been passed down?

To Protect Our Families, We Must Foster Male Spiritual Leadership

> When the LORD saw that Leah was unloved, he enabled her to become pregnant while Rachel remained childless... She replied, "Here is my servant Bilhah! Have sexual relations with her so that she can bear children for me and I can have a family through her." So Rachel gave him her servant Bilhah as a wife, and Jacob had marital relations with her... But Leah replied, "Wasn't it enough that you've taken away my husband? Would you take away my son's mandrakes too?" "All right," Rachel said, "he may sleep with you tonight in exchange for your son's mandrakes."
> Genesis 29:31, 30:3-4, 15

Yes, the sins of the parents showed up in Jacob's family; however, Jacob allowed them to. First, when Laban tricks Jacob, he doesn't pray about whether he should accept this polygamous marriage. He just goes along with it in order to marry Rachel. Then after accepting Leah, he neglects her. Throughout the narrative, it is clear that the wives are running the home. When Rachel wants him to marry her servant, Jacob just obeys. When Leah wants the same, he just goes along with it. When Rachel finds out that Leah has mandrakes, which were

83

considered an ancient aphrodisiac, she asks Leah for some. Leah replies, "Wasn't it enough that you've taken away my husband?" It seems that, at this point, Rachel wouldn't allow Jacob to sleep with Leah. After Leah gives Rachel mandrakes, she allows it. Throughout this narrative, Jacob is the passive male. He is not a spiritual leader at all, which only leads to more sin and dysfunction in the family.

Ephesians 5:22-27 says this about marriage and, specifically, the husband's role:

> Wives, submit to your husbands as to the Lord, because the husband is the head of the wife as also Christ is the head of the church—he himself being the savior of the body. But as the church submits to Christ, so also wives should submit to their husbands in everything. Husbands, love your wives just as Christ loved the church and gave himself for her to sanctify her by cleansing her with the washing of the water by the word, so that he may present the church to himself as glorious—not having a stain or wrinkle, or any such blemish, but holy and blameless.

The husband is to be the spiritual leader of the home. He is called to represent Christ and the wife is called to represent the church. As Christ, the husband is called to love his wife. He should lovingly serve her—not neglect her. He should sacrifice for her, even as Christ died for the church. This means he should sacrifice things like work, friendships, and entertainment in order to minister to his wife. Sadly, many husbands put work, friendships, and entertainment before their wives. Therefore, many wives feel unloved and neglected like Leah. The husband is to love his wife spiritually by washing her with the Word—getting his wife involved in a Bible preaching church, leading family devotions, correcting her when she goes against the Word. All of these things Jacob doesn't do. He doesn't correct Rachel and Leah when they want to bring more wives into the family. His passivity leads to further sin and dysfunction. This is exactly what Adam did at the fall. Scripture seems to indicate that Adam was right next to Eve, as she was tempted by Satan. He doesn't step on Satan's head like Christ eventually did. He doesn't die for his wife, after she sinned, as Christ did for his bride, the church. Instead, Adam passively followed her—leading the world, which was under his leadership, into sin and dysfunction.

Like Adam, Jacob was the stereotypical passive male that wouldn't lead his family—opening the door to drastic consequences.

Application Question: How should we apply the need to foster male, spiritual leadership in the family?

1. *For wives with passive husbands, they shouldn't criticize or belittle them.* They should gently encourage and pray for them. They should help them lead, even by allowing them to make little decisions like what movie to watch or where to go to dinner. As husbands feel comfortable making little decisions, they will feel confident making bigger decisions. When they fail in certain areas, again, wives should avoid criticism, as it will only discourage and push them away. Wives should pray for them, encourage them, and wait on God to change their hearts. Remember, we don't change people, God does.

2. *For husbands who have wives who won't allow them to lead, they should not passively relinquish their role.* We must remember that Scripture doesn't call for husbands to make their wives submit. Abusive male leadership is not biblical—it is a result of sin. Scripture commands husbands to love their wives. As husbands love them like Christ—personally, sacrificially, spiritually, and patiently—eventually, God may change their wives' hearts. With that said, husbands should not passively accept every desire of their wives, like Jacob, especially when those desires are sinful. Passivity may bring short-term peace, but it brings long-term disaster. Again, we can't change people, only God can. We can only love them, pray for them, and be patient with them.

3. *With children, parents must practice biblical gender roles in the family and teach them to eventually do the same.* If parents don't do this, the world will indoctrinate their children and lead them into unbiblical models, like Jacob's, which ultimately lead to dysfunctional families.

Application Question: In what ways have you seen or experienced healthy male spiritual leadership in the home, church, or other places that positively affected you? What are characteristics of it? How have you seen the abuse of male leadership? What are negative effects of bad male leadership, as experienced from a father, husband, or even a pastor?

To Protect Our Families, We Must Pursue Fulfillment in God Alone

When the LORD saw that Leah was unloved, he enabled her to become pregnant while Rachel remained childless. So Leah became pregnant and gave birth to a son. She named him Reuben, for she said, "The LORD has looked with pity on my oppressed condition. Surely my husband will love me now." She became pregnant again and had

another son. She said, "Because the LORD heard that I was unloved, he gave me this one too." So she named him Simeon. She became pregnant again and had another son. She said, "Now this time my husband will show me affection, because I have given birth to three sons for him." That is why he was named Levi. She became pregnant again and had another son. She said, "This time I will praise the LORD." That is why she named him Judah. Then she stopped having children. When Rachel saw that she could not give Jacob children, she became jealous of her sister. She said to Jacob, "Give me children or I'll die!" Jacob became furious with Rachel and exclaimed, "Am I in the place of God, who has kept you from having children?" She replied, "Here is my servant Bilhah! Have sexual relations with her so that she can bear children for me and I can have a family through her."
Genesis 29:31-30:3

Clearly, one of the sources of discord in Jacob's home was the fact that each person was pursuing fulfillment in something other than God, which would never satisfy. Leah pursued her purpose in being loved. In each child's name, one can discern her desperation to be loved by Jacob. Reuben meant "See, a son." She said, "Surely my husband will love me now" (29:32). The second child she named Simeon, which means "hearing." After naming him, she responded, "Because the Lord heard that I was unloved, he gave me this one too" (29:33). The third son she named Levi, which means "attached." In response, she said, "Now this time my husband will show affection to me" (29:34). With the fourth son, Leah seems to briefly find her contentment in God, whether Jacob loves her or not. Judah means "praise." She says, "This time I will praise the Lord" (29:35). Essentially, she says, "Instead of complaining about my difficulties, I will thank God for my blessings."[28] However, after Rachel starts having children, Leah becomes jealous again and pursues children as her purpose, independent from God, causing further dysfunction.

Similarly, Rachel, instead of seeking fulfillment and purpose in her relationship with God, sought it in becoming a mother. In those days, being a mother was seen as the primary purpose of a wife. Children provided labor, protection, and retirement. Therefore, to be barren was extremely shameful. When she couldn't have children, she said to Jacob, "Give me children or I'll die!" (30:1). In response, Jacob became furious and said, "Am I in the place of God, who has kept you from having children?" (30:2). Then, Rachel commanded Jacob to marry her servant, Bilhah, in order to have children through her. This would be an official adoption. In ancient Babylon, this stipulation was often put into marriage contracts. If the wife could not bear children, she would provide her husband with a woman who could.[29] Finally, with Jacob, his fulfillment was found in pleasing Rachel—not pleasing God.

86

With all three, their dysfunctionality was largely a result of God not being their source of fulfillment. When God is not the source of our fulfillment, something or somebody else will be—leading to frustration and discord. Only God can truly make us happy. If we think our spouses will make us happy, we're setting unhealthy expectations, which will keep us constantly frustrated with them. These expectations will also keep our spouses constantly frustrated with us, because they'll always feel like they're failing us. Nobody can fill the place in our hearts that only God can fill. If we rely on friends, work, family, or even the church to make us happy or fulfilled, we will constantly be frustrated. As with Rachel, this frustration will often anger and push those we love away from us instead of drawing them near. Her expectations were misplaced and therefore unfulfilled. Even children couldn't satisfy her, she would just want more. When she finally had a son, she named him Joseph, which means, "May the LORD give me yet another son"—nothing could satisfy her.

Many marriages, and relationships in general, are dysfunctional for this very reason. Children, the husband or wife, the boyfriend or girlfriend, the friend, co-worker, etc., are expected to bring satisfaction. When they don't, it leads to frustration and anger. In response, the unfulfilled person takes out his or her anger on others or even God. In order to truly be satisfied in marriage, friendships, family, or work, we must find our satisfaction and purpose in God. He is the only one who can make us happy and satisfied—not people, things, or circumstances. Our joy and purpose must be in the Lord. Anything else will only lead to discouragement and frustration—resulting in discord.

Like the Psalmist, we must be able to say, "Even if my father and mother abandoned me, the LORD would take me in" (27:10). If God gives me a spouse or not, kids or not, a job or not, a degree or not, if all my friends, family, and co-workers forsake me, I will trust the Lord. He is all that matters. God must be our primary purpose and passion.

Application Question: How can we keep our gifts—like our spouses, friends, or work—in their proper place?

1. *We must prioritize God.* When we constantly abide in God through his Word, prayer, fellowship, etc., it will keep our hearts from idolizing his gifts and living in a constant state of frustration and dissatisfaction. When we're constantly angry and dissatisfied, it probably means our gifts are in the wrong place in our heart. Hebrews 13:5 says, "Your conduct must be free from the love of money and you must be content with what you have, for he has said, 'I will never leave you and I will never abandon you.'" We can only be free of over-loving our gifts if we put God first and find our contentment in him.

2. *We must hold God's gifts with an open hand.* If we don't hold them with an open hand, we will tend to squeeze them too tightly and possibly break them. We must remember our spouses are not ours, they are God's. Our children are not ours, they are, first of all, God's. Our jobs, studies, hobbies, and relationships are all God's gifts, which we are called to steward. We are called to cultivate them for God's purpose. When we hold our gifts with an open hand, it will help keep us from hurting or destroying them and/or hurting or destroying ourselves.

3. *We must give God thanks for his gifts.* This will prevent us from focusing on what we don't have or on the imperfection of our gifts. Unthankfulness often leads to frustration, dissatisfaction, and eventually discord. God's gifts are not meant to satisfy us, but they are meant to make us think of God and give him thanks. Even our gifts' imperfections are meant to help us rely on God more and not seek our ultimate satisfaction in them.

Application Question: In what ways are you tempted to seek fulfillment outside of God? How have you seen or experienced dissatisfaction, anger, and discord, when seeking fulfillment outside of God? How can placing unhealthy expectations on people—such as expectations that belong only to God, like them being perfect (or nearly perfect)—hurt our relationships?

To Protect Our Families, We Must Remember God Ultimately Uses the Bad for Our Good

> When the LORD saw that Leah was unloved, he enabled her to become pregnant while Rachel remained childless... Then God took note of Rachel. He paid attention to her and enabled her to become pregnant. She became pregnant and gave birth to a son. Then she said, "God has taken away my shame." She named him Joseph, saying, "May the LORD give me yet another son."
> Genesis 29:31, 30:22-24

As bad as this narrative is, God's grace runs throughout like a silver lining. Because Leah was unloved, God blessed her. No doubt, she deceived Jacob and, in one sense, deserved to be unloved. For a while, Jacob probably had a difficult time even looking at her, after what she had done. However, God saw her humiliation and shame and blessed her. He gave her seven children; six of them were boys. Two of these boys, Levi and Judah, would become the priestly tribe and the kingly tribe of Israel. Moses and Aaron would come through Levi.

David, Solomon, and Christ would come through Judah. Though deceptive, "unattractive," and broken, God blessed the world through Leah.

With Rachel, she was probably prideful because of her beauty and the fact that her husband worked fourteen years for her. After God humbled Rachel by not allowing her to bear children, he eventually exalted her. He enabled her to give birth to Joseph, who would become a blessing to Egypt and one day save the family during a famine. Eventually, Rachel would also give birth to Benjamin.

This story is a mess, and maybe Moses was sharing this with Israel, while they were in the wilderness, to show them how undeserving they were of God's grace. Their family background was dysfunctional; however, God took their humble beginnings and made them into a great nation—a nation that numbered over two million while enslaved in Egypt.

In the same way, if we are going to protect our family, our lives, and our hearts, we must remember God's grace. God works all things to the good of those who love the Lord (Rom 8:28). He takes our messy family backgrounds, our failures, the failure of others, and uses them for the good. Certainly, there are consequences to sin. We see these throughout this narrative; however, none of our sins or consequences are too big for God. God took the worst thing in the world, the murder of his son, and made it the best thing in the world.

If we remember God's grace, it will keep us from discouragement, hopelessness, and even fighting for our rights, as though God won't defend us. God will defend us; he will work all things out for our good. That's how amazing God is. That's what we see in this family mess. We see God take a dysfunctional family and raise a nation from them, and a messiah, who will bless the world. This messiah, Jesus, eventually dies for the sins of the world, so that all who believe in him will ultimately be saved (John 3:16).

If we don't remember God's grace, especially in difficult times, we will become hopeless and discouraged, leading to more sin, worse consequences, and delayed blessings. But, if we remember God's grace, we will see God's blessing through eyes of faith—helping us respond better, both to God and others, while going through the varied circumstances of our lives, which are all meant for our good.

Are you seeing your trials, failures, and the failures of others with eyes of faith? Where sin abounds, surely, God's grace will abound even more (cf. Rom 5:20). Thank you, Lord!

Application Question: Share a story about how God used your failures or the failures of others for your good. How does God's sovereignty and grace encourage you, as you wrestle with sin and its effects?

Conclusion

How should we protect our families from sin and dysfunctionality?

1. To Protect Our Families, We Must Not Imitate Our Parents' Sins
2. To Protect Our Families, We Must Foster Male Spiritual Leadership
3. To Protect Our Families, We Must Pursue Fulfillment in God Alone
4. To Protect Our Families, We Must Remember God Ultimately Uses the Bad for Our Good

Growing as Kingdom Workers

After Rachel had given birth to Joseph, Jacob said to Laban, "Send me on my way so that I can go home to my own country. Let me take my wives and my children whom I have acquired by working for you. Then I'll depart, because you know how hard I've worked for you." But Laban said to him, "If I have found favor in your sight, please stay here, for I have learned by divination that the LORD has blessed me on account of you." He added, "Just name your wages—I'll pay whatever you want." "You know how I have worked for you," Jacob replied, "and how well your livestock have fared under my care. Indeed, you had little before I arrived, but now your possessions have increased many times over. The LORD has blessed you wherever I worked. But now, how long must it be before I do something for my own family too?" So Laban asked, "What should I give you?" "You don't need to give me a thing," Jacob replied, "but if you agree to this one condition, I will continue to care for your flocks and protect them: Let me walk among all your flocks today and remove from them every speckled or spotted sheep, every dark-colored lamb, and the spotted or speckled goats. These animals will be my wages. My integrity will testify for me later on. When you come to verify that I've taken only the wages we agreed on, if I have in my possession any goat that is not speckled or spotted or any sheep that is not dark-colored, it will be considered stolen." "Agreed!" said Laban, "It will be as you say." So that day Laban removed the male goats that were streaked or spotted, all the female goats that were speckled or spotted (all that had any white on them), and all the dark-colored lambs, and put them in the care of his sons. Then he separated them from Jacob by a three-day journey, while Jacob was taking care of the rest of Laban's flocks. But Jacob took fresh-cut branches from poplar, almond, and plane trees. He made white streaks by peeling them, making the white inner wood in the branches visible. Then he set up the peeled branches in all the watering troughs where the flocks came to drink. He set up the branches in front of the flocks when they were in heat and came to drink. When the sheep mated in front of the branches, they gave birth to young that were streaked or speckled or spotted. Jacob removed these lambs, but he made the rest of the flock face the streaked and

completely dark-colored animals in Laban's flock. So he made separate flocks for himself and did not mix them with Laban's flocks. When the stronger females were in heat, Jacob would set up the branches in the troughs in front of the flock, so they would mate near the branches. But if the animals were weaker, he did not set the branches there. So the weaker animals ended up belonging to Laban and the stronger animals to Jacob. In this way Jacob became extremely prosperous. He owned large flocks, male and female servants, camels, and donkeys.
Genesis 30:25-43 (NET)

How can we grow as kingdom workers—those who expand God's kingdom through their vocations?

After creation, God not only gave humanity a call to be fruitful and multiply but also to work. They were to tend the garden, care for the animals, and rule over the earth. God said to them, "Fill the earth and subdue it!" (Gen 1:28). Often, we tend to think of work with a negative connotation, as though it is a result of the fall, but that is not true. Work was originally one of the ways that humanity was called to build God's kingdom on the earth. Likewise, our call is still to build God's kingdom through work. In Luke 19, the Parable of the Minas, while the master was away, the servants were to work. When the master returned, he would reward them, based on their service, with greater opportunities to serve—overseeing cities in the coming kingdom (v. 11-27). God has called all of us to work and use the gifts and resources he has given us to build his kingdom.

Here in Genesis 30, after Jacob had twelve children (eleven boys and one girl) in seven years, he says to his father-in-law, Laban, that it was time for him to return home. In response, Laban asked him to stay and name his wages. Up to this point, Jacob had only earned two wives and room and board, but now, he would earn a profit to provide for his family long-term.

As we consider this narrative, we must remember that Jacob was not just a laborer. He was a crucial part of redemptive history. God's call was to bless him and his family in order that they would be a blessing to the nations, and this was happening in this story. God used Jacob's work to bless Laban by making him wealthy and also, more importantly, to further introduce him to Yahweh.

For most, instead of being a means to build God's kingdom, work is a way to build their own kingdom. For some, work is their "god"—it takes all of their devotion and focus. For others, it is their identity—their worth rises and falls based on their careers. For others, it is their burden—something that removes joy from their lives. However, for believers, when properly understood, it should be different. Again, work is part of God's creation mandate and a way to establish his rule and kingdom on this earth. Therefore, work is redemptive, and we see this with Jacob's work. God not only blessed Jacob but also others through his work. As we consider Jacob's work partnership with Laban, we learn something about being kingdom workers—those who build God's kingdom through their vocations.

Big Question: What principles can we discern about growing as kingdom workers from Genesis 30:25-43, where Jacob works for Laban for another six years?

As Kingdom Workers, We Must Develop a High Work-Ethic

> After Rachel had given birth to Joseph, Jacob said to Laban, "Send me on my way so that I can go home to my own country. Let me take my wives and my children whom I have acquired by working for you. Then I'll depart, because you know how hard I've worked for you." But Laban said to him, "If I have found favor in your sight, please stay here, for I have learned by divination that the LORD has blessed me on account of you." He added, "Just name your wages—I'll pay whatever you want." "You know how I have worked for you," Jacob replied, "and how well your livestock have fared under my care. Indeed, you had little before I arrived, but now your possessions have increased many times over. The LORD has blessed you wherever I worked…
> Genesis 30:25-30

Jacob had already worked fourteen years for Laban, and Laban had prospered because of it. His livestock fared well and his possessions multiplied. Jacob worked hard for Laban, and he mentioned it during their discussion. In verse 26, he said, "because you know how hard I've worked for you." Laban certainly agreed and therefore tried to secure Jacob's services for a longer period. In response, Laban said, "Just name your wages—I'll pay whatever you want" (v. 28). No reasonable price would have been too much, as Jacob was valuable. Jacob didn't always agree with Laban. In fact, Jacob probably didn't even like him, but that didn't diminish his work-ethic and that must be true for us as well. If we are going to be kingdom workers—those who expand God's kingdom through our work—we must maintain a high work-ethic as well.

Application Question: How can we maintain a high work-ethic, especially in difficult circumstances or while working with difficult people?

1. To maintain a high work-ethic, we must focus on the Lord and not people or circumstances.

For fourteen years, Jacob made no wages. He just worked for room and board and to pay off his marriage debt, which in part, he was cheated into. If he focused on those factors, he probably wouldn't have worked as hard. However, if he focused on the Lord and his promises, then he could be faithful. Jacob knew God was with him—he could see God moving. He said to Laban, "The LORD has blessed you wherever I worked" (v. 30). Jacob, to some extent, was focused on the Lord, and that no doubt motivated him.

This is true for us as well. If we only see our employer, co-workers, low wages, or difficult work environment, often we will lack motivation. Colossians 3:23-24 says, "Whatever you are doing, work at it with enthusiasm, as to the Lord and not for people, because you know that you will receive your inheritance from the Lord as the reward. Serve the Lord Christ." We keep a high work-ethic by focusing on the Lord.

2. To maintain a high work-ethic, we must be goal-oriented.

Earlier in Genesis 29, the narrator said that Jacob's first seven years were like a few days because he loved Rachel so much (v. 19). His goal was to pay her wedding debt, so he could marry her. This initial goal inspired him for fourteen years in total, as the original length was expanded because of Laban's deception. This goal helped him work hard. When Jacob negotiated this new deal, his next goal was to provide long-term for his family. This also enabled him to maintain a high work-ethic.

Likewise, as we're working, we must develop goals that inspire us. They could be short-term goals like finishing a project by lunch or long-term goals like a promotion or getting further training to open up future doors. It also might include ministry goals like witnessing to our co-workers or customers. Proverbs 21:5 says, "The plans of the diligent lead only to plenty." Proverbs 29:18 (KJV) says, "Where there is no vision, people perish." When we don't have God-given goals and plans, then many times we'll struggle with working hard. We may even feel purposeless. We need God-given goals to maintain a high work-ethic.

How is your work-ethic?

Application Question: What are some of your work goals that motivate you? How would you rate your work-ethic on a scale of 1-10 and why? How do you maintain a high work-ethic, especially when working in less than ideal conditions? What factors tend to diminish your work-ethic?

As Kingdom Workers, We Must Work Missionally

But Laban said to him, "If I have found favor in your sight, please stay here, for I have learned by divination that the LORD has blessed me on account of you." He added, "Just name your wages—I'll pay whatever you want." "You know how I have worked for you," Jacob replied, "and how well your livestock have fared under my care. Indeed, you had little before I arrived, but now your possessions have increased many times over. The LORD has blessed you wherever I worked. But now, how long must it be before I do something for my own family too?"
Genesis 30:27-30

It must be noticed that over Jacob's previous fourteen years of work, Laban experienced God's blessing and came to know him in a deeper way. After Jacob asked for permission to leave, Laban said this, "If I have found favor in your sight, please stay here, for I have learned by divination that the LORD has blessed me on account of you." The name "LORD," which Laban used, is God's covenant name Yahweh. Laban knew God more and experienced his favor because of Jacob's dedicated labor.

Similarly, Nebuchadnezzar came to know God more through the faithfulness of his workers—Shadrach, Meshach, and Abednego. Nebuchadnezzar decreed that everybody should bow to his gold statue when the music played; however, the three Hebrews would not, out of obedience to God. Because of this, Nebuchadnezzar threw them into the fire, but God saved them. Afterward, Nebuchadnezzar said this:

"Praised be the God of Shadrach, Meshach, and Abednego, who has sent forth his angel and has rescued his servants who trusted in him, ignoring the edict of the king and giving up their bodies rather than serve or pay homage to any god other than their God! I hereby decree that any people, nation, or language group that blasphemes the god of Shadrach, Meshach, or Abednego will be dismembered and his home reduced to rubble! For there exists no other god who can deliver in this way."
Daniel 3:28-29

As they faithfully served the Lord in an antagonistic environment, God delivered them in such a way that all came to know God. That should be our purpose in the workplace as well. It should be to introduce our God and his kingdom to others. We should pray for our bosses and co-workers. We should look for opportunities to serve and love them. We should also strategically seek opportunities for gospel conversations and invite those at work to church.

Similarly, Paul said this to the slaves in Crete:

95

Slaves are to be subject to their own masters in everything, to do what is wanted and not talk back, not pilfering, but showing all good faith, in order to bring credit to the teaching of God our Savior in everything.
Titus 2:9-10

Verse 10b can also be translated to "make the teaching about God our Savior attractive" (NIV). We must in every way seek to draw people to Christ through our labor. Essentially, that's what Jacob did, as he labored for God while serving Laban. Laban may have never been saved, but he knew of and honored Yahweh because of Jacob's labor. In fact, in Genesis 31:24, God spoke to Laban in a vision about not harming Jacob. Laban's employment of Jacob helped him to know and fear God more. Jacob's labor was missional. As kingdom workers, our labor must be missional as well.

Are you beautifying the teachings of Christ in your workplace?

Application Question: What are some strategic ways to be missional in the workplace? In what ways has God opened doors for you to share God's truth with others to bless them in the workplace?

As Kingdom Workers, We Must Focus on Our Families

Indeed, you had little before I arrived, but now your possessions have increased many times over. The LORD has blessed you wherever I worked. But now, how long must it be before I do something for my own family too?"
Genesis 30:30

It must be noticed that Jacob was not only working so Laban could prosper, but also working to take care of his family. Jacob had just finished a season where he gained two wives and twelve children. After focusing on building his family, Jacob was now going to focus on his financial household. When Laban asked Jacob to stay, he essentially replied, "I've taken care of you, but now I need to take care of my family."

Sadly, many Christians lack this concept of focusing on their family. Some work hard to provide for others at their company, the church, the mission field, or some social justice endeavor but are negligent in providing for their own families. Consequently, their families suffer from financial, emotional, social, or spiritual lack. In 1 Timothy 5:8, Paul said, "But if someone does not provide for his own, especially his own family, he has denied the faith and is worse than an unbeliever." In the context of 1 Timothy 5 and in Genesis 30, the focus is primarily financial; however, believers must also not neglect their families' emotional, social, and spiritual needs. In fact, those might be more important.

Believers must strike the balance between work, serving others, and serving their family. In that balance, our families must be our priority after God. The season we are in may affect what that balance looks like. For example, when children are small, they need greater attention and love from both parents. When they get older, they won't want or need the parents' attention as much. Sadly, many parents miss out on the opportunity to really love on and impart into their young children, by focusing on other endeavors like further education, work, hobbies, etc. As with Jacob, there is a season for everything. There are seasons to prepare for marriage, get married, build a family, build our financial household for retirement, etc. However, some seasons, we will never get back. Our children will only be young for a short season.

Similarly, with newly married couples, I often counsel them to cut back on outside endeavors to focus on one another during their first year of marriage. In Deuteronomy 24:5, husbands were not allowed to go to war during the first year of marriage, so they could please their wives. This, no doubt, was strategic. The first year of marriage is the year with the highest divorce rates. Sadly, many never discern the season and over commit themselves in that first year. Instead of building a strong foundation for the rest of their marriage, they build one with cracks—that doesn't weather storms well. When problems arise, those cracks from the early season of marriage re-emerge.

As kingdom workers, in all seasons, we must focus on our families. We must ask, "What might be best for them in this season?" They are our first ministry before work and church. Jacob had just finished seasons of preparing for marriage and then building his family—fourteen years all together. Now, in these next six years, he was going to focus on building his finances for the future. There is a season for everything—however, in each season, we must prioritize our family.

Application Question: Why is it so hard to find the right balance between work and family? In what ways do people commonly hurt their families by over prioritizing work, education, or some other endeavor? What are some secrets to help us prioritize our families in the various seasons?

As Kingdom Workers, We Must Work in Faith—Trusting God to Provide

> So Laban asked, "What should I give you?" "You don't need to give me a thing," Jacob replied, "but if you agree to this one condition, I will continue to care for your flocks and protect them: Let me walk among all your flocks today and remove from them every speckled or spotted sheep, every dark-colored lamb, and the spotted or speckled goats. These animals will be my wages. My integrity will testify for me later

on. When you come to verify that I've taken only the wages we agreed on, if I have in my possession any goat that is not speckled or spotted or any sheep that is not dark-colored, it will be considered stolen." "Agreed!" said Laban, "It will be as you say."
Genesis 30:31-34

When Jacob replies to Laban about compensation, he sets up a deal that was heavily weighted in Laban's favor. Traditionally, contracted shepherds received about ten to twenty percent of the flock, as well as a percentage of wool and milk products.[30] However, Jacob elects to establish a commission model. He would receive only the dark-colored sheep and the multi-colored goats. Typically, sheep are a white color, and goats are a dark, solid color. Dark sheep and multi-colored goats are rare.[31]

When Laban heard the deal, he quickly agreed. How could he not? While walking away, he probably chuckled to himself, and then when fully away from Jacob, his chuckle probably turned into a roar. This was a tremendous deal for him, but a foolish one for Jacob. However, Jacob's deal reflected his faith in God—God would provide.

Typically, in those days, when negotiations began, one would name an outrageous price, and then the other side would counter-offer. This would go back and forth until a fair price was reached. Something similar happened with Abraham when negotiating to buy a tomb for his deceased wife in Genesis 23. The Canaanite gave him an outrageous price, and in turn, Abraham was supposed to negotiate for a fair price. However, Abraham doesn't. He just accepts it. Abraham was not like the world and neither was Jacob. He was a kingdom worker who operated based on faith instead of fear—Spirit instead of flesh. Jacob had a promise that God's presence and blessing would be with him wherever he went (Gen 28:14-15). When Jacob made this deal, it was made in faith. God was going to provide for him, even if the deal didn't seem to be in his favor.

Likewise, as kingdom workers, we must work in faith—trusting God. Our job, employer, co-workers, or parents don't provide for us. Neither does the economy or the stock market. They may be the means, but God is the Provider. Therefore, we must trust him. When we focus on the means of God's provision instead of the Provider, we will often find ourselves anxious and worried.

In Matthew 6:25-33, Christ told the disciples to stop worrying about their provisions. God provided for the grass and the birds of the air. God, their Father, would provide for them as well. Instead of worrying, they were called to seek first God's kingdom and his righteousness, and all their needs would be provided (Matt 6:33). The disciples did not need to be anxious, and neither do we. We have a promise from God that he will take care of us, as we pursue him first. This doesn't mean that we don't need to work. We do. Scripture says that if we don't work, we shouldn't eat (2 Thess 3:10).

Similarly, Jacob worked, but he didn't need to be anxious about the compensation. God was going to provide. We must remember this as well. It will deliver us from running around like the world—anxiously trying to meet our needs by securing the most advantageous deals. Philippians 4:19 says, "And my God will supply your every need according to his glorious riches in Christ Jesus." God doesn't promise to meet all our wants, but he does promise to meet all our needs. Therefore, we can trust him and operate in faith rather than fear.

Application Question: In what ways do you struggle with anxiety about finances or the future? How is God calling you to trust him—concerning your future provisions? What is the proper balance between trust and being prudent when it comes to securing our provisions? Have you experienced times when God has called you to step out in faith when it comes to work or preparing for the future?

As Kingdom Workers, We Must Expect Conflict and Difficulty

> So that day Laban removed the male goats that were streaked or spotted, all the female goats that were speckled or spotted (all that had any white on them), and all the dark-colored lambs, and put them in the care of his sons. Then he separated them from Jacob by a three-day journey, while Jacob was taking care of the rest of Laban's flocks… Jacob heard that Laban's sons were complaining, "Jacob has taken everything that belonged to our father! He has gotten rich at our father's expense!" When Jacob saw the look on Laban's face, he could tell his attitude toward him had changed… You know that I've worked for your father as hard as I could, but your father has humiliated me and changed my wages ten times. But God has not permitted him to do me any harm.
> Genesis 30:35-36, 31:1-2, 6-7

After striking the deal, Laban immediately had all the dark sheep and multi-colored goats removed, taken three days journey away, and placed under the care of his sons (v. 35-36). What was happening? There are different views on this; however, it seems that, according to the deal, Jacob was supposed to go through the flock and take the unique sheep and goats as his wages (v. 32). In spite of this, Laban takes them. Most likely, Laban was already changing the rules of the deal. After removing the uniquely colored sheep and goats, Laban probably said, "Now, what's left is yours. The deal starts now!" Jacob began this new endeavor with nothing! Laban would continue to do this throughout their partnership. In Genesis 31:7, Jacob says that Laban changed his wages ten times over a six-year period. Working for Laban was difficult—he was unethical and a bully.

This was not the only difficulties Jacob experienced. In Genesis 31:1-2, Laban's sons complained about Jacob because, eventually, he became more prosperous than Laban. Since the sons received portions of Laban's estate as their inheritance, Jacob's success made them jealous and upset. Jacob not only had conflict with Laban but also with Laban's sons.

Similarly, as kingdom workers, we will often experience conflict and difficulty in the workplace. This may happen for a variety of reasons, but it will often happen for faith-based reasons, like spiritual warfare. In Daniel 6, because Daniel was an excellent worker, his government peers sought a way to get him in trouble with the king. Since they couldn't find anything unethical with him, they found something that had to do with his religion and got him thrown into the lion's den (Dan 6). Sometimes, the conflict will come because the workplace's practices are unethical, and we refuse to participate in them. Dishonesty, stealing, laziness, gossip, drunkenness, promiscuity, etc., are all not uncommon practices in the workplace. When one chooses to not participate, they will often be ridiculed, ostracized, or skipped over for promotion. This is commonly the lot of kingdom workers. They are different than the world and are frequently treated as such.

Application Question: How should we respond to conflict and difficulty in the workplace?

1. We must remember to not seek personal vengeance, as God will fight our battles.

Romans 12:19 says, "Do not avenge yourselves, dear friends, but give place to God's wrath, for it is written, 'Vengeance is mine, I will repay,' says the Lord." God promised Jacob that he would protect him (Gen 28:15). In fact, in Genesis 31, God warns Laban in a dream to not harm Jacob. God will fight our battles as well. We must remember this.

With that said, Romans 12:19 primarily refers to not seeking personal vengeance—not judicial vengeance. God has placed authorities at the workplace and within government for the purpose of maintaining justice and punishing evil. Romans 13:4, in referring to governing authorities, says, "for it is God's servant for your good. But if you do wrong, be in fear, for it does not bear the sword in vain. It is God's servant to administer retribution on the wrongdoer." Certainly, there are times when we should report evil that has been done to us to the appropriate authorities. God has placed them in positions of authority for that purpose. At other times, we will choose to just turn the other cheek, as Christ taught (Matt 5:39). We must prayerfully discern how to respond to each circumstance.

100

2. We must remember to overcome evil with good.

Romans 12:20-21 says, "Rather, if your enemy is hungry, feed him; if he is thirsty, give him a drink; for in doing this you will be heaping burning coals on his head. Do not be overcome by evil, but overcome evil with good." Though this is difficult, we must bless our enemies. We should constantly pray for them and find ways to serve them. As we do this, we allow God to work through us to help change their lives and help them grow in the knowledge of God.

3. We must remember that perseverance should be our Spirit-led response to difficulties, including difficulties at work (cf. James 1:4), until God makes it clear otherwise.

Jacob perseveres for six years in this difficult work partnership. Laban cheats him by changing his wages ten times; however, eventually God tells Jacob to leave in a dream (Gen 31). We must persevere until God clearly releases us as well.

Application Question: How have you experienced conflict, difficulty, or injustice in the workplace, especially related to your faith? How did you respond and what were the results? How has God used these work-related difficulties for your good? How is God calling you to currently trust him with work-related difficulties—sometimes relational ones—and to overcome evil with good?

As Kingdom Workers, We Must Work Skillfully

But Jacob took fresh-cut branches from poplar, almond, and plane trees. He made white streaks by peeling them, making the white inner wood in the branches visible. Then he set up the peeled branches in all the watering troughs where the flocks came to drink. He set up the branches in front of the flocks when they were in heat and came to drink. When the sheep mated in front of the branches, they gave birth to young that were streaked or speckled or spotted. Jacob removed these lambs, but he made the rest of the flock face the streaked and completely dark-colored animals in Laban's flock. So he made separate flocks for himself and did not mix them with Laban's flocks. When the stronger females were in heat, Jacob would set up the branches in the troughs in front of the flock, so they would mate near the branches. But if the animals were weaker, he did not set the branches there. So the weaker animals ended up belonging to Laban and the stronger animals to Jacob. In this way Jacob became

extremely prosperous. He owned large flocks, male and female servants, camels, and donkeys.
Genesis 30:37-43

Observation Question: What methods did Jacob use to try to influence the birthing of the flocks?

When Jacob started working for Laban, he used innovative shepherding practices in order to make the deal more advantageous to himself. These included:

1. When the flock was in heat, he set up peeled branches, which looked striped, in the watering troughs. As the sheep and goats mated while looking at the striped branches, the hope was that the visual impression would affect their seed—causing them to be striped and multi-colored (v. 37-39).

2. In addition, Jacob made the normal colored flocks face the uniquely colored ones (v. 40). Again, this was done to impress those colors upon them, so they would bear uniquely colored sheep and goats.

3. Finally, Jacob practiced selective breeding. After seeing that the impression method was working, he used the impressions when breeding the stronger flocks but not with the weaker. Therefore, his flocks became large and strong, while Laban's were weak (v. 41-43).

What was Jacob doing? He was probably using some Canaanite breeding methods to develop these unique flocks.[32] In Amos 1:1, when referring to the shepherds of Tekoa, an area in ancient Israel, the Hebrew word for "shepherd" means "speckled." For this reason, some believe those colored flocks were more desirable in Canaan, and thus, Jacob was using their breeding methods.[33]

Most commentators say there is no scientific basis for these methods and that they were just superstitious—like Rachel's belief in the mandrakes as an aphrodisiac (Gen 29:14-15). However, these types of functional practices are not uncommon among Eastern cultures. For example, with many Eastern medicinal practices, though they may work, the Western scientific community cannot completely explain why. Either way, whether superstitious or not, as Jacob used the innovative shepherding practices of that day, God blessed them. Soon after, Jacob had a dream where God spoke to him. In that dream, he saw streaked, speckled, and spotted flocks mating (Gen 31:10-13). Essentially, God was saying to him, "I gave you those flocks!" Jacob was innovative, and God blessed his innovation.

102

Similarly, wherever God places us vocationally, we must seek to become skillful masters of our trades. In order to honor God and make his teachings attractive, we must continue to develop skills in our fields by securing knowledge through reading, experimenting, asking questions, being mentored, and modeling others. We must aim to be excellent. As we do this, God will often bless the labor of our hands.

Are you still trying to grow in your vocation—whether that be as a student, educator, homemaker, businessman, minister, or in any other field? We must constantly aim for excellence, as we seek to expand God's kingdom through work.

With the making of the tabernacle, God gave Bezalel the gift of craftsmanship to make beautiful structures (Ex 31:2-5). God gave Samson strength to protect and judge Israel. God gave Solomon wisdom to rule Israel. Similarly, God made Daniel ten times wiser than all the king's wise men (Dan 1:22). God wants to empower us and give us wisdom for whatever task he has called us to. However, Scripture says, we have not because we ask not (James 4:2). It also says, if we lack wisdom, we should ask God, for he gives liberally (James 1:5). Are you asking? Are you seeking God for wisdom and empowerment to better perform your craft for his glory and kingdom?

Application Question: In what ways have you experienced God's wisdom, empowerment, and favor to do some job or hobby God called you to? How is God calling you to seek his empowerment for whatever task he currently has you doing?

As Kingdom Workers, We Must Work with Integrity

My integrity will testify for me later on. When you come to verify that I've taken only the wages we agreed on, if I have in my possession any goat that is not speckled or spotted or any sheep that is not dark-colored, it will be considered stolen." "Agreed!" said Laban, "It will be as you say." ...When the stronger females were in heat, Jacob would set up the branches in the troughs in front of the flock, so they would mate near the branches. But if the animals were weaker, he did not set the branches there. So the weaker animals ended up belonging to Laban and the stronger animals to Jacob. In this way Jacob became extremely prosperous. He owned large flocks, male and female servants, camels, and donkeys.
Genesis 30:33-34, 41-43

Finally, we can discern our need to work with integrity from Jacob's contract with Laban. Initially, Jacob created a contract with stipulations which made sure his work was done with integrity. The dark lambs and mixed goats were his—

not the white lambs and solid colored goats. Because of this, Laban could come and check his flocks any time and discern what was not Jacob's (30:33). This plan kept him free from accusation.

However, there is a diversity of opinion on whether Jacob's practices after initiating the deal were completely free of deception or not. Obviously, in order for the deal to be beneficial to him, he needed to find ways to produce a uniquely colored flock. Even with using the impression method, it was not guaranteed. The chances of producing a uniquely colored flock were stacked against him. God had to bless his labor, which he did. For that reason, many commentators think Jacob's actions were within the bounds of the structured business deal and therefore were ethical. Matthew Henry called them "the honest improvement of a fair bargain."[34] Others disagree.

Either way, it is clear either from Jacob's faithfulness or unfaithfulness that, as kingdom workers, we must demonstrate integrity in our practices. If we don't, it will push people away from God and ultimately lead to God's discipline. Colossians 3:23-25 says,

> Whatever you are doing, work at it with enthusiasm, as to the Lord and not for people, because you know that you will receive your inheritance from the Lord as the reward. Serve the Lord Christ. For the one who does wrong will be repaid for his wrong, and there are no exceptions.

God will repay us for our good but also for our wrong. Therefore, we must work for God with a reverent fear of his displeasure and discipline. Similarly, in Ephesians 6:5-6, Paul said:

> Slaves, obey your human masters with fear and trembling, in the sincerity of your heart as to Christ, not like those who do their work only when someone is watching—as people-pleasers—but as slaves of Christ doing the will of God from the heart.

This means our work must be free of complaining and bitterness, as we're working for the Lord, who primarily cares about our heart motives. We must also offer a full-day's work—not only working when our employers are watching us. As kingdom workers, we must labor with integrity for we are working for the Lord and not for men.

Are you working with integrity, as unto the Lord and not for men?

Application Question: Why is it at times difficult to work with integrity, while in the workplace? How have you experienced work environments with a lack of integrity? How is God calling you to maintain your integrity, regardless of where you work or serve?

104

Conclusion

As we consider this narrative, we must remember that Jacob was a crucial part of redemptive history. God's call was to bless him and his family in order that the world would be blessed through them. This promise also applied to his work—his work was not free of trouble, but it was redemptive. Laban came to know God more through Jacob's work, and it should be the same with our labor. Others should be blessed through our work, and God should be glorified through it. How can we grow as kingdom workers—those who build God's kingdom through their vocations?

1. As Kingdom Workers, We Must Develop a High Work-Ethic
2. As Kingdom Workers, We Must Work Missionally
3. As Kingdom Workers, We Must Focus on Our Families
4. As Kingdom Workers, We Must Work in Faith—Trusting God to Provide
5. As Kingdom Workers, We Must Expect Conflict and Difficulty
6. As Kingdom Workers, We Must Work Skillfully
7. As Kingdom Workers, We Must Work with Integrity

Faithfully Following God

Jacob heard that Laban's sons were complaining, "Jacob has taken everything that belonged to our father! He has gotten rich at our father's expense!" When Jacob saw the look on Laban's face, he could tell his attitude toward him had changed. The LORD said to Jacob, "Return to the land of your fathers and to your relatives. I will be with you." So Jacob sent a message for Rachel and Leah to come to the field where his flocks were. There he said to them, "I can tell that your father's attitude toward me has changed, but the God of my father has been with me. You know that I've worked for your father as hard as I could, but your father has humiliated me and changed my wages ten times. But God has not permitted him to do me any harm. If he said, 'The speckled animals will be your wage,' then the entire flock gave birth to speckled offspring. But if he said, 'The streaked animals will be your wage,' then the entire flock gave birth to streaked offspring. In this way God has snatched away your father's livestock and given them to me. "Once during breeding season I saw in a dream that the male goats mating with the flock were streaked, speckled, and spotted. In the dream the angel of God said to me, 'Jacob!' 'Here I am!' I replied. Then he said, 'Observe that all the male goats mating with the flock are streaked, speckled, or spotted, for I have observed all that Laban has done to you. I am the God of Bethel, where you anointed the sacred stone and made a vow to me. Now leave this land immediately and return to your native land.'" Then Rachel and Leah replied to him, "Do we still have any portion or inheritance in our father's house? Hasn't he treated us like foreigners? He not only sold us, but completely wasted the money paid for us! Surely all the wealth that God snatched away from our father belongs to us and to our children. So now do everything God has told you." So Jacob immediately put his children and his wives on the camels. He took away all the livestock he had acquired in Paddan Aram and all his moveable property that he had accumulated. Then he set out toward the land of Canaan to return to his father Isaac. While Laban had gone to shear his sheep, Rachel stole the household idols that belonged to her father. Jacob also deceived Laban the Aramean by not telling him that he was

leaving. He left with all he owned. He quickly crossed the Euphrates River and headed for the hill country of Gilead…
Genesis 31 (NET)

How can we faithfully follow God?

In Genesis 28, when Jacob left his family to pursue a wife, God appeared to Jacob and told him that he would be with him and bring him back to Canaan. Now, twenty years, two wives, twelve children, and many flocks later, it was time for Jacob to return. While overseeing Laban's flocks for the last six years, Jacob used innovative techniques to help the flocks bear dark colored sheep and multi-colored goats, which were his according to his business deal with Laban. Because of this, Jacob became wealthy—in fact, he became wealthier than Laban (v. 1). Though he was prospering, God spoke to him in a dream and told him to return home.

In this narrative, Jacob looks like an Abrahamic figure—obeying God and leaving Haran for the promised land (Gen 12). As we consider this passage, we learn principles about how we can faithfully follow God as well.

Big Question: What principles can we discern about faithfully following God from Jacob's leaving Laban to return home?

To Faithfully Follow God, We Must Discern God's Will

Jacob heard that Laban's sons were complaining, "Jacob has taken everything that belonged to our father! He has gotten rich at our father's expense!" When Jacob saw the look on Laban's face, he could tell his attitude toward him had changed. The LORD said to Jacob, "Return to the land of your fathers and to your relatives. I will be with you." So Jacob sent a message for Rachel and Leah to come to the field where his flocks were. There he said to them, "I can tell that your father's attitude toward me has changed, but the God of my father has been with me. You know that I've worked for your father as hard as I could, but your father has humiliated me and changed my wages ten times. But God has not permitted him to do me any harm. If he said, 'The speckled animals will be your wage,' then the entire flock gave birth to speckled offspring. But if he said, 'The streaked animals will be your wage,' then the entire flock gave birth to streaked offspring. In this way God has snatched away your father's livestock and given them to me…
Genesis 31:1-16

108

While Jacob was working for Laban, Laban's sons began to complain against him. They declared that Jacob had taken everything away from their father and gotten rich off him (v. 1). Of course, that wasn't true. Jacob had a fair deal with Laban and had profited from the deal. What was really happening was the sons were jealous. Sons typically would receive their father's inheritance, and since Jacob was earning many of Laban's flocks, the sons saw their inheritance diminishing. But not only were Laban's sons upset, so was Laban. His countenance changed towards Jacob (v. 2).

As Jacob discerns this, he calls for his two wives to meet with him in the field. He shares how God told him to return to his homeland. He also shares how he had worked hard for Laban, but Laban changed his wages ten times. The women replied that Laban had treated them like foreigners. He sold them and used up all the money he gained without giving them any (v. 15). It seems the daughters were hoping that the money would be used as a dowry instead of a bride price. With a dowry, the money would eventually be given to the daughters to help with their marriage[35] or kept for them in case their husband died. However, Laban spent the fourteen years of Jacob's earnings. Rachel and Leah agreed, probably for the first time since they married Jacob—it was time to go!

In order for Jacob to follow God, he needed to clearly discern God's will, which was for him to leave Laban and return to Canaan. We must also clearly discern God's will in order to faithfully follow him. "What university should we go to? What major should we choose? Who should we marry? What job should we take? What type of schooling should we give our children?" In order to follow God's will, we must many times discern God's answers to questions like these.

Application Question: What principles about discerning God's will can be gained from Genesis 31?

1.   To discern God's will, we must consider our hearts' desires.

In Genesis 30, Jacob approached Laban and said, "Give me my wives and children and let me go home" (v. 25 paraphrase). After that, Laban encouraged him to stay by offering to make him a partner in the business. However, Jacob's desire to leave Haran and return home, never left him.

This is one of the ways that God guides us into his perfect will—he places certain desires in our hearts. Philippians 2:12-13 says,

> So then, my dear friends, just as you have always obeyed, not only in my presence but even more in my absence, continue working out your salvation with awe and reverence, for the one bringing forth in you both the desire and the effort—for the sake of his good pleasure—is God.

109

God works in us first by giving us the desire to do something and then the power (or effort) to do it. Jacob's desire to return home was put in his heart by God six years earlier and was later confirmed. Often God does the same with us. He gives us a desire to study his Word more, pray more, and serve in various ways. He also works in our hearts to help us make "major" decisions like who to marry, what job to take, or where to live. Finally, he gives us power to complete those works.

With that said, we must recognize that our hearts can be led astray, and their desires are not always godly. In fact, our hearts' desires often are against God's will. Jeremiah 17:9 says, "The heart is deceitful above all things and beyond cure. Who can understand it?" It is not only deceitful but often confusing. However, when we are walking with God, living in prayer, his Word, and obedience, God often speaks through our hearts. Psalm 37:4 (ESV) says, "Delight yourself in the Lord, and he will give you the desires of your heart." Therefore, in discerning God's will, we must consider our desires.

In my counseling, I often come across students who are worried God has given them the gift of singleness and that they will be single all their lives. So I ask them, "Do you desire to be single and serve God without any distractions, like a spouse or children?" When they say, "No!" I tell them most likely that's not their gifting, and if it is, God will give them those desires later. It's the same with a call to ministry. Yes, initially, we may say, "No!" But God continues to work on our hearts until we are willing, and it's our pleasure.

As we're seeking to discern God's will, we must ask ourselves, "What are my desires?"

2. To discern God's will, we must consider our circumstances.

With Jacob, God, in his sovereignty, allowed Laban's sons to become jealous of him and for Laban's countenance to change towards him. Sure, God was prospering Jacob, which might have seemed like a reason to stay, but his relationships had become toxic. This was part of the way God was leading Jacob to return home.

It's the same with us. God leads us to his will not only by changing our desires but often by changing our circumstances. Ephesians 1:11 says God "accomplishes all things according to the counsel of his will." God uses all circumstances to accomplish his will, and therefore, circumstances are often like guide posts for us. God guides us by opening and closing doors. That relationship that ended—most likely wasn't the one to marry. That job which wasn't offered—probably wasn't the right job. Closed doors are especially instructive. Instead of being discouraged by them, we should look at them as God's guidance and give God thanks for them. Through them he says, "I have something better!"

110

3. To discern God's will, we must consider God's Word.

As mentioned, while working, Jacob had a dream in which God called him to return to his homeland. Since the Scriptures were not yet written during that time, God often spoke in more charismatic ways. God may still speak through charismatic ways today; however, the primary way God speaks to us is through Scripture. Even our seemingly divine promptings must be tested and confirmed by Scripture, as God will never contradict his Word (cf. 1 Cor 4:6, 12:3, 14:29). Again, God primarily speaks to us through his Word. In Psalm 119:105, David said, "Your word is a lamp to walk by, and a light to illumine my path." While we are in God's Word, God turns the lights on, so we can better discern his direction. When we're not faithfully studying God's Word, we will lack clarity.

Are you living in God's Word?

4. To discern God's will, we must seek godly counsel.

With Jacob, though he had strong desires, circumstances, and a Divine dream, he still sought the counsel of his wives. Rachel and Leah confirmed Jacob's discernment; it was time to leave. In the same way, for us to discern God's will, we must seek the counsel of others. God has made the church a body, and therefore, we are dependent upon one another. The eye can't say to the hand I don't need you. Many times, God will use somebody else in the body to be our eyes—to help us see our circumstances differently and to help us discern the best possible route to take. Proverbs 20:18 says, "Plans are established by counsel, so make war with guidance." Proverbs 11:14 says, "there is success in the abundance of counselors."

Who are your counselors who help you discern God's will and have success?

Apart from Scriptures' clear leading on moral issues, the other avenues by which God leads us must be tested and not taken absolutely. Difficult circumstances don't always mean it's time to quit. Peace doesn't always mean it's time to stay. Nor does the counsel of others always constitute God's will. We must weigh all of these together—often God will guide us through a combination of these. With Jacob, all of these combined to give him strong confirmation of God's will. Many times, God will do the same with us.

Application Question: In what ways have you experienced God's guidance through a combination of desires, circumstances, his Word, and godly counsel? In what ways are you currently seeking God's direction? Who are your counselors, whom you go to for help in discerning God's will?

To Faithfully Follow God, We Must Be Careful of Fear

> While Laban had gone to shear his sheep, Rachel stole the household idols that belonged to her father. Jacob also deceived Laban the Aramean by not telling him that he was leaving. He left with all he owned. He quickly crossed the Euphrates River and headed for the hill country of Gilead..."I left secretly because I was afraid!" Jacob replied to Laban. "I thought you might take your daughters away from me by force.
> Genesis 31:19-21, 31

With Jacob and his family, instead of firmly telling Laban that they would be leaving for Canaan, they deceptively packed up and immediately left. Even Moses, the narrator, says Jacob "deceived Laban" (v. 20). They had lived together for twenty years, were business partners, and were family. However, Jacob quickly leaves without saying "good bye." It is possible to do God's will in a sinful way. Sometimes God may lead us to confront somebody in sin; however, it is probably not God's will for us to yell at that person or, worse, slap him in the face. Jacob obeys God but in a deceptive way, which brought negative consequences. He could have lost his favorite wife Rachel, who stole Laban's household gods (v. 19). When Laban catches them, Jacob swears that whoever stole the gods would die. It is interesting that though Rachel wasn't caught, not many years later, she dies while giving birth to Jacob's thirteenth child, Benjamin (Gen 35).

The way Jacob left was not an act of faith but an act of fear. Isaiah 28:16 says, "...The one who maintains his faith will not panic." In fact, it seems that Rachel's stealing of Laban's gods was an act of fear as well. Some believe her stealing of the gods meant that she still worshiped them and was seeking their protection. Evidence for this might be seen in Genesis 35:2-5 where Jacob later commands the members of his household to burn all their idols—which seems to represent a family repentance. This would demonstrate Jacob's continual passiveness with his wives and lack of spiritual leadership (cf. Gen 29:31-30:24). However, others believe that the theft may have been more of an insurance policy. The Syrian root of the word for "household gods" (teraphim) means "to inquire."[36] Laban probably used these idols to inquire and seek direction. Earlier, Laban said that he had learned through "divination" that God was blessing him because of Jacob (Gen 30:25). So Rachel, instead of trusting God, might have been trying to keep Laban from discerning their whereabouts through divination. Another possibility is that she took them, as proof of their property rights. Tablets from an ancient Mesopotamian tribe called the Nuzis showed that household gods were used to demonstrate who was the heir to the family's property.[37] Again, if that was the reason, Rachel was making sure that nobody could say that Jacob stole the flocks from Laban or was planning for Jacob to eventually claim all of Laban's property.

Either way, both Jacob and Rachel's actions were not based on faith but fear. Jacob later shares that he left without confirming for fear that Laban would keep his wives (v. 31). Rachel, probably, feared the wrath of her father and the loss of their property. Neither trusted God.

Colossians 3:15 (NIV) says, "Let the peace of Christ rule in our hearts." Fear will lead us away from doing God's will, instead of into God's will. Sadly, many are ruled by fear instead of God's peace. They are worried about the economy. They are worried about finding a spouse. They are worried about their health. Many times, their fears lead them into irrational thinking and then ungodly decisions. Fear guides them instead of God's peace.

When Abraham was afraid of losing his wife, he lied and said she was his sister (Gen 12). In the Parable of the Talents, the servant with one talent, instead of investing to make a profit, because of fear, hid it in the ground. He said,

> ...'Sir, I knew that you were a hard man, harvesting where you did not sow, and gathering where you did not scatter seed, so I was afraid, and I went and hid your talent in the ground. See, you have what is yours.
> Matthew 25:24-25

Fear kept him from faithfully following the master and doing his will. This is often true for us. Fear keeps us from taking steps of faith and trusting God. Fear of failure and incompetency keeps us from serving. When God approached Moses about leading Israel, it was fear that almost kept him from his blessings. Moses said, "But God, I can't speak, and I can't lead" (Ex 4). After God approached Gideon about leading Israel, he replied, "I'm from the least tribe in Israel, and I'm the least in my family. I'm a nobody! God you've got the wrong guy!" (Judges 6). Fear almost kept them from faithfully following God. It often does the same with us.

Are you being led by fear or by faith?

Application Question: What types of fear do you struggle with that potentially could hinder your walk with the Lord? How should we conquer our fears?

To Faithfully Follow God, We Must Be Careful of the World's Influence

> Three days later Laban discovered Jacob had left. So he took his relatives with him and pursued Jacob for seven days. He caught up

with him in the hill country of Gilead. But God came to Laban the Aramean in a dream at night and warned him, "Be careful that you neither bless nor curse Jacob." Laban overtook Jacob, and when Jacob pitched his tent in the hill country of Gilead, Laban and his relatives set up camp there too. "What have you done?" Laban demanded of Jacob. "You've deceived me and carried away my daughters as if they were captives of war! Why did you run away secretly and deceive me? Why didn't you tell me so I could send you off with a celebration complete with singing, tambourines, and harps? You didn't even allow me to kiss my daughters and my grandchildren good-bye. You have acted foolishly! I have the power to do you harm, but the God of your father told me last night, 'Be careful that you neither bless nor curse Jacob.' Now I understand that you have gone away because you longed desperately for your father's house. Yet why did you steal my gods?" …
Genesis 31:22-42

After three days, Laban realized that Jacob left. Immediately, Laban gathered his relatives and pursued Jacob for seven days and finally caught up with him. However, in a dream at night, the Lord warned Laban, saying, "Be careful that you neither bless nor curse Jacob" (v. 24). This Hebrew expression, in the context, seems to mean, "Don't use either flattery or threats to try to persuade Jacob to return."[38] Laban's original plan must have been to make Jacob return either by blessing, like a sweeter business deal, or a curse, like taking Jacob's wives and children. However, God forbade him from doing so. God kept Laban from hindering Jacob's obedience.

Laban is a picture of the world. He lived for money and riches and was willing to deceive and hurt others in order to get them—including hurting his family. He had a form of religion—an awareness of God—but didn't follow him. In fact, he worshiped many gods. He did appeal to the true God when it was convenient, as he said earlier to Jacob, "I've been blessed by Yahweh because of you" (Gen 30:27). Laban was a manipulator. He made promises to Jacob throughout their relationship and continually backed out of them. He manipulated and attempted to control Jacob by promises and threats.

The world does the same with us. It will offer us blessings, like wealth, popularity, or promotion, if we'll follow and turn away from God. If not, it will threaten us, whether by harassment, the loss of riches or opportunities for it, imprisonment, death, etc. As an example, Satan offered Christ the world if he would only bow down and worship him. When he didn't, Satan used the world to put Christ on the cross. Judas betrayed Christ for money. Demas deserted Paul because of love for the world. Like Laban, the world continually seeks to keep us away from doing God's will, and it uses blessings or threats to do so.

Consider the following verses: Romans 12:2 says,

Do not be conformed to this present world, but be transformed by the renewing of your mind, so that you may test and approve what is the will of God—what is good and well-pleasing and perfect.

The world aims to press and mold us into its image. When we conform—through adopting its language, thought-processes, and practices—the less we are able to test and approve God's will. Not only will we be unable to follow God, we won't even be able to discern his will.

Second Corinthians 6:14-18 says,

Do not become partners with those who do not believe, for what partnership is there between righteousness and lawlessness, or what fellowship does light have with darkness? And what agreement does Christ have with Beliar? Or what does a believer share in common with an unbeliever? ... Therefore "come out from their midst, and be separate," says the Lord, "and touch no unclean thing, and I will welcome you, and I will be a father to you, and you will be my sons and daughters," says the All-Powerful Lord.

Paul speaks to the Corinthians and calls for them to separate from the world and not partner with it. If they obeyed this, God would welcome them and be a father to them. Since the Corinthian church was already believers, this referred to intimacy, answered prayer, and God's blessing. Many believers are missing God's best because of their partnership with a system and people who hate God. The entertainment they listen to and watch teaches sexual immorality and ungodliness. The people they admire, fellowship with, and aim to model, do the same. Because of these worldly partnerships and their negative influence, many believers lack intimacy with God, their Father.

If we are going to follow God, we must be careful of worldly influences—whether they come from friends, family, or employers, like Laban. We must be in the world but not of it. We must minister to it and yet be separate from it. Many fail to faithfully follow God because of the world's negative influence—whether it be from the world's promises of blessings or curses.

Are you separating from the world or partnering with it? Are you influencing the world or being conformed to it?

Application Question: In what ways does the world promise blessings if we conform to it and curses if we don't? How can we be in the world and positively influence it, and yet practice a healthy separation from it? How have you experienced stagnation in your spiritual life because of enjoying the world and its promises instead of God and his promises?

115

To Faithfully Follow God, We Must Trust Him

...So now, come, let's make a formal agreement, you and I, and it will be proof that we have made peace." So Jacob took a stone and set it up as a memorial pillar. Then he said to his relatives, "Gather stones." So they brought stones and put them in a pile. They ate there by the pile of stones. Laban called it Jegar Sahadutha, but Jacob called it Galeed. Laban said, "This pile of stones is a witness of our agreement today." That is why it was called Galeed. It was also called Mizpah because he said, "May the LORD watch between us when we are out of sight of one another. If you mistreat my daughters or if you take wives besides my daughters, although no one else is with us, realize that God is witness to your actions." "Here is this pile of stones and this pillar I have set up between me and you," Laban said to Jacob. "This pile of stones and the pillar are reminders that I will not pass beyond this pile to come to harm you and that you will not pass beyond this pile and this pillar to come to harm me. May the God of Abraham and the god of Nahor, the gods of their father, judge between us." Jacob took an oath by the God whom his father Isaac feared. Then Jacob offered a sacrifice on the mountain and invited his relatives to eat the meal. They ate the meal and spent the night on the mountain. Early in the morning Laban kissed his grandchildren and his daughters goodbye and blessed them. Then Laban left and returned home.
Genesis 31:30-55

After Laban tracked down Jacob, he confronted him, saying he wanted to throw a party and kiss his daughters and children goodbye—probably not true—and that Jacob acted foolishly (v. 27-28). He later says, "Why did you take my gods?" (v. 30). Jacob, unaware that Rachel stole them, foolishly declared that whoever had them would die. Laban searches everything Jacob had—all of his tents and yet found nothing. When he reaches Rachel, who is sitting on her camel, she asks for permission to not stand because it was her time of month. Laban doesn't distrust her—probably because he assumes that she would never sit on the family's deities, which would have been, to them, blasphemous.

When Laban couldn't find his gods, Jacob challenges him in front of their relatives (v. 36-42). Twenty years of frustrations came out of his mouth. Laban had changed his wages ten times. Every time a lamb was taken, Laban charged Jacob for it. Jacob worked day and night, in hot and cold, to care for Laban's flocks, and the only reason Laban hadn't hurt Jacob was out of fear of Isaac and Isaac's God.

After a mutual sharing of complaints, Laban requests a nonaggression agreement (v. 44). Jacob gathers stones together as witnesses of this agreement. He names them "Galeed," which in Hebrew means "the heap of witness." Laban named it "Jegar-sahadutha," which in Aramaic means the same (v. 47). The stone memorial was also called "Mizpah," which means "watchpost" (v. 49).[39] There Laban swore to the God of Abraham and the god of Nahor, and Jacob swore to the God whom Isaac feared—the true God (v. 53).

By swearing, Jacob promised to not mistreat Laban's daughters or take other wives. He also promised to never return to Haran and try to harm Laban. Laban promised the same. If either one of them broke these promises, it was believed that the deities they swore by would judge them. After their oaths, they ate together, which, in the East, represented a binding agreement.

Laban's oath was superstitious, as he believed in many gods, but Jacob's was based on true faith in Yahweh, God. In Genesis 28, at Bethel, God promised to be with him, bless him, and bring him back to the land. God was faithful and had protected Jacob. When Jacob acted hastily and left Laban, God warned Laban in his sleep to not harm him. Jacob had seen God's faithfulness and believed that God would continue to be faithful. God would be with Jacob, protect him, and curse those who mistreated him (cf. Rom 12:19). Therefore, Jacob's memorial was an act of faith in God.

Similarly, if we are going to follow God, we must trust his promises. He will protect us; he will be with us; he will bless us; he will use everything, including bad things, for our good. The very reason many of us aren't faithfully following God is because we don't trust him. We don't trust that he has good plans for us. Eve sinned against God because she doubted his goodness. We often do the same.

If we are going to faithfully follow God along life's winding road, we must settle in our hearts to trust him. Trusting him starts with receiving Christ as our Lord and Savior (Rom 10:9-10). Because God loves us, he sent Christ to live on this earth and die for us to pay the penalty for our sins. All of us have sinned against God and because of that we deserve death (Rom 3:23, 6:23). However, God paid the penalty, so we can have a relationship with him and spend eternity with him (John 17:3). When we accept Christ as our Lord, we become God's children (John 1:12). God promises that he will never leave us nor forsake us (Matt 28:20) and that he will use all our circumstances, even bad ones, for our good—to make us into Christ's image (Rom 8:28-29). God has good plans for his children, but we have to trust and follow him. Psalm 37:3-5 says,

> Trust in the LORD and do what is right! Settle in the land and maintain your integrity! Then you will take delight in the LORD, and he will answer your prayers. Commit your future to the LORD! Trust in him, and he will act on your behalf.

When we trust God, he will act on our behalf. Faith is the key to unlocking all of God's promises including salvation, having our needs met, and being used by him. Have you followed Christ as your Lord? Are you willing to follow him wherever he leads? If so, God will act on your behalf and use you for his purposes. If we don't trust God fully, we will miss God's best and will be prone to sin and rebellion.

Application Question: In what areas do you struggle with trusting God most and why? How can we grow in our faith, so that we trust God more?

To Faithfully Follow God, We Must Live at Peace with Others

> So now, come, let's make a formal agreement, you and I, and it will be proof that we have made peace."
> Genesis 31:44

It must be noticed that God does not allow Jacob to return to Canaan without making things right with Laban. After the pact, they weren't best friends, but at least, there was mutual respect and an agreement to not harm each other. In the next chapters, God opens the door for Jacob to reconcile with Esau, who Jacob swindled out of his birthright twenty years earlier.

Similarly, if we are going to faithfully follow God, we must reconcile our relationships as well. This is emphasized throughout the New Testament. In Matthew 5:23-24, Christ taught that if while offering a gift to God, we recognize that somebody has something against us, we should leave the gift, reconcile, and then offer the gift to God. In Matthew 6:15, Christ taught that if we didn't forgive others, God would not forgive us. In 1 Peter 3:7, Peter cautioned husbands to be considerate of their wives, lest their prayers be hindered.

Our horizontal relationships affect our vertical relationship. If we are out of fellowship with others, we will not be in right fellowship with God, and vice versa. Romans 12:11 says, "If possible, so far as it depends on you, live peaceably with all people." We can't change people's hearts, but we can do our part to live at peace, even if that means being separate from one another as Jacob and Laban chose to do.

What relationship is God calling you to reconcile, so you can faithfully follow him?

Application Question: In what ways have you experienced discord with others hindering your relationship with God? Are there any relationships God is calling you to reconcile?

Conclusion

In Genesis 31, Jacob follows God's call to leave Haran for the promised land. Like his grandfather Abraham, he takes a step of faith. Leaving wasn't easy, but it was God's will for his life. As we consider this, it teaches us principles about how we can faithfully follow God—despite our circumstances.

1. To Faithfully Follow God, We Must Discern God's Will
2. To Faithfully Follow God, We Must Be Careful of Fear
3. To Faithfully Follow God, We Must Be Careful of the World's Influence
4. To Faithfully Follow God, We Must Trust Him
5. To Faithfully Follow God, We Must Live at Peace with Others

Seeking Reconciliation

So Jacob went on his way and the angels of God met him. When Jacob saw them, he exclaimed, "This is the camp of God!" So he named that place Mahanaim. Jacob sent messengers on ahead to his brother Esau in the land of Seir, the region of Edom. He commanded them, "This is what you must say to my lord Esau: 'This is what your servant Jacob says: I have been staying with Laban until now. I have oxen, donkeys, sheep, and male and female servants. I have sent this message to inform my lord, so that I may find favor in your sight.'" The messengers returned to Jacob and said, "We went to your brother Esau. He is coming to meet you and has four hundred men with him." Jacob was very afraid and upset. So he divided the people who were with him into two camps, as well as the flocks, herds, and camels. "If Esau attacks one camp," he thought, "then the other camp will be able to escape." Then Jacob prayed, "O God of my father Abraham, God of my father Isaac, O LORD, you said to me, 'Return to your land and to your relatives and I will make you prosper.' I am not worthy of all the faithful love you have shown your servant. With only my walking stick I crossed the Jordan, but now I have become two camps. Rescue me, I pray, from the hand of my brother Esau, for I am afraid he will come and attack me, as well as the mothers with their children. But you said, 'I will certainly make you prosper and will make your descendants like the sand on the seashore, too numerous to count.'" Jacob stayed there that night. Then he sent as a gift to his brother Esau two hundred female goats and twenty male goats, two hundred ewes and twenty rams, thirty female camels with their young, forty cows and ten bulls, and twenty female donkeys and ten male donkeys. He entrusted them to his servants, who divided them into herds. He told his servants, "Pass over before me, and keep some distance between one herd and the next." He instructed the servant leading the first herd, "When my brother Esau meets you and asks, 'To whom do you belong? Where are you going? Whose herds are you driving?' then you must say, 'They belong to your servant Jacob. They have been sent as a gift to my lord Esau. In fact Jacob himself is behind us.'" He also gave these instructions to the second and third servants, as well as all those who were following the herds, saying, "You must say the same thing to

Esau when you meet him. You must also say, 'In fact your servant Jacob is behind us.'" Jacob thought, "I will first appease him by sending a gift ahead of me. After that I will meet him. Perhaps he will accept me." So the gifts were sent on ahead of him while he spent that night in the camp.
Genesis 32:1-21 (NET)

How should we seek reconciliation with those we've hurt or who have hurt us?

With the advent of sin, relationships became fractured. God prophesied to Adam and Eve that there would be discord in their marriage. Genesis 3:16 says, "You will want to control your husband, but he will dominate you." Ultimately, their fractured marriage led to broken children. Their oldest son, Cain, killed the younger, Abel.

Similarly, Jacob came from a dysfunctional home. Isaac favored Esau and Rebekah favored Jacob. In order to secure the oldest son Esau's birthright, Jacob dressed like his brother and deceived his blind father. Since then, Esau harbored resentment for his brother, and like Cain, plotted to kill him. In order to save Jacob's life, Rebekah sent him away to Haran to find a wife. She promised that after Esau's anger had subsided, she would send for him (Gen 27:43-45). Twenty years passed, Jacob gained two wives, twelve children, and great wealth while working for his uncle Laban. However, while working there, Jacob also had a difficult relationship with his uncle—so much so, that he ran away with his family at night. Laban searched after him for seven days and caught up to him. If God had not rebuked Laban in a dream, he might have harmed Jacob. Instead, they made a covenant before God to not hurt one another (Gen 31).

Jacob came from a dysfunctional family. His relationship with his brother was broken. His relationship with his uncle was unhealthy. In this narrative, after having some sort of reconciliation with Laban, Jacob now seeks to address his broken relationship with Esau.

Since we have sin in our hearts and live in a sinful world, we will commonly hurt others and others will hurt us. Therefore, we'll commonly need to seek reconciliation. Christ said if we don't forgive others, God won't forgive us (Matt 6:14). Also, in the Parable of the Merciless Servant, Christ taught that if we didn't forgive, God would discipline us (Matt 18:35). In 1 Peter 3:7, Peter said if husbands aren't considerate of their wives, it would hinder their prayers. Discord not only affects our relationships with others but also our relationship with God. Therefore, we must be quick to seek reconciliation, lest we give the devil a foothold in our lives and communities (Eph 4:26-27).

In Genesis 32:1-21, we see Jacob's attempt to reconcile with his brother Esau, after twenty years of division. As we consider it, we'll learn principles about seeking reconciliation with others.

122

Big Question: What principles can we discern about seeking reconciliation from Jacob's attempt to reconcile with Esau in Genesis 32:1-21?

To Seek Reconciliation, We Must Continually Abide in God's Presence

> So Jacob went on his way and the angels of God met him. When Jacob saw them, he exclaimed, "This is the camp of God!" So he named that place Mahanaim.
> Genesis 32:1-2

After Jacob made a peace treaty with Laban and continued on his way to Canaan, God's angels met with him. We don't know exactly what this looked like. But it must be noted that it doesn't say that angels "appeared to him," but that they "met him." It seems that God's angels, who are usually invisible, not only appeared but also ministered to Jacob—probably similar to how angels ministered to Christ after his temptation in the wilderness (Matt 4:11). Hebrews 1:14 says that angels are spirits sent by God to serve those who will inherit salvation. They are always ministering to believers, even when we don't see them. Psalm 91:11-12 says, "For he will order his angels to protect you in all you do. They will lift you up in their hands, so you will not slip and fall on a stone." Christ warned that nobody should despise God's little ones—referring to young believers—because their angels always see the face of God (Matt 18:10). They are always waiting for God's command to act on behalf of believers.

When God's angels met with Jacob, he exclaimed, "This is the camp of God!" The word "camp" can also be translated "host," "army," or "group of people."[40] It seems that this was not just a few angels but a great number of them. Jacob names the place Mahanaim, which means "two camps." Commentators are divided on what Mahanaim referred to. Some believe it referred to the camp of angels and Jacob's camp. Others believe that Jacob encounters two camps of angels—a great angelic army. If there were two camps of angels, then it probably pictured how God was protecting Jacob from the two dangerous situations. He was protecting Jacob from Laban on one side and Esau on the other. We saw something similar when Elisha was surrounded by an army of Syrians and his servant was afraid. Therefore, Elisha prayed for God to open the eyes of his servant, so he could know the help God had provided. After the prayer, the servant sees fiery angels protecting them from the Syrians (2 Kings 6:15-17). Again, Scripture says this is not uncommon for believers. Psalm 34:7 says, "The LORD's angel camps around the LORD's loyal followers and delivers them." In Job 1:10, Satan proclaims that God put a hedge

123

of protection around Job—probably referring to angels. The Lord is always protecting and ministering to believers through angels.

It must be noticed that the first time Jacob encountered angels was when he left his home in Canaan for Haran (Gen 28). As he was obediently seeking a wife, God revealed himself through a heavenly ladder with angels ascending and descending upon it. Now, as Jacob is returning home, in obedience to God, he similarly experiences God's grace. Often, we will encounter God's presence and grace in the midst of our obedience as well. He gives us special mercies to encourage and strengthen us for the tasks ahead. Initially, God encouraged Jacob before he would enter a difficult twenty years of service with Laban. And now, God ministers to Jacob twice before he encounters Esau. God reveals angels to him and later appears to him in physical form as a wrestler (Gen 32:24-32)—all to encourage and empower Jacob for reconciliation.

Through meeting with God, God also gives grace to us. When we're abiding in him, through his Word and prayer, we'll find energy, strength, and desire to reconcile with others. When we're not, we'll often hold on to grudges and negative memories. The acts of flesh are "hostilities, strife, jealousy, outbursts of anger, selfish rivalries, dissensions, factions, envying, murder" (Gal 5:20-21). However, the fruits of the Spirit are "love, joy, peace, patience, kindness, goodness, faithfulness, gentleness, and self-control" (Gal 5:22-23). These fruits only come when we live in the Spirit (Gal 5:16)—when we are abiding in God's presence, even as Jacob was. He met with angels, representing God, and he also met with God, in human form, before he reconciled with Esau.

Are you continually meeting with God and receiving his ministry? Or are you walking in flesh? When we continually meet with God, he encourages us to seek reconciliation with others and empowers us to do so.

Application Question: How have you experienced desire and empowerment to seek reconciliation when abiding in God? How have you experienced hardness of heart towards others when neglecting time with God? Are there any people God is calling you to seek reconciliation with or to help reconcile?

To Seek Reconciliation, We Must Humble Ourselves and Give Up Our Rights

Jacob sent messengers on ahead to his brother Esau in the land of Seir, the region of Edom. He commanded them, "This is what you must say to my lord Esau: 'This is what your servant Jacob says: I have been staying with Laban until now. I have oxen, donkeys, sheep, and

male and female servants. I have sent this message to inform my lord, so that I may find favor in your sight.'"
Genesis 32:3-5

After meeting with the angels, Jacob seeks reconciliation with his estranged brother, who was living in the land of Seir. The fact that he knew where Esau was located probably meant he had received some word from home—though not telling him that Esau's anger had subsided. Jacob sent messengers to Esau in order to seek his favor and reconciliation. He said this to Esau through his servants, "I have been staying with Laban until now. I have oxen, donkeys, sheep, and male and female servants. I have sent this message to inform my lord, so that I may find favor in your sight" (v. 4-5). This statement not only showed Jacob's desire for reconciliation, but also the fact that he wasn't laying claim to his right of leadership over Esau. Jacob called Esau, "Lord"—humbling himself before him as a servant. The fact that Jacob mentions his wealth means that he wasn't trying to claim any of Esau's wealth.

When seeking reconciliation with others, we must do the same. We must humble ourselves before them and serve them. In Philippians 2:3-4, Paul says this to a congregation struggling with discord (cf. Phil 4:2):

Instead of being motivated by selfish ambition or vanity, each of you should, in humility, be moved to treat one another as more important than yourself. Each of you should be concerned not only about your own interests, but about the interests of others as well.

Instead of selfishly claiming our rights, we should humble ourselves before others by seeking their desires over our own. The primary reason for most discord is simply pride—two people want their own way and won't focus on the other's viewpoint or desires. Therefore, the primary way that we seek reconciliation is by humbling ourselves before others and serving them.

When Jacob calls Esau, "Lord," again, it implies that Jacob is his servant and that he won't be exercising his right as Isaac's heir. Something similar happened in Genesis 13, when Abraham's and Lot's servants were fighting with one another. Though Abraham was the patriarch, he humbles himself before Lot and says, "Take your pick of the land. Whatever direction you go, I will go the other." Culturally Abraham had the right to the best of the land and spiritually he had the right, as God promised the land to him. This was also true with Jacob. Isaac gave the right of firstborn to Jacob, and God had promised that Esau would serve Jacob, even before they were born. However, Jacob doesn't claim his rights—he simply humbles himself before his brother.

We must do the same if we are going to seek reconciliation. Yes, we might have the right to be angry. Yes, they did us wrong. However, we must humbly give up our rights and serve them. Paul said this to the Corinthians who were going to court and suing one another in 1 Corinthians 6:7. "The fact that you have lawsuits among yourselves demonstrates that you have already been defeated. Why not rather be wronged? Why not rather be cheated?" Again, Paul's argument is, "Why not just humble yourself and give up your rights in order to seek reconciliation? Why not turn the other cheek like Christ taught?"

Sadly, instead of humbling ourselves and giving up our rights, many of us hold on to our pride and our rights—allowing, sometimes, years to go by without reconciliation, like Jacob did. During this time, he not only lacked a relationship with his brother, but it also cost him many years of intimacy with his father and mother. Our broken relationship with someone often negatively affects other relationships as well.

Proverbs 15:1 says, "A gentle response turns away anger, but a harsh word stirs up wrath." To seek reconciliation, instead of responding in anger towards others, we must humble ourselves and speak and act gently towards them, like Jacob did, in hopes of reconciliation.

Are you holding on to your pride and offense—as you stay at odds with others? Or are you humbling yourself and giving up your rights in order to seek reconciliation? Humbling ourselves and giving up our rights doesn't mean that we don't at times seek justice or even peacefully separate, as seen with Jacob and Laban. But it does mean that we take the necessary steps to resolve the tension in a godly manner.

Application Question: In what ways is pride often the biggest culprit in discord? In what ways can we practically humble ourselves before others in order to seek reconciliation? Should we always give up our rights, including rights for justice? If not, when should we pursue our rights?

To Seek Reconciliation, We Must Realize that It Might Not Happen Immediately

The messengers returned to Jacob and said, "We went to your brother Esau. He is coming to meet you and has four hundred men with him." Jacob was very afraid and upset. So he divided the people who were with him into two camps, as well as the flocks, herds, and camels. "If Esau attacks one camp," he thought, "then the other camp will be able to escape."
Genesis 32:6-8

Unfortunately, Jacob's attempt at reconciliation doesn't seem to be welcomed. Esau doesn't give positive words to Jacob's servants; he immediately gathers four hundred men and rides out to meet Jacob. When Jacob hears this, he is immediately overcome with fear (v. 7). He forgot that God had two armies of angels around him. All he could focus on was the small army coming towards him and his family. It seems that Jacob's attempt for reconciliation failed, and Esau still intended to harm him. Therefore, Jacob separates his camp into two—thinking that if Esau attacked one, the other could still escape.

We don't know for sure if Esau's initial plan was to harm Jacob, but all the evidence seems to point towards that. Given their past history, gathering such a large contingent to meet Jacob, surely would be taken negatively. Also, Jacob's mother never sent word that Esau's intentions had changed, as she promised (Gen 27:43-45). Therefore, all the evidence pointed towards the fact that Esau was still harboring a deadly grudge.

Similarly, when we take steps towards reconciliation, we must also recognize that our attempts might not be met kindly. It's often said that time heals all wounds, but that is not always true. Often time only more firmly cements the wounds, leaving people crippled. Often people go throughout life holding onto their unforgiveness and bitterness. Certain experiences like seeing the person, hearing about their prosperity, or hearing about a similar situation, only bring back all their raw emotions. For many when they talk about their experience many years later, it's like it's fresh—like it happened recently. Time doesn't heal all wounds. However, God can, when we forgive and seek reconciliation—otherwise those wounds tend to cement.

Romans 12:18 says, "If possible, so far as it depends on you, live peaceably with all people." Whether others are ready to reconcile or not, we must do our part. This means forgiving them, praying for them, reaching out to them, and also waiting for them.

If we don't realistically consider that our attempts at reconciliation might be rejected, we might get discouraged or give up when they are. Often reaching out is just the first step, then there are smaller ones that help build trust. God may still need to do more work in them or us first before reconciliation occurs. Either way, we can't change people's hearts, but we can do our part, while trusting God.

Application Question: Why does reconciliation often take time? In what ways have you experienced delays while pursuing full reconciliation? What should we do in the waiting season?

To Seek Reconciliation, We Must Labor in Prayer

> Then Jacob prayed, "O God of my father Abraham, God of my father Isaac, O LORD, you said to me, 'Return to your land and to your relatives and I will make you prosper.' I am not worthy of all the faithful love you have shown your servant. With only my walking stick I crossed the Jordan, but now I have become two camps. Rescue me, I pray, from the hand of my brother Esau, for I am afraid he will come

and attack me, as well as the mothers with their children. But you said, 'I will certainly make you prosper and will make your descendants like the sand on the seashore, too numerous to count.'"
Genesis 32:9-12

After dividing into two camps, Jacob prays. Interestingly, this is Jacob's first recorded prayer.[41] Though God met with Jacob at Bethel (Gen 28), later gave him a dream calling him to return to Canaan (Gen 31), and allowed him to experience two camps of angels (Gen 32), Scripture never says Jacob prayed as a response. He might have made vows, named the places, and responded in obedience, but Scripture doesn't say he prayed. Maybe, that was part of the reason that Jacob was very weak spiritually—prone to walk in the flesh instead of the Spirit. He had a weak prayer life, which led to bad decisions and deceitful practices. However, it was through prayer that God was going to give Jacob wisdom and help bring reconciliation.

No doubt, God orchestrated these circumstances to help Jacob grow in his prayer life. Laban was behind him and Esau was in front of him. There was nothing else to do but pray. Often this is how God trains us to pray as well. He allows us to go through a very difficult circumstance to create a deeper dependence upon God and prayer. Jacob was very afraid, and this fear, instead of leading him to hopelessness, led him to hope in God. God could deliver him. There are five aspects to Jacob's prayer from which we can learn:

1. *In prayer, we must pray God's Word.* In verse 9, Jacob declares how God said to him, "Return to your land and to your relatives and I will make you prosper," and in verse 12, he reiterates God's promise to make his children like the sands of the seashore. He essentially says to God, "You promised to take care of me and bless my family!" In the same way, we must pray God's promises. God said that he will never leave us nor forsake us (Matt 28:20). He promises to meet all our needs, as we seek first his kingdom (Matt 6:33). He promises us peace, as we reject anxiety and live in thanksgiving and prayer (Phil 4:6-7). He promises to give us wisdom if we ask for it (Jam 1:5). If we are going to pray effectively, we must know God's Word. The very reason many of us are weak in prayer is because we don't know it. God's Word prompts and empowers prayer. Are you living in God's Word?

2. *In prayer, we must humble ourselves before the Lord and depend on his grace.* Jacob says, "I am not worthy of all the faithful love you have shown your servant" (v. 10). In Luke 18:9-14, Christ gave the Parable of the Pharisee and the Tax Collector. Before God, the Pharisee boasted about his righteousness, but the tax collector confessed his sin and unworthiness. Christ said the tax collector went home justified

128

but the Pharisee did not (Lk 18:14). Sadly, many of our prayers are unproductive because they are rooted in pride and what we think we deserve, instead of recognizing God's grace—his unmerited favor upon sinners. Many people have angry prayers that blame God, as they don't recognize their own sin and guilt. The humble person receives God's blessing and the prideful person only receives God's discipline. God opposes the proud but gives grace to the humble (Jam 4:6). Are you humbling yourself before God or pridefully claiming what you think you deserve?

3. *In prayer, we must declare God's faithfulness.* In verse 10, Jacob declares, "With only my walking stick I crossed the Jordan, but now I have become two camps." When he left Canaan for Haran, he had nothing. Now his people were like two armies. God had truly blessed him, and Jacob affirms that in prayer. Psalm 107:2 says, "Let those delivered by the Lord speak out, those whom he delivered from the power of the enemy." In fact, many of the Psalms are simply God's people recounting God's past works—he delivered Israel from Egypt, split the Red Sea, conquered their enemies, etc. We would do well to do this often in prayer, as it honors God and strengthens our faith. We must remember times when he delivered us, strengthened us, and used us for his glory. In one sentence, Jacob encapsulates twenty years of God's faithfulness. When he began following God, he had nothing and now he had much. Are you giving God thanks in your prayers—remembering his faithful works?

4. *In prayer, we must bring our petitions before the Lord.* In verse 11, he says, "Rescue me, I pray, from the hand of my brother Esau." Jacob brings a specific petition before the Lord—asking for deliverance from Esau. Similarly, when coming to God, we must bring our petitions. The Lord's Prayer is six petitions—for God's name to be hallowed, his kingdom to come, his will to be done, our daily bread, forgiveness, and protection. Therefore, in prayer, we must continually bring our requests. We should not be timid in bringing them before God for he loves to bless his children. James says we have not because we ask not (James 4:2). This means that there are many good things we don't have, simply because we've never asked God for them. Are you bringing your petitions before God?

5. *In prayer, we must honestly share our thoughts and emotions with God.* In verse 12, Jacob says, "for I am afraid he will come and attack me, as well as the mothers with their children." Many of the Psalms are just like this—God's people pouring out their fears, doubts, complaints,

confusions, and praises before God. Typically, we only share things with people who we trust and know us well, because we're afraid of what people will do with our secrets. However, with God, he already knows our hearts and is trustworthy, so he's the perfect person to share with. We must continually bring our thoughts and raw emotions before the Lord. As we do this, we allow God to transform our hearts. He turns our fears into peace, our doubts into faith, and our anger into love. Sadly, many of us miss this ministry, as we rarely honestly share with God. First Peter 5:7 says, "Cast your cares before the Lord for he cares for you" (paraphrase). Are you bringing your worries and anxieties before the Lord? We should because he cares and has power to heal our hearts, fix our situations, and restore our relationships. Are you being transparent and honest with the Lord or hiding from him?

In order to seek reconciliation and deliverance, like Jacob, we must labor in prayer. Only God can transform us and those we care about. He is the reconciler. He sent Christ to die for our sins to reconcile us both to God and one another. Reconciliation is God's business, and therefore, we must continually come before him, asking for grace over our relationships.

Are you allowing difficult relationships (and situations) to draw you to prayer? That is one of God's purposes in allowing difficulties to happen. His grace is available to those who humbly ask for it (James 4:6).

Application Question: What aspect of prayer stood out to you most in Jacob's prayer and why? How is God calling you to grow in your prayer life?

To Seek Reconciliation, We Must Bless Those Separated from Us

Jacob stayed there that night. Then he sent as a gift to his brother Esau two hundred female goats and twenty male goats, two hundred ewes and twenty rams, thirty female camels with their young, forty cows and ten bulls, and twenty female donkeys and ten male donkeys. He entrusted them to his servants, who divided them into herds. He told his servants, "Pass over before me, and keep some distance between one herd and the next." He instructed the servant leading the first herd, "When my brother Esau meets you and asks, 'To whom do you belong? Where are you going? Whose herds are you driving?' then you must say, 'They belong to your servant Jacob. They have been sent as a gift to my lord Esau. In fact Jacob himself is behind us.'" He also gave these instructions to the second and third servants, as

well as all those who were following the herds, saying, "You must say the same thing to Esau when you meet him. You must also say, 'In fact your servant Jacob is behind us.'" Jacob thought, "I will first appease him by sending a gift ahead of me. After that I will meet him. Perhaps he will accept me." So the gifts were sent on ahead of him while he spent that night in the camp.
Genesis 32:13-21

Next, Jacob seeks to pacify Esau with gifts. It is an ingenious plan. He sends over 550 animals, in three separate caravans, spaced evenly apart. [42] With the passing of each caravan, the servants would say to Esau, "They belong to your servant Jacob. They have been sent as a gift to my lord Esau. In fact Jacob himself is behind us" (v. 18). The hope was that these gifts and gentle words would soften Esau's heart. Some commentators think that Jacob is not trusting God. He has prayed, but now, he is acting in the flesh. However, it seems that Jacob's actions were acts of faith—inspired by his prayer. Matthew Henry said, "When we have prayed to God for any mercy, we must second our prayers with our endeavors; else, instead of trusting god, we tempt him."[43] Certainly, there are times when we should pray and simply wait to see God's glory, but most times, it shows a lack of faith to not act. We should pray for a job and also apply for one. We should pray for reconciliation but also show acts of kindness in seeking it, which is exactly what Jacob does.

Similarly, if we are going to seek reconciliation, we must do so by showing acts of kindness to the offended party. In Romans 12:19-21, Paul said:

> Do not avenge yourselves, dear friends, but give place to God's wrath, for it is written, "Vengeance is mine, I will repay," says the Lord. Rather, if your enemy is hungry, feed him; if he is thirsty, give him a drink; for in doing this you will be heaping burning coals on his head. Do not be overcome by evil, but overcome evil with good.

Instead of seeking vengeance or fighting for our rights, we must overcome evil with good. We should pray for our enemies and kindly serve them. As we do this continually, it will often change their hearts towards us. The acts of kindness overcome evil. This is exactly what Jacob did to Esau. In Genesis 33, eventually, they embrace each other and weep together. Through Jacob's trust in God, humility, prayer, and acts of kindness, God changed Esau's heart.

How are you responding to those who have hurt you or you've hurt? Are you overcoming evil with good or returning evil for evil? If we are going to pursue reconciliation, like Jacob, we must in faith and obedience to God's Word, bless those separated from us.

Application Question: What types of acts of kindness should we show towards others to overcome evil with good and to seek reconciliation? In what ways have you seen God bring reconciliation through this method?

Conclusion

How should we seek reconciliation with others?

1. To Seek Reconciliation, We Must Continually Abide in God's Presence
2. To Seek Reconciliation, We Must Humble Ourselves and Give Up Our Rights
3. To Seek Reconciliation, We Must Realize that It Might Not Happen Immediately
4. To Seek Reconciliation, We Must Labor in Prayer
5. To Seek Reconciliation, We Must Bless Those Separated from Us

What Is God's Purpose in Our Trials?

During the night Jacob quickly took his two wives, his two female servants, and his eleven sons and crossed the ford of the Jabbok. He took them and sent them across the stream along with all his possessions. So Jacob was left alone. Then a man wrestled with him until daybreak. When the man saw that he could not defeat Jacob, he struck the socket of his hip so the socket of Jacob's hip was dislocated while he wrestled with him. Then the man said, "Let me go, for the dawn is breaking." "I will not let you go," Jacob replied, "unless you bless me." The man asked him, "What is your name?" He answered, "Jacob." "No longer will your name be Jacob," the man told him, "but Israel, because you have fought with God and with men and have prevailed." Then Jacob asked, "Please tell me your name." "Why do you ask my name?" the man replied. Then he blessed Jacob there. So Jacob named the place Peniel, explaining, "Certainly I have seen God face to face and have survived." The sun rose over him as he crossed over Penuel, but he was limping because of his hip. That is why to this day the Israelites do not eat the sinew which is attached to the socket of the hip, because he struck the socket of Jacob's hip near the attached sinew.
Genesis 32:22-32 (NET)

What is God's purpose in our trials and struggles?

In this context, Jacob is experiencing many difficulties. After working for his uncle Laban for twenty years, he flees in the middle of the night with his family and possessions. Laban was a difficult employer and relative. He deceived Jacob many times. After Jacob left with his family, Laban caught up to him with a small band, probably, planning to harm Jacob. However, God warned Laban in a dream to not speak anything good or bad to Jacob. After meeting, Jacob and Laban made a nonaggression pact—to not harm one another (Gen 31).

Right after this pact, Genesis 32:1-2 says that a large army of angels met with Jacob. Jacob calls the place Mahanaim, which means two camps. There were probably two angelic armies. God sent them, no doubt, to encourage and strengthen Jacob. But, they were also there to show Jacob that God had protected him and his family and was going to continue to protect him.

Probably motivated from his encounter with God's angels, Jacob decides to reconcile a twenty-year, broken relationship with Esau, his brother. Previously, Jacob had swindled Esau out of his birthright, and in response, Esau wanted to kill him. It was that fractured relationship that initially prompted Jacob to seek refuge with Laban in Haran and to find a wife. After contacting Esau and seeking favor with him, Esau responds by coming to meet Jacob with four hundred men on horses. Jacob, probably, rightly assumes Esau is still angry and wants to take his life.

Jacob sends three caravans of gifts before him to try to appease Esau. Then in this text, after a night of no sleep, he sends his family across the Jabbok river. Because of the powerful rushing waters, this would have been very dangerous to do at night; however, having one more barrier between Esau and his family seemed less dangerous.

After sending them across the river, Jacob stays on the other side—probably to pray and spend time with God. Then while alone, he is attacked by a man in the middle of the night. This man is God, in angelic form, wrestling with Jacob (cf. Hos 12:3-4, Gen 32:30). Sometimes this text is taught with a focus on us wrestling with God in prayer. However, it must be noticed in verse 24 that the man wrestled with Jacob and not vice versa. Initially, God was seeking something from Jacob, and then towards the end of the night, after Jacob was, essentially, defeated when his hip was dislocated, Jacob seeks a blessing from the man.

What is happening in this text? First, it must be noticed that this bares some similarities with how God appeared as a man at other times in Scripture. With Abraham, who was a pilgrim from Ur dwelling in Canaan, God appeared as a pilgrim and went to his house (Gen 18). With Joshua, who was Israel's general, God appeared as a soldier (Josh 5:13-15). And here, with Jacob, whose name means "heel-grabber," who had tried to trip people up like a wrestler throughout his life (i.e. his brother, father, and uncle), God appeared as a wrestler. As Jacob had previously tried to wrestle things from others, God wanted something from Jacob. Throughout his life, God had always been wrestling with Jacob—seeking his submission, obedience, and trust. Psalm 18:26 says, "You prove to be reliable to one who is blameless, but you prove to be deceptive to one who is perverse." Since Jacob was a wrestler by nature, God met Jacob as one.[44]

In this specific circumstance, as Jacob anticipates an encounter with murderous Esau, it seems that God's wrestling with Jacob was symbolic of what was happening in the natural world (cf. 32:28 and 33:4). Previously, God showed Jacob how, in the spiritual world, angels were protecting him in his encounter with Laban (Gen 32:1-2). But now God is showing him that though he is in turmoil, awaiting murderous Esau, it was God who was actually allowing the turmoil in his life. Through the circumstances, God was wrestling with Jacob to bring changes in his life. The same is true with us. We may never physically see God or his angels working behind our circumstances, but they are there. God particularly uses trials and struggles for transformative purposes in our lives (Heb 12:7).

One person said, "God whispers to us in our pleasures but shouts at us in our trials." A.W. Tozer said, "The Lord cannot fully bless a man until He has first conquered him."[45] F. B. Meyer said,

> This is life; a long wrestle against the love of God, which longs to make us royal. As the years go on, we begin to cling where once we struggled; and as the morn of heaven breaks, we catch glimpses of the Angel-face of love...[46]

Therefore, as we consider God's wrestling with Jacob, we learn principles about God's purposes in trials and how we should respond to them. Jacob had a struggle with Esau, but behind this struggle was a struggle with God, who was seeking to transform Jacob's life.

Big Question: What principles can we learn about God's purposes in our trials and how we should respond to them?

God's Purpose in Our Trials Is for Us to Focus on Him

> During the night Jacob quickly took his two wives, his two female servants, and his eleven sons and crossed the ford of the Jabbok. He took them and sent them across the stream along with all his possessions. So Jacob was left alone. Then a man wrestled with him until daybreak.
> Genesis 32:22-24

Though the NET says Jacob "quickly took his wives," the NIV says Jacob "got up" and the ESV says he "arose." It seems that Jacob had already gone to bed but couldn't sleep. He sends his family and possessions across the river but stays by himself, most likely to think or pray.

Jacob oversaw a large camp of people. In fact, in his earlier prayer, he calls it "two camps" (Gen 32:10). He had two wives, twelve children, and enough flocks to spare over 550 of them as gifts to Esau. There was always plenty of work, plans, and decisions to be made, which was good. However, it probably had a tendency to crowd out God and prayer. It was when Jacob was intentionally alone that he could really focus on God, which was probably one of God's purposes in the trial.

This is also true with us. Busyness and life circumstances tend to hinder our time with God. It is often through trials that God encourages us to separate from the crowd and busyness to focus on him. Again, as mentioned, it seems this wrestling was symbolic of what was happening in the natural world. Behind Jacob's trial with Esau was God's wrestling with Jacob. God wanted to do something in Jacob's life through this trial, but in order to do it, God had to get him alone and appear to him in a dramatic way.

Sadly, many of us spend our time focusing on "Esau" in our trial by being consumed with people or circumstances, and therefore, missing God's hand in it. We miss his "reaching" out to us, as he reached out to Jacob. If we are going to respond well to our trials, we must see God in them and his desire to draw us to himself and for us to intentionally choose to focus on him. Our trials are not accidental or haphazard, but part of God's sovereign plan to make us into his image (cf. Eph 1:11, Rom 8:28-29). We must focus on him—through prayer, studying his Word, and obedience. God desires to change us and if we need to go through a trial to draw our focus to him, then he is willing to allow one. In this circumstance, God had Jacob all alone, and it was time to do work in his life. God desires to get us alone and bring change in us as well.

Are you drawing near God in the midst of your trial? Are you seeking his face? Is the discipline of solitude—being alone with God—a regular part of your life? Don't let busyness choke out your time with God. When we do that, sometimes a trial is the only way for God to get our attention and our obedience. Psalm 46:10 (NIV) says, "Be still and know that I am God."

Application Question: Why is it so easy to let busyness crowd God out of our lives? How has God used trials to help you focus on him more? How do you practice the discipline of solitude—daily getting alone with God? How is God calling you to grow in this discipline?

God's Purpose in Our Trials Is for Us to Develop Perseverance

So Jacob was left alone. Then a man wrestled with him until daybreak. Genesis 22:34

After the man grabs Jacob, they wrestle till day break. This is a phenomenal task. How did Jacob last so long? Wrestling is grueling. Six minutes of intense wrestling will wear most people out. But Jacob wrestles all night—maybe for six or seven hours. This is a greater workload than running a marathon, which for most takes four to five hours—elite runners can do it in two. From this alone, we can tell that God provided a special grace for Jacob to continue throughout the night. But then, we must ask the question, "Why did God provide grace for

Jacob to wrestle so long? Also, we must ask, "If God's primary purpose was to defeat Jacob, why did he not just end it quickly?" We know the man was powerful enough to do this. When it nears daybreak, the man simply touches Jacob's hip and it dislocates. Some versions say it shrank. He could have won at any time. Why does he wrestle with Jacob all night and potentially provide grace so it could continue?

It seems one of the purposes was to teach Jacob perseverance—though he, no doubt, felt like quitting. Similarly, God allowed Jacob to go through twenty years of a difficult relationship with Laban. He was tricked and cheated many times. God could have ended that trial at any time, but he waited twenty years to do so. Of course, there were many things God was doing through Jacob's trial with Laban, and there were many things God was doing as he wrestled with Jacob throughout the night. But one of the main things God was doing was developing perseverance in him.

God often does the same thing with us. He provides grace for us to continue under difficult circumstances and ends the situation at the proper time. He does this to teach us perseverance. Consider the following verses:

And let endurance have its perfect effect, so that you will be perfect and complete, not deficient in anything.
James 1:4

Not only this, but we also rejoice in sufferings, knowing that suffering produces endurance, and endurance, character, and character, hope.
Romans 5:3-4

God uses endurance or perseverance to complete us—meaning to make us mature. When we persevere—meaning to bear up under a heavy weight—it develops our character and helps us trust in God.

This happens in parenting all the time. A parent puts a child into a sport or club, but when the child encounters difficulty, he immediately wants to quit. If the parent allows the child to quit, quitting will often become part of his character. When circumstances get tough, he will want to quit relationships, jobs, hobbies, etc., throughout his life. He may never develop perseverance. But wise parents understand the benefit of perseverance. If the child continues, even though he emotionally wants to quit, he will develop the ability to persevere in the various difficulties of life—in the work force, marriage, parenting, church, etc.

God isn't trying to develop spoiled children who want to quit every time they go through something hard. He is trying to develop mature children who not only can persevere but also can help others persevere through the difficulties of life. He develops ministers from his trials.

Are you persevering in your trial? Often like David, we have to pray, "Renew a steadfast spirit within me" (Psalm 51:10 NASB). Lord, help us to stand, even when we feel like quitting!

Application Question: Why is perseverance such an important virtue to develop? In what ways is God calling you to persevere in your current season? What are some disciplines that help with developing a "steadfast spirit" while going through trials (Ps 51:10)?

God's Purpose in Our Trials Is for Us to Recognize Our Weakness and Need for Him

> When the man saw that he could not defeat Jacob, he struck the socket of his hip so the socket of Jacob's hip was dislocated while he wrestled with him. Then the man said, "Let me go, for the dawn is breaking." "I will not let you go," Jacob replied, "unless you bless me."
> …
> Genesis 32:25-26

While Jacob and the man wrestled, Jacob would not give up. Therefore, God touched Jacob's hip and dislocated it. In wrestling, the hips and legs are where the strength is. That's why wrestlers typically have very muscular lower bodies. When the hip was dislocated, the fight was over. Jacob lost.

God often does this with us as well. It is often our strengths that keep us away from God and obedience to him. We feel competent for our work load, relationships, future, etc.—therefore, we are not as dependent upon God as we should be, if at all. So God often has to touch our strengths—our places of confidence—to help us depend on him. For some, he touches their intelligence, others their body, others their finances, others their family or friendships. Wherever our pride, strength, and focus are, outside of God, God often touches it, so we see our weakness.

To the Church of Laodicea, God said:

> 'I know your deeds, that you are neither cold nor hot. I wish you were either cold or hot! So because you are lukewarm, and neither hot nor cold, I am going to vomit you out of my mouth! Because you say, "I am rich and have acquired great wealth, and need nothing," but do not realize that you are wretched, pitiful, poor, blind, and naked
> Revelation 3:15-17

The church had wealth, thought they were right before God, and that they didn't need anything. This created a spiritual lukewarmness—they weren't

138

passionate about God at all. However, God said they were really "wretched, pitiful, poor, blind, and naked" (3:17). They didn't know how weak they were, so God was going to "vomit" them out of his mouth (3:16)—which probably referred to some type of judgment or trial. The trial was going to show them how weak they really were and how they needed God.

Often God does the same to us. He has to touch us, and sometimes injure us, so we know our weakness. Previously, we didn't feel like we needed to read God's Word, go to church or small group, pray, or serve, but after our trial, we realize that we need God desperately. That's what God was doing to Jacob.

In fact, from this point on, Jacob was no longer wrestling, all he could do was cling to the man and not let go. All he could do was hold onto God—he barely had enough strength with one leg to hold himself up. God does the same to us. Through trials and the pain experienced in them, he helps us cling to him.

With Paul, God allowed him to experience a demonic thorn in the flesh which made him weak. We don't know exactly what it was, but most believe it was a sickness. When Paul asked for God to remove it, God replied, "My grace is enough for you, for my power is made perfect in weakness" (2 Cor 12:9). As Paul was weak, he also began to cling to God more and therefore experience power in his weakness. In response to this, Paul said,

> So then, I will boast most gladly about my weaknesses, so that the power of Christ may reside in me. Therefore I am content with weaknesses, with insults, with troubles, with persecutions and difficulties for the sake of Christ, for whenever I am weak, then I am strong.
> 2 Corinthians 12:9b-10

In our trials, God often touches our perceived strength, so we can know our true weakness and cling to God's power. Where are your strengths outside of God located? How have you experienced God's touch and therefore the revealing of your weakness?

Application Question: What are your areas of strength which you have a tendency to neglect God in or because of? In what ways have you experienced God touching your strength, so that you cling more dearly to him and experience his power?

God's Purpose in Our Trials Is for Us to Grow in Prayer

> Then the man said, "Let me go, for the dawn is breaking." "I will not let you go," Jacob replied, "unless you bless me." ...
> Genesis 32:26

As mentioned, at this point, Jacob is no longer wrestling in his strength, he is simply clinging to God in weakness. While doing this, Jacob begins to pray. The man says, "Let me go," but Jacob replies, "I will not let you go unless you bless me." This sounds like a command, but it really wasn't. Jacob had lost. He was defeated. Hosea 12:3-4, while summarizing Jacob's life, describes Jacob's request this way: "In the womb he attacked his brother; in his manly vigor he struggled with God. He struggled with an angel and prevailed; he wept and begged for his favor. He found God at Bethel, and there he spoke with him!"

Jacob weeps and begs for this man's favor. He is in pain and at this man's mercy. He cries out, "No, I won't let you go. Please bless me." We don't know at what point Jacob discerned he was wrestling with God. Maybe, he knew immediately, but if not, he certainly knew when the man easily dislocated his hip. Later, he calls the place Peniel because he had seen God's face and survived (v. 30).

Jacob was not a man of prayer. Jacob's narrative begins in Genesis 25; however, we never see him pray until Genesis 32. When he hears that Esau is coming to meet him with 400 men, he prays. He claims God's promises of prospering him and making his descendants numerous (v. 9-12). Again, he prays as he wrestles with God (v. 26). Jacob prays twice in this one chapter. He humbly begs the Lord with tears for a blessing.

Throughout Jacob's narrative, desiring God's blessing has been his greatest attribute. The problem is he always sought it the wrong way. He swindled his brother and deceived his father for it. When he married—a crucial part of his receiving Abraham's blessing—he married two women instead of one, which wasn't part of God's perfect will for his life. Of course, his circumstances were not ideal, as Laban deceived him; however, that was no excuse to accept the deception and live in sin. Jacob desired God's blessing but always sought it the wrong way. But now, God was training him through trials how to receive the blessing properly—it was through laboring in prayer. When Esau was going to receive the blessing instead of him, he should have prayed. When Laban tricked him by giving him Leah, he should have prayed. Prayer was the missing ingredient in his life. God was aiming to correct that through this trial.

In the same way, God often trains us to labor in prayer through our trials. Before experiencing trials, we spent little time in prayer. We prayed at meals and before bed, but we rarely, if at all, isolated ourselves to spend quality time in prayer. Through weakening and breaking Jacob, God was training him to become a man of prayer and not just of action.

Are you daily drawing near the Lord in prayer? Are you allowing trials to help you seek God's blessing—his deliverance, his empowerment, and his direction?

Application Question: Why do most people struggle with their prayer lives and being faithful in it? What are some strategies that might help people pray more often and better? How is God calling you to cling to God in prayer and seek his blessing? What blessings are you currently seeking God for?

God's Purpose in Our Trials Is for Us to Recognize and Confess Our Sin

> The man asked him, "What is your name?" He answered, "Jacob."
> Genesis 32:27

After Jacob asked for a blessing, the man replies, "What is your name?" Obviously, God knew the answer to that, since he is omniscient. When God asks a question in Scripture, it is not to gain information. It is typically for the other's benefit and realization. When God asked Adam if he ate from the Tree of the Knowledge of Good and Evil, it was not because God didn't know the answer. It was because he wanted Adam to recognize his sin and confess it.

When Jacob answered by sharing his name, it was meant to help Jacob realize, he had lived out his name. He had been deceitfully wrestling with people his whole life. His name meant "deceiver" or "heel grabber." It has a wrestling connotation to it. He deceived his brother, father, and uncle. God was using the trial to help Jacob see his sin and be free from it.

When Jacob answered God with his name, in his heart, it appears to have been a form of confession. He was saying:

> I have been a deceiver. When my father asked who I was, I said, "Esau." I deceived him. When you told me to leave Laban, I didn't trust you. I deceived Laban by quickly leaving in the middle of the night. Laban's and Esau's seeking to harm me is all my fault. I have been a Jacob. Forgive me and please bless me.

It's the same for us. God often uses trials to help us recognize our failures and repent of them. In Deuteronomy 8:2 (NIV), Moses said the reason God led Israel into the wilderness was to reveal what was in their hearts—to see if they would obey God. He said, "Remember how the LORD your God led you all the way in the wilderness these forty years, to humble and test you in order to know what was in your heart, whether or not you would keep his commands."

What does our response in trials say about our hearts? Do we run away from God or to him in our trials? Do we run to some addiction, idol, or sin before God—a relationship, work, alcohol, lying, complaining, or self-pity?

141

We tend to think of our enemies as our circumstances or certain people. However, our biggest enemy is our hearts—their love for sin and lack of trust in God. Therefore, by God's grace, he allows trials to reveal the sin in our hearts, so we can repent of it. First John 1:9 says, "But if we confess our sins, he is faithful and righteous, forgiving us our sins and cleansing us from all unrighteousness."

Are you confessing your sin in the midst of your trial, or are you clinging to it instead of God? Are you fighting with God—holding on to your independence and self-reliance—instead of laying everything down to cling to him?

Application Question: If our sinful tendencies typically show up in trials (lying, complaining, addictions, love for the world, lack of trust in God, etc.), what sinful tendencies of yours often show up in the midst of trials? Are there specific ones that you are struggling to fully repent of?

God's Purpose in Our Trials Is to Change Our Character

"No longer will your name be Jacob," the man told him, "but Israel, because you have fought with God and with men and have prevailed." Genesis 32:28

After Jacob told God his name, God renamed him "Israel." Naming represented at least two things in that culture: ownership and a change of character or destiny. Sometimes kings would rename their subjects. For example, Daniel and his three Hebrew friends were all given Babylonian names when they became subjects of Babylon. Jacob, who commonly lived for himself, was now, even more so, going to live for God. In fact, many translate the name "Israel" as "God rules," "God commands," "God prevails," or "God strives." Those who prefer this translation say every time the name of God is coupled with a verb, God is always the subject.[47] For example, Daniel means "God judges" not "he judges God," and Samuel means "God heard" not "he heard God." Others translate "Israel" as "strives with God" or "prevails with God." They would take this meaning by how the narrator explains the naming. Jacob had fought with God and men and prevailed (v. 28). Others translate it "Prince of God."

How did Jacob prevail with God? Certainly, he didn't win the battle. By the end of it, his hip was dislocated, and he was clinging to the angel. In fact, after Jacob named the site Peniel, he said he had seen God's face and "survived" (v. 30). He barely survived—he was not the victor. Therefore, in what way, did Jacob prevail with God? In this way, previously, Jacob operated in his strength—deceiving and manipulating people and situations—but, with the angel, he succeeded in receiving the blessing, as he cried out in his weakness and prayer. This would be the increased means by which Jacob would achieve

142

victory in the future. When the narrator talked about "prevailing with men," this was about his future. God would deliver Jacob from Esau (33:4). By weakness and prayer, Jacob found success.

Jacob's battle and renaming marked a character change in Jacob. He would still, at times, operate in his flesh by depending on his fleshly wisdom instead of God's. However, depending on God would begin to identify him more.

In the same way, that is what God aims to achieve through our trials. He wants to change us more into his image. Again, Romans 5:3-4 says we rejoice in tribulation because it produces perseverance and then character. Our character changes as we learn perseverance in our trials, patience with people, love for the unlovable, and trust in God, rather than doubting him. God doesn't waste our trials but uses them to the best end.

Application Question: How have you grown in character, as you've experienced past trials? What aspects of your character do you believe God is working on now through the trials or difficulties you're experiencing?

God's Purpose in Our Trials Is for Us to Know God Better

> Then Jacob asked, "Please tell me your name." "Why do you ask my name?" the man replied.
> Genesis 32:29

After being renamed, Jacob politely asked to know the man's name. But the man simply replied, "Why do you ask my name?" Why does the man not answer Jacob? The reason seems to be that Jacob already knew who he was. Jacob knew the man was God and that is why he named the place Peniel—"face of God" (v. 30).

Similarly, one of God's primary purposes in trials is to help us know him more by revealing different characteristics of himself. In Genesis 12, when Abraham was called to leave his home and family, God revealed himself as Yahweh—the covenant God. In leaving his home and family, he would learn that God was faithful—he was a God of covenant. In Genesis 17, when God told Abraham he was going to have a child in his old age, God's name was El Shaddai. He was the all-powerful God—the one who does miracles. Likewise, God revealed himself as Yahweh to Jacob at Bethel when he first left his father's house. Yahweh protected him from Laban and was protecting him now from Esau. Jacob knew his name and was experiencing the covenant God in a more intimate way, as he wrestled with him and received his blessing.

In the same way, when we go through trials, one of God's purposes is for us to know him more—to know his name and character, to know that he is faithful, loving, just, merciful, and all-powerful.

143

Application Question: What aspect(s) of God's character has he been revealing to you recently through Scripture or your trials?

God's Purpose in Our Trials Is to Bless Us

Then Jacob asked, "Please tell me your name." "Why do you ask my name?" the man replied. Then he blessed Jacob there.
Genesis 32:29

After renaming Jacob, the man blesses him. We don't know exactly what this entailed. Most likely, the angel restated the promises of Abraham and Isaac over him, just as God had done at Bethel (Gen 28). God was going to make him into a great people and prosper him. Certainly, this blessing also included protection, as was needed in his current situation with Esau.

Similarly, God's purpose in our trials is to bless us. This means not only changing our character and allowing us to know God more, but also much more. With Joseph, after losing his family and experiencing slavery and imprisonment, God exalted him to second-in-command over Egypt, where he could save many people including his family. With Job, after he lost his family, health, and career, ultimately God restored double of all he lost. With Daniel, who was taken away from his home and family to Babylon, God favored him and placed him in government positions to bless the nations.

Through being faithful in trials, God promises that he will expand our ministry to others, as he did with Joseph and Daniel. In 2 Corinthians 1:3-5, Paul said:

Blessed is the God and Father of our Lord Jesus Christ, the Father of mercies and God of all comfort, who comforts us in all our troubles so that we may be able to comfort those experiencing any trouble with the comfort with which we ourselves are comforted by God. For just as the sufferings of Christ overflow toward us, so also our comfort through Christ overflows to you.

In our trials, as we seek the Lord, we experience his comfort, so we can in turn comfort others with it. It has often been said that our misery often becomes our ministry. We minister out of our sufferings and the comfort received during them.

If we're faithful in our sufferings, God not only blesses us with an expanded ministry, but also promises to bless us richly in heaven. Consider the following verses:

144

Happy is the one who endures testing, because when he has proven to be genuine, he will receive the crown of life that God promised to those who love him.
James 1:12

Blessed are you when people insult you and persecute you and say all kinds of evil things about you falsely on account of me. Rejoice and be glad because your reward is great in heaven, for they persecuted the prophets before you in the same way.
Matthew 5:11-12

God promises eternal rewards as we faithfully endure trials. We must remember that God has good plans for us, even though it may seem hard to believe when encountering difficulties. Through Christ's sufferings, he paid the penalty for our sins, so that anyone who trusts in him can be saved (John 3:16). He was also made perfect through his sufferings, so he could have an eternal ministry as our high priest—sympathizing with our weaknesses, praying for us, and giving grace in our time of need (cf. Heb 2:10, 4:15-16, 7:25). He also has been given a name, which is above every name, that at the name of Jesus, every knee would bow and every tongue confess that Jesus is Lord (Phil 2:6-11). God's plan is to bless those who faithfully suffer.

Are you trusting that God has good plans for you in your suffering? We need to realize this if we are going to stand. Those who hope in the Lord shall renew their strength, they shall mount up on the wings of eagles, run and not grow weary, and walk and not faint (Isaiah 40:31). We must trust that God's ultimate plan is to bless us and not hurt us.

Application Question: In what ways have you experienced God's blessing after faithfully going through a trial? How can we, in faith, hold on to this truth while suffering?

God's Purpose in Our Trials Is for Us to Become Better Witnesses

So Jacob named the place Peniel, explaining, "Certainly I have seen God face to face and have survived." The sun rose over him as he crossed over Penuel, but he was limping because of his hip. That is why to this day the Israelites do not eat the sinew which is attached to the socket of the hip, because he struck the socket of Jacob's hip near the attached sinew.
Genesis 32:30-32

145

After this experience, Jacob named the place Peniel, which means "face of God."[48] Since his limp continued after this experience, Israelites chose to not eat the meat around the hip, in remembrance of Jacob's encounter with God. This is still observed by some orthodox Jews today.

What this implies is that Jacob shared this experience. He shared it with his wives, children, and servants. It was passed down by the Jews, first through oral history and then through Scripture. He shared his wrestling experience at Peniel with others. His injury and the place it happened were both memorials of God's work.

Similarly, though trials may be hard, discouraging, and, at times, shameful, they are not our stories to keep to ourselves. They are God's stories of how he protected us, challenged us, helped us grow, and even used our wounds for his glory. We must share them with others, so God receives honor. Also, it is by sharing them with others that we receive full healing and often process exactly what God has done in our lives. James 5:16 says, "So confess your sins to one another and pray for one another so that you may be healed. The prayer of a righteous person has great effectiveness."

Sadly, many never share their stories and therefore never experience God's grace. They don't experience God's healing, don't allow God to heal others through them, and therefore, rob God of his glory.

Don't keep your trials to yourself! Share them with others. Allow God to heal you, heal others, and glorify himself. Psalm 107:2 (NIV) says, "Let the redeemed of the Lord tell their story."

Application Question: Why do people often not share their testimonies with others? How can we grow in transparency in order to receive healing, help others heal, and give glory to God?

Conclusion

As we consider God's wrestling with Jacob, it was a picture of his current trial with Esau. Often, we only see our natural circumstances and forget there is a spiritual reality that oversees them. In this story, God pulls back the curtain: Jacob's struggle was not only with Esau, it was also with God and with himself. God wanted to change Jacob through his difficulties. God had always been wrestling with Jacob, seeking to get his will done in his life. Similarly, God has always been lovingly wrestling with us, seeking our submission to his will and kingdom.

What is God's purpose in our trials and struggles?

1. God's Purpose in Our Trials Is for Us to Focus on Him
2. God's Purpose in Our Trials Is for Us to Develop Perseverance

146

3. God's Purpose in Our Trials Is for Us to Recognize Our Weakness and Need for Him
4. God's Purpose in Our Trials Is for Us to Grow in Prayer
5. God's Purpose in Our Trials Is for Us to Recognize and Confess Our Sin
6. God's Purpose in Our Trials Is to Change Our Character
7. God's Purpose in Our Trials Is for Us to Know God Better
8. God's Purpose in Our Trials Is to Bless Us
9. God's Purpose in Our Trials Is for Us to Become Better Witnesses

Living Out Our New Identity in Christ

Jacob looked up and saw that Esau was coming along with four hundred men. So he divided the children among Leah, Rachel, and the two female servants. He put the servants and their children in front, with Leah and her children behind them, and Rachel and Joseph behind them. But Jacob himself went on ahead of them, and he bowed toward the ground seven times as he approached his brother. But Esau ran to meet him, embraced him, hugged his neck, and kissed him. Then they both wept. When Esau looked up and saw the women and the children, he asked, "Who are these people with you?" Jacob replied, "The children whom God has graciously given your servant." The female servants came forward with their children and bowed down. Then Leah came forward with her children and they bowed down. Finally Joseph and Rachel came forward and bowed down. Esau then asked, "What did you intend by sending all these herds to meet me?" Jacob replied, "To find favor in your sight, my lord." But Esau said, "I have plenty, my brother. Keep what belongs to you." "No, please take them," Jacob said. "If I have found favor in your sight, accept my gift from my hand. Now that I have seen your face and you have accepted me, it is as if I have seen the face of God. Please take my present that was brought to you, for God has been generous to me and I have all I need." When Jacob urged him, he took it. Then Esau said, "Let's be on our way! I will go in front of you." But Jacob said to him, "My lord knows that the children are young, and that I have to look after the sheep and cattle that are nursing their young. If they are driven too hard for even a single day, all the animals will die. Let my lord go on ahead of his servant. I will travel more slowly, at the pace of the herds and the children, until I come to my lord at Seir." So Esau said, "Let me leave some of my men with you." "Why do that?" Jacob replied. "My lord has already been kind enough to me." So that same day Esau made his way back to Seir. But Jacob traveled to Succoth where he built himself a house and made shelters for his livestock. That is why the place was called Succoth. After he left Paddan Aram, Jacob came safely to the city of Shechem in the land of Canaan, and he camped near the city. Then he purchased the portion of the field where he had pitched his tent; he bought it from the sons of Hamor, Shechem's

father, for a hundred pieces of money. There he set up an altar and called it "The God of Israel is God."
Genesis 33 (NET)

How can we live out our new identity in Christ?

In Genesis 32:22-32, Jacob wrestled with God, and after wrestling, God gave him a new name, Israel, which means "God commands," "God prevails," or "the one who prevails with God." The changing of his name meant a change of character and destiny. Previously Jacob trusted in his wisdom and strength instead of God's, but now he was to be marked by obeying God's commands and relying on God's strength instead of his own.

However, as we continue studying Jacob's narrative, we certainly see growth, but we also see him continually fall back into old habits. He wasn't the same old Jacob, but he didn't always live like Israel either. In fact, it's interesting to consider that when God gave Abraham a new name in Genesis 17, he is always called by that name in the Genesis narrative from that point on. But for Jacob, after being named Israel, the narrator, Moses, calls him Jacob twice more than Israel throughout his narrative (Gen 33-50).[49] Since the Holy Spirit inspired every part of Scripture, we can have no doubt that this was intentional. Jacob, though experiencing God and being renamed, commonly didn't live out his new identity. Arthur Pink said this: "It is one thing to be privileged with a special visitation from or manifestation of God to us, but it is quite another to live in the power of it."[50]

Sadly, this is commonly true for us. As believers, we have been called children of God, saints, co-heirs with Christ, co-workers with God, and new creations. Scripture also teaches us that our old man, our old nature, died with Christ and that we are no longer slaves of sin but slaves of righteousness (Rom 6). However, many of us live as slaves of sin instead of slaves of righteousness and as sinners instead of saints. We look like Jacob instead of Israel.

How can we live out our new identity in Christ? As Jacob meets with Esau, it is clear that he is not the same man that he was, but at the same time, he is not who he should have been. As we consider Jacob's struggle to live as Israel, we'll learn more about how to live out our new identity in Christ.

Big Question: What can we learn about living out our identity in Christ, as we consider how Jacob struggled to live out his new name in Genesis 33?

To Live Out Our New Identity, We Must Be Careful of Our Spiritual Weaknesses

Jacob looked up and saw that Esau was coming along with four hundred men. So he divided the children among Leah, Rachel, and the two female servants. He put the servants and their children in front, with Leah and her children behind them, and Rachel and Joseph behind them... Let my lord go on ahead of his servant. I will travel more slowly, at the pace of the herds and the children, until I come to my lord at Seir." So Esau said, "Let me leave some of my men with you." "Why do that?" Jacob replied. "My lord has already been kind enough to me." So that same day Esau made his way back to Seir. But Jacob traveled to Succoth where he built himself a house and made shelters for his livestock. That is why the place was called Succoth.
Genesis 33:1-2, 14-17

Even though God has changed our names and given us new identities, we still have certain propensities and weaknesses. Some of them are passed down generationally (Ex 20:5) and some of them come from our practice of certain sins. The more we practice a certain sin, the more vulnerable we are to fall back into it later on in life. With Jacob, one of his weaknesses was favoritism. As seen throughout his narrative, his parents played favorites between him and his brother, Esau, causing animosity between them. When Jacob married two women, he favored Rachel.

Though, Jacob had just wrestled with God and prevailed, he falls right back into the habit of favoritism when he sees Esau. He orders his family to line up based on rank/importance: first the servants and their children, then Leah and her children, and finally Rachel and her son, Joseph. If the servants and their children were attacked, the others could flee. Everybody in the family knew their rank. It probably re-opened a wound for Leah, who had struggled with being unloved throughout the marriage (Gen 29). In addition, all the children knew who Jacob's favorite child was—it was Joseph.

Later, this seed sown in the children would bear fruit. In Genesis 37, Jacob would give Joseph a robe of many colors—again showing all the other children who his favorite was. This caused the other brothers to hate Joseph and sell him into slavery. Though Jacob was renamed and changed, favoritism was his default setting—like a computer program. He often fell back into it, with disastrous results.

However, this was not Jacob's only negative default. He also was a deceiver. That's actually what his name meant. After reconciling with his brother, Esau, he lies to him—saying that he would meet Esau in Seir—Esau's home. However, when Esau goes south, Jacob goes north, towards Succoth. That was Jacob's default setting. He lied both to get what he wanted and to protect himself. This was something passed down generationally. Abraham struggled with lying. He lied about his wife being his sister twice—both times leading to her being taken by powerful men. Isaac, Jacob's father, also lied about his wife. Later,

Jacob's eleven sons would lie to him for years—saying that Joseph was killed by an animal, when they had really sold him into slavery.

If we are going to walk in our new nature and identity in Christ, we must recognize our spiritual weaknesses—the areas we are most prone to fall into sin. David's weakness was women. Moses tended to take strong actions in his flesh. Early on, he killed an Egyptian—trusting in his own strength to deliver Israel. Later, when God told him to speak to a rock, so water would flow out, he was so frustrated with Israel, he hit the rock; and therefore, God judged him. He was prone to rely on his own strength. That was his default setting.

What is your weakness? If you are going to walk in your new identity, you must identify it and be careful of it. Is it complaining when things are difficult? Is it wanting to quit in the midst of adversity? Is it unforgiveness—cutting people off who have failed you? Whatever negative things you tend to practice when stressed, angry, or threatened is probably your default setting. If you're going to walk in your new identity, you must be careful of your spiritual weaknesses.

Application Question: What are your spiritual weaknesses—the areas of sin, which you are particularly prone to fall into, especially in times of difficulty? How do you protect yourself from falling into those weaknesses?

To Live Out Our New Identity, We Must Labor to Live at Peace with Others

> But Jacob himself went on ahead of them, and he bowed toward the ground seven times as he approached his brother. But Esau ran to meet him, embraced him, hugged his neck, and kissed him. Then they both wept... Esau then asked, "What did you intend by sending all these herds to meet me?" Jacob replied, "To find favor in your sight, my lord." But Esau said, "I have plenty, my brother. Keep what belongs to you." "No, please take them," Jacob said. "If I have found favor in your sight, accept my gift from my hand. Now that I have seen your face and you have accepted me, it is as if I have seen the face of God. Please take my present that was brought to you, for God has been generous to me and I have all I need." When Jacob urged him, he took it.
> Genesis 33:3-4, 8-11

When Jacob sees Esau, he bows down seven times. As discovered from ancient Egyptian tablets, this was protocol for honoring a king.[51] Jacob humbles himself as a servant before his brother. After embracing each other and weeping, Jacob insists that Esau take his luxurious gift of over 550 cattle. Even though Esau refused, it was important to Jacob for him to take the gift. In ancient times, it was known that one would not accept a gift from an enemy but only from a friend. Therefore, by accepting the gift, Esau would further confirm that their enmity was over and that he had favored Jacob.[52]

In verse 10, when Jacob said, "'If I have found favor in your sight, accept my gift from my hand. Now that I have seen your face and you have accepted me, it is as if I have seen the face of God,'" he was connecting his wrestling with God and seeing God's face to seeing Esau's face.[53] When God blessed Jacob after their wrestling, Jacob and Esau's restoration was a fruit of that.

Similarly, our relationship with others is also connected to our relationship with God. In Matthew 5:23-24, Christ said,

> So then, if you bring your gift to the altar and there remember that your brother has something against you, leave your gift there in front of the altar. First go and be reconciled to your brother and then come and present your gift.

For this reason, to be out of fellowship with others is to be out of fellowship with God. Our old nature is prone to discord and unforgiveness and our new nature is prone to peace (cf. Gal 5:19-23). Therefore, to live out our new identity in Christ, we must always seek to live at peace with others, as much as depends on us (Rom 12:18).

In order to seek restoration, Jacob humbles himself as a servant, when he bows seven times to Esau—honoring him as a king. He also offered restitution through his generous gift. We must do the same if we are going to live out our new natures in Christ.

Are there any relationships God is calling you to seek to restore? How is God calling you to humble yourself to pursue reconciliation?

Application Question: Are there any strained relationships in your life that God is calling you to seek to restore? What steps should be taken to restore relationships, as modeled in Jacob's reconciliation with Esau?

To Live Out Our New Identity, We Must Put Our Confidence in God's Grace and Not Human Strength

> When Esau looked up and saw the women and the children, he asked, "Who are these people with you?" Jacob replied, "The children whom God has graciously given your servant." The female servants came forward with their children and bowed down. Then Leah came forward with her children and they bowed down. Finally Joseph and Rachel came forward and bowed down. Esau then asked, "What did you

intend by sending all these herds to meet me?" Jacob replied, "To find favor in your sight, my lord." But Esau said, "I have plenty, my brother. Keep what belongs to you." "No, please take them," Jacob said. "If I have found favor in your sight, accept my gift from my hand. Now that I have seen your face and you have accepted me, it is as if I have seen the face of God. Please take my present that was brought to you, for God has been generous to me and I have all I need." When Jacob urged him, he took it.
Genesis 33:5-11

Twice while talking with Esau, Jacob recognized God's gracious provisions in his life. When Esau asked who all the people were with him, Jacob replied, "The children whom God has graciously given your servant" (v. 5). After Esau asked about all the herds that were sent to meet him, again Jacob replied by recognizing God's grace. In verse 11, Jacob said, "Please take my present that was brought to you, for God has been generous to me and I have all I need.'"

Jacob recognized that all twelve of his children were gifts of God—only God had power over the womb, not him or his wives. He also recognized all his wealth came from God. It was not because of all his diligent labor—it was God's grace. God made all of Laban's flocks bear striped and dark colored offspring, which were Jacob's according to his deal with Laban. Jacob's confidence was in God's grace and not in his strength or wisdom. This was a marked change for Jacob, who had depended on his ability to manipulate others throughout his life in order to get his way. Now, he realized that God was the giver of every good gift and that he needed to put his confidence in him.

Having confidence in God's grace and not our strength is a mark of our new nature. In Philippians 3:3 (NIV), Paul said it this way, "For it is we who are the circumcision, we who serve God by his Spirit, who boast in Christ Jesus, and who put no confidence in the flesh." The Judaizers, who invaded the Philippian congregation, relied on their works for salvation—specifically circumcision. However, true believers rely on God's grace, as salvation comes through God and not our works. All religions declare something similar to the Judaizers—salvation comes from what we do and not what was done for us. Christianity, properly understood, teaches that salvation comes only by grace—God's unmerited favor. Ephesians 2:8-9 says, "For by grace you are saved through faith, and this is not from yourselves, it is the gift of God; it is not from works, so that no one can boast."

Therefore, those who are truly saved and made new in Christ put their confidence in God's grace, even as Jacob did—not just for salvation but for all things. In Philippians 2:12-13, it says that God works in us to will and do of his good pleasure. All of our good works are simply manifestations of God's grace. In 1 Corinthians 4:7, Paul said, "'For who concedes you any superiority? What do you have that you did not receive? And if you received it, why do you boast as though you did not?" How can we boast, if God has given us everything—such as intelligence, health, gifts, and opportunities? All has come from God. It all represents God's grace.

Since the world has not experienced God's Spirit and true salvation, they find their identity and boast in their works—their wealth, accomplishments, resumes, and degrees. John calls this the "pride of life" (1 John 2:16 NIV). This often leads to judging those with less accomplishments or secular status. However, for those walking in the Spirit, it should not be that way. Our experience of grace should make us gracious towards others.

What do you boast in—your flesh, such as accomplishments and strengths, or God's grace, his unmerited favor on your life? What you boast in shows where your confidence is. As "Jacob," his confidence was in his strength and ability to manipulate others, but as "Israel," his confidence was in God's grace and his grace alone. Confidence in our flesh leads to pride or insecurity and misjudging others. Confidence in God's grace leads to humility and the edification of others. Which identifies you? To live out our new identities in Christ, we must put our confidence in God's grace and not our strength or others.

Application Question: Why are we so prone to boast in our achievements and successes and miss God's hand in them? How can we grow in recognizing God's grace and giving him thanks for it? In what ways do you struggle with a prideful/critical spirit?

To Live Out Our New Identity, We Must Learn to Trust God

> So that same day Esau made his way back to Seir. But Jacob traveled to Succoth where he built himself a house and made shelters for his livestock. That is why the place was called Succoth. After he left Paddan Aram, Jacob came safely to the city of Shechem in the land of Canaan, and he camped near the city.
> Genesis 33:16-18

Jacob traveled to Succoth, the opposite direction of Esau's home in Seir. Seir was south, and Succoth was northwest.[54] Not only did Jacob deceive Esau, but also disobeyed God. When God called Jacob to leave his uncle's house, he was supposed to return to the land of his fathers, Canaan (Gen 31:3). However, Succoth was outside of the promised land. We can surmise that Jacob stayed there for a few years, since he built a house and made shelters for his livestock. Afterward, he moved to Shechem, which was in the promised land.

Why did Jacob delay obedience? It seems that he still feared Esau. This is implied in Genesis 33:18 when the narrator said Jacob came "safely" to the city of Shechem. Even though Jacob and Esau reconciled, Jacob still didn't trust him. He went the opposite direction out of fear. However, this fear really meant Jacob didn't trust God. In Genesis 28:15, God promised to protect Jacob and bring him back from Haran to Canaan. In Genesis 31:3, God told Jacob to leave Haran and return to his fathers' land and that God would be with him. And in Genesis 32:28, after wrestling with God, God said that he had prevailed with God and men; this prevailing with men referred, at least in part, to Esau. Though Jacob had many promises of God's blessings and protection, he didn't trust them wholly. This kept him from living out his identity as Israel—the one God commands.

Similarly, a lack of trust in God will keep us from living out our identity. It was when Eve doubted God that she fell away from him. If we don't trust God's promises to us, we will sin against him and miss his best as well. God promises that as we seek first his kingdom all things will be added unto us (Matt 6:33). He promises that as we acknowledge him in all our ways, God will direct our paths (Prov 3:6). He promises that as we confess our sins to one another and pray for one another, we'll find healing (James 5:16). He promises if we practice generous giving, God will generously give to us (2 Cor 9:6-10). He promises that if we delight in his word and meditate on it day and night, he will prosper us (Ps 1:1-3). His promises to us are legion. However, because we don't trust God and his promises, we often delay obedience and live in our old nature instead of our new one. Therefore, like Jacob, we delay in Succoth; like Israel, we wander in the wilderness; like Abraham, we run down to Egypt instead of living in the land of promise.

In what ways are you not trusting God and therefore delaying obedience? Many say to God, "One day, I will wholeheartedly follow you, one day I'll give you all I have, but first I want to get married, first I have to take care of my career, first I want to have fun..." Obedience just keeps getting delayed, when we don't fully trust God. Are you trusting God and therefore obeying, or doubting him and delaying?

Application Question: Are there any areas of delayed or partial obedience in your life? How is God calling you to remedy them? What are your fears that threaten your reception of God's promises and keep you from obedience? How can we further develop our faith?

To Live Out Our New Identity, We Must Be Bold Worshipers

> Then he purchased the portion of the field where he had pitched his tent; he bought it from the sons of Hamor, Shechem's father, for a hundred pieces of money. There he set up an altar and called it "The God of Israel is God."
> Genesis 33:19-20

156

When Jacob purchased a field in Shechem, it was an act of faith. God had promised him and his descendants the land, and therefore, he not only returned to it, but also purchased land in it. Shechem was also the first place that Abraham went when entering the promised land (Gen 12:6). After purchasing property, Jacob built an altar there and called it, "The God of Israel is God." Not only would this be a place of worship for his family, but it was also a declaration of monotheism to the surrounding pagans—declaring there was no other God. Jacob was a bold worshiper. His grandfather, Abraham, did the same thing when he came to Shechem. In Genesis 12:6-7, Abraham built an altar right next to the "tree of Moreh"—which means the "tree of teaching." Canaanites would often build sanctuaries in trees. It was probably a place where pagan prophets taught. However, it didn't matter to Abraham. He boldly proclaimed his God there, and Jacob did the same. The God of Israel is God!

Similarly, if we are going to live out our identity in Christ, we must be bold worshipers. This is much truer in the New Covenant than in the Old Covenant. In the Old, they were called to worship at the tabernacle and then the temple; however, in the New, God has made our bodies his temple. First Corinthians 6:19 says, "Or do you not know that your body is the temple of the Holy Spirit who is in you, whom you have from God, and you are not your own?" Therefore, since we are God's temple, we should worship at all times, as we are not limited by location. We should worship at church, at home, at work, and while at leisure. For the believer, every place must become an altar and opportunity to express our appreciation to God and tell others about him. First Corinthians 10:31 says, "So whether you eat or drink, or whatever you do, do everything for the glory of God."

In addition, it must be remembered that when Jacob made a nonaggression pact with Laban, he swore by "the God whom his father Isaac feared" (Gen 31:53). Now, he calls God, "the God of Israel." His identity is now found in God and not just the God of his father. He is unashamed and bold. God blessed him while in Haran, protected him from Laban, and now protected him from Esau. God was his God, and he would boldly proclaim his glory.

Are you boldly worshiping God and proclaiming his glory? We need to do this both individually and corporately. In Matthew 18:20, Christ taught that when two or more are gathered in his name, he is in the midst. This means that though God is always with us, he is with us in a special way when gathered with other worshipers to honor God's name. If we are going to live out our new identity as children of God, we must live a lifestyle of worship—seeking him individually through prayer and devotion, but also meeting with saints for prayer and praise, gathering in small groups and large groups for worship. In Acts 2, when Peter preached and 3,000 were saved, they immediately started gathering every day from house to house and at the temple court for worship. The new Christians gathered where all the Jews worshiped, even though they

157

were persecutors of the faith. They were bold worshipers, like Abraham and Jacob.

Are you a bold worshiper? Are you sharing your faith, unashamedly, with others? In Romans 1:16, Paul said, "For I am not ashamed of the gospel, for it is God's power for salvation to everyone who believes, to the Jew first and also to the Greek."

If you are a quiet worshiper, who never shares your faith, you might not be a worshiper at all. When people are truly excited about something, they tell people. They talk with excitement about the new movie they just saw or the new restaurant they recently dined at. They often tell all who will listen. They post on social media for all to see. When we are truly worshiping God, that's how we are with our faith. Every place becomes the foundation of an altar.

Are you a bold worshiper? Are you living out your new identity as a worshiper of Christ? You are the temple of God and therefore every place you go should essentially become an altar. Thank you, Lord. Amen!

Application Question: How do you practice weekly worship, both individually and corporately? How is God calling you to grow in your worship of him? In what ways are you tempted to be quiet about your faith instead of sharing it? Are there any ways God is calling you to grow in your boldness?

Conclusion

After Jacob wrestled with God, God gave him a new name and identity; however, after receiving this great blessing, he often failed to live according to it. He fluctuated between being the deceiver, Jacob, and the one God commands, Israel. He wasn't the same, but he wasn't where he should have been. We often are like this as well. God calls us saints, but we often live as sinners. God calls us new creations in Christ, but we often live like our old selves. How can we live out our new identities in Christ?

1. To Live Out Our New Identity, We Must Be Careful of Our Spiritual Weaknesses
2. To Live Out Our New Identity, We Must Labor to Live at Peace with Others
3. To Live Out Our New Identity, We Must Put Our Confidence in God's Grace and Not Human Strength
4. To Live Out Our New Identity, We Must Learn to Trust God
5. To Live Out Our New Identity, We Must Be Bold Worshipers

Consequences of Neglecting God

Now Dinah, Leah's daughter whom she bore to Jacob, went to meet the young women of the land. When Shechem son of Hamor the Hivite, who ruled that area, saw her, he grabbed her, forced himself on her, and sexually assaulted her. Then he became very attached to Dinah, Jacob's daughter. He fell in love with the young woman and spoke romantically to her. Shechem said to his father Hamor, "Acquire this young girl as my wife." When Jacob heard that Shechem had violated his daughter Dinah, his sons were with the livestock in the field. So Jacob remained silent until they came in. Then Shechem's father Hamor went to speak with Jacob about Dinah. Now Jacob's sons had come in from the field when they heard the news. They were offended and very angry because Shechem had disgraced Israel by sexually assaulting Jacob's daughter, a crime that should not be committed. But Hamor made this appeal to them: "My son Shechem is in love with your daughter. Please give her to him as his wife. Intermarry with us. Let us marry your daughters, and take our daughters as wives for yourselves. You may live among us, and the land will be open to you. Live in it, travel freely in it, and acquire property in it." Then Shechem said to Dinah's father and brothers, "Let me find favor in your sight, and whatever you require of me I'll give. You can make the bride price and the gift I must bring very expensive, and I'll give whatever you ask of me. Just give me the young woman as my wife!" Jacob's sons answered Shechem and his father Hamor deceitfully when they spoke because Shechem had violated their sister Dinah. They said to them, "We cannot give our sister to a man who is not circumcised, for it would be a disgrace to us. We will give you our consent on this one condition: You must become like us by circumcising all your males. Then we will give you our daughters to marry, and we will take your daughters as wives for ourselves, and we will live among you and become one people. But if you do not agree to our terms by being circumcised, then we will take our sister and depart." Their offer pleased Hamor and his son Shechem. The young man did not delay in doing what they asked because he wanted Jacob's daughter Dinah badly. (Now he was more important than anyone in his father's household.) So Hamor and his son Shechem went to the gate of their city and spoke to the men of their city, "These men are at peace with us. So let them live in the land and travel freely in it, for the land is wide enough for them. We will take their daughters for wives, and we will give them our daughters to marry. Only on this one condition will these men consent to live with us and become one people: They demand that every male among us be circumcised just as they are circumcised. If we do so, won't their livestock, their property, and all their animals become ours? So let's consent to their demand, so they will live among us." All the men who assembled at the city gate agreed with Hamor and his son Shechem. Every male who assembled at the city gate was circumcised. In three days, when they were still in pain, two of Jacob's sons, Simeon and Levi, Dinah's brothers, each took his sword and went to the unsuspecting city and slaughtered every male. They killed Hamor and his son Shechem with the sword, took Dinah from Shechem's house, and left. Jacob's sons killed them and looted the city because their sister had been violated. They took their flocks, herds, and donkeys, as well as everything in the city and in the surrounding fields. They captured as plunder all their wealth, all their little ones, and their wives, including everything in the houses…

Genesis 34 (NET)

What are consequences of neglecting God?

Genesis 34 is one of the more tragic chapters in the Bible. In the narrative, Jacob's only daughter Dinah was raped by a prince in the land of Shechem. After the assault, the young man (also named Shechem) realized that he loved Dinah and sent his father to arrange a marriage between the families. Jacob's sons agreed on the condition that the men of Shechem circumcise themselves. Because of the potential to gain great wealth through the partnership, the men of the town agreed and went through with the procedure. On the third day after their circumcision, when the pain probably was the worst, two of Jacob's sons murdered all the men in the town.

The story is tragic. Many might question, "Why is this story in the Bible?" and "What can we learn from it?" There are many things: For one, stories like this give evidence of the Divine authorship of Scripture. From a human perspective, adding this story makes no sense. If Moses, the author of Genesis, was simply trying to encourage Israel before they entered the promised land, this story would have been left out, as it displays the Jews in an unflattering light. Even the Canaanites look more righteous than Israel in this story. Human authors would not have added this story. But, since God is the ultimate author of Scripture, he doesn't hide the flaws of his people. David had flaws. Moses had flaws. Abraham had flaws. Jacob had flaws, and the Israelites had flaws.

160

In fact, this demonstrates that all are sinners—Jews and Gentiles. However, God can change flawed people and use them for his purposes, which he eventually does with Israel. In one sense, this chapter should give us all hope.

In addition, not only does this story demonstrate the Divine authorship of Scripture, but also shows us what happens when God is neglected. In the previous narrative, Jacob had worked for his uncle Laban for twenty years, and while working for him, he was cheated and abused. When Jacob fled from Laban, God rescued him. After God resolved that situation, Jacob sought reconciliation with his brother Esau; however, Esau responded with bringing 400 men to meet him. His response appears to be hostile. However, God delivered Jacob from that situation as well—bringing reconciliation.

After a long period of time living in the land of Succoth, Jacob finally brought his family to the land of Shechem in Genesis 33. While there, Jacob built an altar—declaring that the God of Israel was God (Gen 33:20). For twenty years of hostile service in Haran, God protected and prospered Jacob. When he was about to encounter his angry brother, God protected him again. But now in Shechem, Jacob was threatened by a much more difficult problem—ease and prosperity. Though his major struggles seemed to be over, his most difficult struggle appeared—maintaining faith in ease and prosperity. This is why Scripture says we should rejoice in various trials and tribulations, as they test our faith (Jam 1:2). It is much harder to be faithful to God in ease than in difficulty. And it appears that Jacob and his family began to neglect God in this season.

How can we tell that Jacob and his family neglected God?

In Genesis 35, after this terrible narrative, Jacob led his family in repentance. Consider what he says to his household and all who were with him, "Get rid of the foreign gods you have among you. Purify yourselves and change your clothes" (v. 2). While in Shechem and living in prosperity, his family had started worshiping pagan gods. In fact, Josephus, a Jewish historian, said that Dinah went into the city, not only to see the ladies, but also to go to a pagan festival.[55] It appears that while neglecting God, Jacob's family began to conform to the world and worship the idols of the world. This is exactly how Paul describes the pagan world in Romans 1:21-23:

> For although they knew God, they did not glorify him as God or give him thanks, but they became futile in their thoughts and their senseless hearts were darkened. Although they claimed to be wise, they became fools and exchanged the glory of the immortal God for an image resembling mortal human beings or birds or four-footed animals or reptiles.

When the world denies the knowledge of God, as seen in creation or Scripture, people naturally find something to worship, even if it's themselves. Humanity was made to worship God, and if we don't worship him, we will

161

worship something else. We don't just see this in the world around us, but we see this in ourselves, as believers. When we're neglecting God, he is replaced by some idol—something that gets most of our attention: social media, video games, career, money, relationships, etc.

In Romans 1:28, Paul adds: "And just as they did not see fit to acknowledge God, God gave them over to a depraved mind, to do what should not be done." When people neglect God, their thinking becomes depraved—leading to depraved actions. That's just what we see in this chapter—the consequences of neglecting God, both among pagans and believers.

Something else that may imply the neglect of God in this narrative is the fact that this is one of the few chapters in the Bible where God is never mentioned.[56] In the book of Esther, God is never mentioned either, but his sovereign and positive influence is seen throughout the pages. In Genesis 34, though God is not mentioned, we know he is present, but he seems to be present for judgment. He is handing people over to a "depraved mind" as they've neglected him—allowing them to commit sin and reap the terrible consequences of it.

This is the tragic story of society, as we see these consequences happening all around us and often in our own lives. In this story, a pagan rapes Dinah, and in return, the Israelites deceive and kill all the men in the city—committing a worse sin. Sadly, that often happens in our world as well, when believers neglect God. They neglect God—leading to being conformed to the world and often committing worse sins than the world, impacting society negatively. Though redeemed, believers still have a sinful nature that must be subdued by living in the Spirit (Gal 5:16-22).

As we study this narrative, we must be sober and aware that these unfortunate consequences of neglecting God can happen in our nations, communities, churches, and homes. Let us consider them and be warned, which, no doubt, is the narrator's purpose in sharing this story.

Big Question: What are the consequences of neglecting God, as demonstrated in the Genesis 34 narrative?

When God Is Neglected, Sexual Immorality Saturates Society

Now Dinah, Leah's daughter whom she bore to Jacob, went to meet the young women of the land. When Shechem son of Hamor the Hivite, who ruled that area, saw her, he grabbed her, forced himself on her, and sexually assaulted her. Then he became very attached to Dinah, Jacob's daughter. He fell in love with the young woman and spoke romantically to her. Shechem said to his father Hamor, "Acquire this

young girl as my wife." When Jacob heard that Shechem had violated his daughter Dinah, his sons were with the livestock in the field. So Jacob remained silent until they came in. Then Shechem's father Hamor went to speak with Jacob about Dinah. Now Jacob's sons had come in from the field when they heard the news. They were offended and very angry because Shechem had disgraced Israel by sexually assaulting Jacob's daughter, a crime that should not be committed. But Hamor made this appeal to them: "My son Shechem is in love with your daughter. Please give her to him as his wife. Intermarry with us. Let us marry your daughters, and take our daughters as wives for yourselves. You may live among us, and the land will be open to you. Live in it, travel freely in it, and acquire property in it." Then Shechem said to Dinah's father and brothers, "Let me find favor in your sight, and whatever you require of me I'll give. You can make the bride price and the gift I must bring very expensive, and I'll give whatever you ask of me. Just give me the young woman as my wife!"
Genesis 34:1-12

As the story begins, Dinah, Jacob's only daughter, goes to the city to meet with the young ladies of the land and is raped by Shechem, the prince of the land. Most likely, Dinah was around fourteen to sixteen years old. In the ancient world, it was known that unaccompanied ladies were vulnerable to being assaulted by men. Henry Morris says, "Unattached young women were considered fair game in cities of the time, in which promiscuity was not only common but, in fact, a part of the very religious system itself."[57] This was particularly true of the Canaanites, who were corrupt and known for their sexual immorality (cf. Lev 18). Unaccompanied women were often violently taken by the leaders of the land. This happened twice with Abraham, as his wife was taken into Pharaoh's and Abimelech's harems (12:15; 20:2). Both times, aware of this tragic cultural reality, Abraham lied and said that she was his sister to protect himself from being killed because of her. Isaac, Jacob's father, also lied about his wife, afraid someone would take her and kill him (Genesis 26:7). Why Dinah's father or brothers are not with her is unclear.

But to further demonstrate the gravity of the gross immorality in Shechem, when Hamor, the prince's father, approached Jacob about Dinah marrying his son, he doesn't apologize or even mention the issue. It was as if it wasn't a big deal. Maybe, Hamor thought, "Oh, boys will be boys!" This shows how acceptable the rape of a young lady was. In the ancient world, sexual immorality was a part of religious worship—people would have all types of gross sex to please the gods and seek prosperity. Therefore, sex wasn't special, and it wasn't necessarily to be preserved for one's spouse—especially if one was a man.

163

This is what happens in a society that disregards God. In Romans 1:24-27, Paul describes this:

Therefore God gave them over in the desires of their hearts to impurity, to dishonor their bodies among themselves...For this reason God gave them over to dishonorable passions. For their women exchanged the natural sexual relations for unnatural ones, and likewise the men also abandoned natural relations with women and were inflamed in their passions for one another. Men committed shameless acts with men and received in themselves the due penalty for their error.

Sexual immorality and homosexuality are results of denying God. When God is denied, sexual immorality saturates society. We see this happening all around us. Sex is emphasized on TV, movies, music, and the Internet. It is used to sell all types of products. Pornography is one of the biggest industries in the world. Sex trafficking is a growing illegal industry. In the US, one out of six females are victims of an attempted or completed rape.[58] Similarly, one out of four females on college campuses experience sexual assault.[59] In addition, the acceptance of homosexuality has grown. It is commonly promoted on the TV, news, college campuses, and city parades. Even polygamy, having multiple marriage partners, is growing in acceptability. When God is neglected in a society, sexual immorality saturates it.

But this is not just a problem for society, it is also a problem for believers. When we are neglecting God, we will often find ourselves struggling with lustful thoughts and images—consequently, making us more prone to fall into sexual actions. In Genesis 38, Judah, Jacob's son, will visit a prostitute. David, the king of Israel, will not only have many wives and concubines, but will also commit adultery (2 Sam 11). When God is neglected in our lives, often, lust will rear its ugly head in some form or another. We must be careful of this.

Because of this danger, Paul said, "Flee sexual immorality! 'Every sin a person commits is outside of the body'—but the immoral person sins against his own body" (1 Cor 6:18). It's so dangerous, we must run from it. Turn off the TV! Cut off the Internet! End the relationship! We must be zealous and brutal to stay pure in a world that is being increasingly sexualized.

Are you guarding yourself and others against sexual immorality?

Application Question: In what ways have you seen or experienced the growing promotion and acceptance of sexual immorality in society? How should Christians protect their minds and bodies from this very present danger?

When God Is Neglected, Parents Neglect Their Children

Now Dinah, Leah's daughter whom she bore to Jacob, went to meet the young women of the land... When Jacob heard that Shechem had violated his daughter Dinah, his sons were with the livestock in the field. So Jacob remained silent until they came in... Jacob's sons answered Shechem and his father Hamor deceitfully when they spoke because Shechem had violated their sister Dinah. They said to them, "We cannot give our sister to a man who is not circumcised, for it would be a disgrace to us. We will give you our consent on this one condition: You must become like us by circumcising all your males. Then we will give you our daughters to marry, and we will take your daughters as wives for ourselves, and we will live among you and become one people. But if you do not agree to our terms by being circumcised, then we will take our sister and depart."
Genesis 34:1, 5, 13-17

In this narrative, one of the sad realities is the lack of parental involvement and leadership. As mentioned, it was common and accepted in that society for unaccompanied females to be sexually assaulted. In some areas, even unaccompanied men might be raped (cf. Gen 19, Judges 19)! Why was Jacob's teenage daughter even allowed to go to the city by herself? Where were the parental boundaries?

In addition to this, after the rape, Jacob is quiet and uninvolved. He doesn't charge Shechem with wrong and doesn't even get involved with the negotiation. He allows his sons to handle it. To make this even worse, it is clear from the narrative that Dinah wasn't at home with Jacob but was being held captive by this family (Gen 34:26). When his sons agreed to intermarry with the Hivites on the condition of circumcision, Jacob doesn't say, "No." This was a major spiritual failure on Jacob's part. To intermarry with the Canaanites would have threatened God's promise. Abraham wouldn't allow Isaac to marry a Canaanite. Isaac wouldn't allow Jacob to marry a Canaanite. This would have led to compromise and the Israelites further adopting the sins of that culture. Jacob fails his children practically and spiritually. Why was he so uninvolved?

With Dinah, Jacob is probably quiet because she wasn't his priority. This is sad to say, but Jacob was known for playing favorites. He favored Rachel's children over Leah's. Also, because sons were favored over daughters during that period of time, Dinah might have been his least favorite. She was a child of Leah, and she wasn't a boy. Maybe, Jacob doesn't say anything because he knows that he is responsible. He didn't protect her by loving her and establishing appropriate boundaries for her. This was a sad situation.

However, this situation is very common when God is neglected. When God is neglected, parents neglect their responsibilities to their children. (1) They don't establish appropriate boundaries for them. Many of our kids are exposed to things they shouldn't be exposed to on the Internet, TV, video games, books, music, etc. Many parents set no appropriate boundaries, which allows the enemy to tempt and influence them negatively. Some parents even say things like, "Well, I don't want to shelter my kids and protect them from the world!" In Romans 16:19, Paul said, "But I want you to be wise in what is good and innocent in what is evil." We should prepare our children for the world by teaching them the truth about sin, what they will encounter in the world, and how they should respond. If we don't do that, the world will expose them in a negative way—it will be done in a way that promotes evil and lures them into sin, instead of away from it. We must train our children to be wise and at the same time innocent. The world only plans to corrupt them and take away their innocence.

(2) In a society where people neglect God, not only will parents neglect their responsibilities by not setting appropriate boundaries, but they also will tend to not discipline their children at all. Often disciplining children will be looked down upon, as if left alone, children will naturally blossom into maturity and wisdom. Proverbs 22:15 says, "Folly is bound up in the heart of a child, but the rod of discipline will drive it far from him." Proverbs 19:18 (GNT) says, "Discipline your children while they are young enough to learn. If you don't, you are helping them destroy themselves." Without appropriate discipline, children will grow up wild and rebellious. When there is no discipline in the home, the children will disrespect and rebel against the parents. This leads to children disrespecting teachers, bosses, government leaders, and even God—creating increased dishonesty, crime, and anarchy in society.

Why do parents neglect their children, other than the fact they're neglecting God? Some neglect their children simply because they were neglected as children, and therefore, they don't know how to properly parent. Their father or mother wasn't around or involved for whatever reasons. The sins of the parents show up in the children's lives and therefore are repeated (cf. Ex 20:5). Another common reason parents neglect their children is simply for career purposes. In order to have a higher standard of living, kids are handed off to schools, coaches, and tutors for training. Often these people don't have any Christian values at all. When a worldly environment gets our children for eight or more hours a day (especially if we include television, music, etc.), then the one or two hours a day with parents and one hour of church on Sunday won't be very influential.

In this narrative, Jacob didn't only fail Dinah, he also failed his sons, who committed unjust murders. They were right to seek justice; however, murdering a whole village of men for the sins of one was hardly just. Since Jacob did nothing, his sons reacted. Finally, when Jacob rebukes his sons, he only focuses on what they did to "him" (v. 30)—not God or others.

When God is neglected in a society or a home, parents typically neglect their responsibilities—to the demise of their children.

Application Question: In what ways have you witnessed this growing trend of parents neglecting their children by not loving them, disciplining them, and setting boundaries for them? Why is this happening? How should it be remedied?

When God Is Neglected, Religion Is Abused

Jacob's sons answered Shechem and his father Hamor deceitfully when they spoke because Shechem had violated their sister Dinah. They said to them, "We cannot give our sister to a man who is not circumcised, for it would be a disgrace to us. We will give you our consent on this one condition: You must become like us by circumcising all your males. Then we will give you our daughters to marry, and we will take your daughters as wives for ourselves, and we will live among you and become one people. But if you do not agree to our terms by being circumcised, then we will take our sister and depart."
Genesis 34:13-17

In response to Hamor's and Shechem's offer, Jacob's sons said that it would be disgraceful for Dinah to marry someone uncircumcised. Therefore, they promised to give consent if all the males of the city became circumcised. If they did that, then the two tribes could intermarry.

It is clear that Jacob's sons had no plan to intermarry with these people. This deal was deceptive. But what makes this deception even worse is the fact that they used their sign of faith to secure the deal. In Genesis 17, God called Abraham to circumcise himself and the males in his household as a sign of faith. This was to be a perpetual sign of their covenant with God for generations. Therefore, by asking the men to circumcise themselves—they were asking them to participate in Israel's religion. Most likely, they further explained the symbolic nature of circumcision. This is what made their act even more evil.

This is also common when God is neglected in our world today; religion becomes abused for selfish and evil reasons. (1) Sometimes religion is used for financial gain. In 1 Timothy 6:5, Paul warned Timothy about those who used godliness as "a way of making a profit." Many churches and Christian organizations are just money-making businesses. Profit has eroded their sense of mission and integrity. (2) Religion is also used to control and abuse people—as often seen in cults. In 2 Timothy 3:5-6 (NIV), Paul describes abusive spiritual leaders:

having a form of godliness but denying its power. Have nothing to do with such people. They are the kind who worm their way into homes and gain control over gullible women, who are loaded down with sins and are swayed by all kinds of evil desires

167

With this abuse of religion, many will fall away from the church in droves. The false teaching, hunger for power and money, and manipulation of people will drive many away.

(3) Religion is also abused when it primarily focuses on people securing their "passions," like lust or wealth, instead of holiness. In 2 Timothy 4:2-4 (ESV), Paul warns Timothy of this:

> Preach the word; be ready in season and out of season; reprove, rebuke, and exhort, with complete patience and teaching. For the time is coming when people will not endure sound teaching, but having itching ears they will accumulate for themselves teachers to suit their own passions, and will turn away from listening to the truth and wander off into myths.

Not only will the leaders neglect God and abuse the people, but also the people won't want God and his Word. Religion will be used primarily to comfort people in sin and even encourage it, instead of to warn and challenge them to holiness. Congregations will find teachers who make them feel good by preaching myths. When God is neglected, the abuse of religion will be comprehensive—developing many false believers and false teachers.

When God was neglected in Shechem, religion was used for personal gain. The men agreed to circumcision, not because of faith, but to gain the wealth of Israel (v. 20-24). Religion was also abused for vengeance. Jacob's sons murdered the men of the city after they were circumcised. Sadly, when God is neglected, religion will be abused—leading to tragic results in our societies as well.

Application Question: How have you seen or experienced the abuse of religion in the church and society in general? How should true believers seek to remain faithful in times like these?

When God Is Neglected, Violence Increases

> In three days, when they were still in pain, two of Jacob's sons, Simeon and Levi, Dinah's brothers, each took his sword and went to the unsuspecting city and slaughtered every male. They killed Hamor and his son Shechem with the sword, took Dinah from Shechem's house, and left. Jacob's sons killed them and looted the city because their sister had been violated. They took their flocks, herds, and donkeys, as well as everything in the city and in the surrounding fields. They captured as plunder all their wealth, all their little ones, and their wives, including everything in the houses.

168

Genesis 34:25-29

While the Hivites were in pain from their circumcision, two of Jacob's son's, Simeon and Levi, murdered all the men of the village. Most likely, they had some servants help with this slaughter. After the murder, they also plundered the city and surrounding fields—taking the wealth, children, and women.

This is also common in society and church when God is neglected. Romans 1:28-32 says:

> And just as they did not see fit to acknowledge God, God gave them over to a depraved mind, to do what should not be done. They are filled with every kind of unrighteousness, wickedness, covetousness, malice. They are rife with envy, murder, strife, deceit, hostility. They are gossips, slanderers, haters of God, insolent, arrogant, boastful, contrivers of all sorts of evil, disobedient to parents, senseless, covenant-breakers, heartless, ruthless. Although they fully know God's righteous decree that those who practice such things deserve to die, they not only do them but also approve of those who practice them.

Paul says when people don't acknowledge God, it leads to murder, hostility, insolence, ruthlessness, and even approval of such evils. Sadly, we live in societies where abortions happen more than live births. People declare the rights of parents to murder their children. Generations are being wiped out because of inconvenience. When Paul says "heartless" (Rom 1:31), it can also be translated "without natural affection" (KJV). It is normal for parents to love their children. However, when people neglect God, abortions become common place because love comes from God. Self-love is the default of our flesh, and when someone gets in the way of our comfort—hurting them is acceptable.

In a society where God is neglected, senseless violence becomes common—suicide, the murder of innocents in schools and businesses, genocide, war, etc. Even our entertainment will be violent, as people apart from God love violence. The video games, movies, and music will be filled with it. Artists who sing about their abuse of women, drug selling, and gang banging will go platinum and get movie deals. As the entertainment world promotes violence, our young people will become even more violent.

This is the world we live in, and sadly, these acts of violence will at times be seen amongst the church. When James writes the Hebrew Christians who were scattered because of persecution, he rebukes them for murdering one another. James 4:1-3 says,

> Where do the conflicts and where do the quarrels among you come from? Is it not from this, from your passions that battle inside you? You desire and you do not have; you murder and envy and you cannot

obtain; you quarrel and fight. You do not have because you do not ask; you ask and do not receive because you ask wrongly, so you can spend it on your passions.

Hatred and anger are seeds of murder; therefore, when Christians allow those emotions to foster, they lead to acts of violence. Husbands beat their wives. Children fight with their parents, and church members continually hurt one another—behaving worse than pagans. The sins of Jacob's children did not draw pagans to God; it only further pushed them away. Like Paul said, "the name of God is being blasphemed among the Gentiles because of you" (Rom 2:24). The people of Israel were no better than the world around them. In fact, they were probably worse.

Sadly, in many places, Christians don't have great testimonies either. Instead of returning good for evil (Rom 12:21), they return eye for eye and tooth for tooth. Sometimes like Jacob's sons, they go even farther than that— returning face for tooth and body for finger. Instead of justice, they seek vengeance—turning many away from Christ.

Application Question: How have you seen or experienced violence increasing in the world? Why is it so prevalent? In what ways have you seen or experienced it in the church?

When God Is Neglected, He Brings Discipline to Help Us Repent

In Genesis 35:1-3, we see that God uses this difficult event to turn Jacob and his family back to God. It says:

> Then God said to Jacob, "Go up at once to Bethel and live there. Make an altar there to God, who appeared to you when you fled from your brother Esau." So Jacob told his household and all who were with him, "Get rid of the foreign gods you have among you. Purify yourselves and change your clothes. Let us go up at once to Bethel. Then I will make an altar there to God, who responded to me in my time of distress and has been with me wherever I went."

Often God has to do the same with us. He will use tragedy in a person's life, family, or nation to draw people to repentance. Hebrews 12:5-6 and verse 8 says,

> And have you forgotten the exhortation addressed to you as sons? "My son, do not scorn the Lord's discipline or give up when he corrects you.

For the Lord disciplines the one he loves and chastises every son he accepts." ... But if you do not experience discipline, something all sons have shared in, then you are illegitimate and are not sons.

In what ways is God drawing you back to himself through discipline? God loves us too much to allow us to continue to neglect him and go our own way. When Jonah ran from God, God brought a storm in his life to turn him back (Jonah 1). When David committed adultery and murder, Scripture says God's hand was heavy upon him until he repented (Psalm 32:3-5 ESV). When the Corinthian church was abusing the Lord's Supper, God disciplined some with sickness, depression, and even death (1 Cor 11:28-30). God loved them too much to allow them to continue in sin.

God does the same with us. He uses discipline to help us repent and turn back to him. If we are without discipline, we are not true children of God.

Application Question: In what ways have you experienced strong discipline, including the consequences of sin, which turned you from sin back to God? How do you see God's discipline operating in the church and society?

Application

Application Question: In understanding the consequences of neglecting God, how should we respond?

1. We must be careful of times of ease and prosperity.

It wasn't when things were bad that Jacob's family neglected God and committed treacherous acts; it was when things were good. It was after God delivered them from Laban and Esau. It was when they were prosperous and admired by others that they neglected God (cf. Gen 35:2)—leading to great sins. In the same way, when things are good, we tend to neglect God and fall into sin as well. Be careful of those times.

2. We must be spiritually disciplined.

A major fall away from God doesn't happen at once. It happens gradually. It happens as we stop attending church faithfully, reading our Bibles, praying, and having Christian fellowship. Soon we find ourselves far away from God and his people, and doing things we never thought we would do again or worse. To stop this gradual fall, we must be faithful and disciplined. We must practice regular spiritual disciplines, have accountability, and put God first before everything.

3.   We must be hopeful because God is greater than our broken situations.

Though God is never mentioned in this terrible narrative—hope in him is implied. God eventually takes this blasphemous and murderous family and makes them the twelve tribes of Israel. They become the authors and stewards of God's Word. They build the tabernacle and temple and become witnesses to the pagan world. Jesus said salvation comes from the Jews (John 4:22). God eventually uses these people greatly, and God can do the same with us. He can turn around our lives, churches, and nations. He can bring light out of darkness and beauty out of ugliness. He can take our thorns and make them our greatest boasts (2 Cor 12:7-9). Therefore, as we consider our dark and desperate situations, we must be hopeful. Our God is greater! Thank you, Lord.

Conclusion

After God delivers Jacob and his family from Laban and Esau and they arrive safely in Canaan, it seems they neglected God. In Genesis 35, we see that the family picked up many idols while dwelling in Canaan. God stopped being their priority and there were terrible consequences because of this. In addition, the Hivites, who were pagans, were already experiencing the results of not acknowledging the true God. Sadly, many of these consequences can be seen in our societies, churches, and individual lives. What are consequences of neglecting God? It is important to know them, so we can repent of them.

1.   When God Is Neglected, Sexual Immorality Saturates Society
2.   When God Is Neglected, Parents Neglect Their Children
3.   When God Is Neglected, Religion Is Abused
4.   When God Is Neglected, Violence Increases
5.   When God Is Neglected, He Brings Discipline to Help Us Repent

Experiencing Revival in Our Lives and Communities

Then God said to Jacob, "Go up at once to Bethel and live there. Make an altar there to God, who appeared to you when you fled from your brother Esau." So Jacob told his household and all who were with him, "Get rid of the foreign gods you have among you. Purify yourselves and change your clothes. Let us go up at once to Bethel. Then I will make an altar there to God, who responded to me in my time of distress and has been with me wherever I went." So they gave Jacob all the foreign gods that were in their possession and the rings that were in their ears. Jacob buried them under the oak near Shechem and they started on their journey. The surrounding cities were afraid of God, and they did not pursue the sons of Jacob. Jacob and all those who were with him arrived at Luz (that is, Bethel) in the land of Canaan. He built an altar there and named the place El Bethel because there God had revealed himself to him when he was fleeing from his brother. (Deborah, Rebekah's nurse, died and was buried under the oak below Bethel; thus it was named Oak of Weeping.) God appeared to Jacob again after he returned from Paddan Aram and blessed him. God said to him, "Your name is Jacob, but your name will no longer be called Jacob; Israel will be your name." So God named him Israel. Then God said to him, "I am the sovereign God. Be fruitful and multiply! A nation—even a company of nations—will descend from you; kings will be among your descendants! The land I gave to Abraham and Isaac I will give to you. To your descendants I will also give this land." Then God went up from the place where he spoke with him. So Jacob set up a sacred stone pillar in the place where God spoke with him. He poured out a drink offering on it, and then he poured oil on it. Jacob named the place where God spoke with him Bethel. They traveled on from Bethel, and when Ephrath was still some distance away, Rachel went into labor—and her labor was hard. When her labor was at its hardest, the midwife said to her, "Don't be afraid, for you are having another son." With her dying breath, she named him Ben-Oni. But his father called him Benjamin instead. So Rachel died and was buried on the way to Ephrath (that is, Bethlehem). Jacob set up a marker over her grave; it is the Marker of Rachel's Grave to this day. Then Israel

173

traveled on and pitched his tent beyond Migdal Eder. While Israel was living in that land, Reuben had sexual relations with Bilhah, his father's concubine, and Israel heard about it. Jacob had twelve sons: The sons of Leah were Reuben, Jacob's firstborn, as well as Simeon, Levi, Judah, Issachar, and Zebulun. The sons of Rachel were Joseph and Benjamin. The sons of Bilhah, Rachel's servant, were Dan and Naphtali. The sons of Zilpah, Leah's servant, were Gad and Asher. These were the sons of Jacob who were born to him in Paddan Aram. So Jacob came back to his father Isaac in Mamre, to Kiriath Arba (that is, Hebron), where Abraham and Isaac had stayed. Isaac lived to be 180 years old. Then Isaac breathed his last and joined his ancestors. He died an old man who had lived a full life. His sons Esau and Jacob buried him.
Genesis 35 (NET)

How can we experience revival in our lives and communities?

Genesis 35 comes right after the terrible story of Genesis 34. There Jacob's daughter Dinah was raped by the prince of Shechem. Then Jacob's sons seek vengeance by killing all the men in Shechem. If someone was reading the Bible for the first time, he might ask, "God is going to bless all the nations through this family? The messiah is going to come through them?"

In Genesis 35, God immediately goes to work to further transform Jacob and his family into a people, God can use greatly. If Genesis 34 was a desert, Genesis 35 is an oasis. In Genesis 34, God is never mentioned. Throughout the narrative God is neglected by both Jacob's family and the Hivites. But in Genesis 35, the name "God" is mentioned eleven times. It is also mentioned twelve more times in names like Israel, Bethel, and El Shaddai (Sovereign God or God Almighty).[60] His name and influence saturate this chapter. Jacob and his family experience a revival in their lives—preparing them for greater works for God.

As we consider this chapter, it demonstrates how to experience revival in our lives and communities. Many of us can look back at times when we were more on fire for God, hungrier for his Word, and more passionate to serve him. But now, those times are simply distant memories. Similarly, many of our well-known churches, Christian universities and organizations are really just monuments of the past—times when God moved in special ways. How can we experience and maintain personal and corporate revival? We can discern this from the revival Jacob and his family experienced in Genesis 35.

Big Question: What principles about experiencing revival can be discerned from Genesis 35?

To Experience Revival, We Must Recognize Our Desperate Need for God

> Then God said to Jacob, "Go up at once to Bethel and live there. Make an altar there to God, who appeared to you when you fled from your brother Esau." So Jacob told his household and all who were with him, "Get rid of the foreign gods you have among you.
> Genesis 35:1-2

In order for Jacob and his family to experience revival, God needed to shake them. He needed to shake them by revealing how bad their spiritual lives had become. Typically, a fall doesn't happen at once. It's gradual as small compromises begin to manifest in our lives—leading to larger ones. As displayed in this chapter, Jacob's family had begun to gather idols (Gen 35:4). When Jacob initially moved to Shechem, he erected an altar named "the God of Israel is God" (Gen 33:20). However, idolatry eventually became a stronghold in his family—eroding their morals and spirituality. They worshiped God and the gods of the nations. In many ways, they were just like the world. Therefore, God allowed them to experience tragedy to show them how far they had fallen and remind them of their deep need for him.

The tragedy was meant to break them. Dinah had been defiled, the men of the city had been murdered, and now they were in fear of the other nations coming after them (Gen 34:30). The revelation was meant to reveal their need to get right with God. Through all this, they should have recognized, they were sinful before God and just as ungodly, if not worse than, the world around them. They were broken and therefore right where God needed them to be, so he could move in their lives in a special way and change them. Psalm 34:18 says, "The Lord is near the brokenhearted; he delivers those who are discouraged." Matthew 5:3 says, "Blessed are the poor in spirit, for the kingdom of heaven belongs to them."

Other than through trials, God often helps us recognize our great need for him by giving us a special revelation of himself. With Isaiah, he saw God high and lifted up, and in response, he confessed his sins and those of his people (Is 6). Seeing God's light, showed him the darkness in his heart and the darkness around him. Similarly, it's interesting to consider that right after God called Jacob to return to Bethel, Jacob immediately told his people to get rid of their idols, even though God never mentioned them. Like Isaiah, when Jacob experienced God, he saw his sin and the sin around him. Through both his family trial and his revelation of God, Jacob knew his and his family's great need for God and therefore was ready for revival.

In understanding this, we can tell why many of us aren't experiencing revival. We don't see our need for it. We don't recognize how broken and sinful we are. We don't recognize our need for God's Word, prayer, Christian fellowship, and repentance. This is why we often lack a desire for these things and neglect them. Therefore, God has to help us see our need—either through a trial, special revelation, or both.

Are you recognizing your desperate need for God? Are you ready to experience personal revival?

Application Question: In what ways have you experienced revival after a trial or special revelation of God? How can we keep a recognition of our desperate need for God, even when not experiencing trials or special revelations? How can we grow spiritually even in mundane times?

To Experience Revival, We Must Hear and Respond to God's Word

Then God said to Jacob, "Go up at once to Bethel and live there. Make an altar there to God, who appeared to you when you fled from your brother Esau." … and they started on their journey. The surrounding cities were afraid of God, and they did not pursue the sons of Jacob. Genesis 35:1, 5

As mentioned, in Jacob's brokenness, God spoke to him. He called him to return to Bethel, where God initially appeared to Jacob when he fled Esau (Gen 28), and build an altar there. After Jacob's family left Shechem, the fear of God fell on the surrounding peoples, as God protected Jacob's family. Psalm 34:7 says, "The LORD's angel camps around the LORD's loyal followers and delivers them." As they were obedient, God delivered them.

In the same way, revival cannot happen apart from our hearing and responding to God's Word. Consider the following verses: Psalm 19:7 (ESV) says, "The law of the LORD is perfect, reviving the soul." James 1:25 says, "But the one who peers into the perfect law of liberty and fixes his attention there, and does not become a forgetful listener but one who lives it out—he will be blessed in what he does."

When we hear and obey God's Word, God blesses us. There is no revival apart from God's Word. Therefore, if we are going to experience revival, we must give great attention to reading Scripture, listening to it, memorizing it, and obeying it. Because many neglect God's Word, they never experience revival. It bores them. They would rather watch TV, play video games, listen to music, hang out with friends, or a host of other things—anything but spending time in the Bible. Therefore, revival tarries.

In Nehemiah 8, when Israel experienced a great revival, it began with them listening to the Word of God read and preached from dawn till noon—six

176

hours! And the whole time they heard it, they stood. When they meditated on God's Word and honored it, the Lord brought a great revival. They cried, repented, and committed to following God's laws. Revivals throughout history have followed the same pattern. They were marked by a deep reverence for God's Word. Sadly, in most churches today, if the preacher goes over thirty minutes, people start fidgeting, falling asleep, or getting angry. We don't honor God's Word corporately or individually, and therefore, revival tarries.

Instead of protecting us, as seen with God's terror falling on the surrounding peoples, God often intentionally allows threats in our lives—meant to shake us and turn us to his Word. Psalm 119:67 says, "Before I was afflicted I used to stray off, but now I keep your instructions."

Are you devoted to God's Word? How is God calling you to study it, listen to it, meditate on it, and obey it more? This is a step towards revival that can't be missed.

Application Question: In what ways is revival attached to studying, obeying, and honoring God's Word? How have you experienced revival in times when you were most devoted to Scripture? How is God calling you back to a special devotion to Scripture?

To Experience Revival, We Must Remove All Spiritual Hindrances

> So Jacob told his household and all who were with him, "Get rid of the foreign gods you have among you. Purify yourselves and change your clothes... So they gave Jacob all the foreign gods that were in their possession and the rings that were in their ears. Jacob buried them under the oak near Shechem
> Genesis 35:2, 4

After God told Jacob to return to Bethel and before departing, Jacob immediately called his family to repent. They were to get rid of their foreign gods, purify themselves, and change their clothes. What gods was Jacob referring to? When Rachel left Haran, she stole her father's idols (Gen 31:19). It seems that Jacob never took them from her. She was syncretic—worshiping Yahweh and other gods. Over time, this, no doubt, spread throughout Jacob's household and especially to Rachel's children and servants. Probably, when Jacob's sons raided Shechem—taking their goods—they probably also took the idols. They even were carrying special earrings, which represented the various gods and were used for divine protection.[61]

Though Jacob was aware of all this, it seems he never previously commanded his family and servants to get rid of them. He just allowed idolatry to exist in his home. The people of Israel had started to look like the pagans surrounding them. When Jacob calls his household to purify themselves and change their clothes, these acts were symbolic of a change of character (cf. Eph 4:22-24, Jude 23). When they purified themselves, they probably washed their bodies. Jacob's household was to start anew.

We must do the same. To experience revival, we must get rid of all spiritual hindrances in our lives. We must get rid of any idols. Idols aren't necessarily tiny figurine gods that we worship. Idols are anything that draw our focus and attention away from God. Anything we put our trust in over him. Sometimes they can be pleasures like entertainment, a hobby, or sports. Sometimes they can be people like friends, family, or a dating relationship. Sometimes they can be things like a job, car, or money.

In order to experience revival, everything must be in its proper place—under God. God uses our jobs to provide for us. But we must never look at our job as our Provider. God is the one who gave us the job, and he is the one who will lead us to a new one when it's time. He is the one who provides for our future—giving direction and meeting our present and future needs. That's why we can seek first the kingdom of God and his righteousness, and all things will be added to us (Matt 6:33). As long as we are doing God's will, we will experience God's provisions.

There is always a danger of idolizing our gifts instead of the Giver of every good gift (Jam 1:17). For this reason, we must guard our hearts (Prov 4:23). Like the rich man, sometimes we need to give away certain things, as their influence is too strong on us (Matt 19). At other times, we simply must give less time to those things and not be engrossed in them (1 Cor 7:31). At all times, God must be first.

First Peter 2:1-2 says, "So get rid of all evil and all deceit and hypocrisy and envy and all slander. And yearn like newborn infants for pure, spiritual milk, so that by it you may grow up to salvation." We must rid ourselves of all evil, so we can "yearn"—meaning hunger for the things of God. Many of us lack hunger for the things of God because we are clinging to things that are sinful and worldly.

What are your spiritual hindrances? What keeps you from hungering for the things of God—his Word, prayer, church, worship, and serving—and experiencing revival?

Application Question: What are the idols in your life—areas of undue influence or pleasure that threaten and hinder your relationship with God? How is God calling you to bury your idols, wash your body, and change your clothes in order to re-focus on him?

To Experience Revival, We Must Practice the Discipline of Worship

He built an altar there and named the place El Bethel because there God had revealed himself to him when he was fleeing from his brother... So Jacob set up a sacred stone pillar in the place where God spoke with him. He poured out a drink offering on it, and then he poured oil on it. Jacob named the place where God spoke with him Bethel... Jacob set up a marker over her grave; it is the Marker of Rachel's Grave to this day.
Genesis 35:7, 14-15, 20

When Jacob returned to Bethel, he built an altar in obedience to God's command. He called it El Bethel, which means "God of Bethel" (v. 7). The Israelites had many sacred places. They were sacred because of something God had done at those places—Mount Sinai, Jerusalem, the Jordan River, Bethel, etc. However, Jacob, who seems to have grown in maturity, is not as concerned with the place of experiencing God, but with God himself. That's why he renamed it, "God of Bethel." Both the altar and the renaming of the place represented Jacob's worship—his desire to honor God. Though he had just experienced tragic events and was despised and threatened by the pagans around him, Jacob worshiped the living God in the midst of his difficulties.

While at Bethel, God spoke to him again (v. 10-12). After hearing the Divine message, Jacob set up a sacred pillar and poured a drink offering and oil on it (v. 14). He consecrated it as a place of worship. Immediately after, "Jacob named the place where God spoke with him Bethel" (v. 15). Since he had previously named the area Bethel (Gen 28:19), this probably was a public declaration. Everybody else needed to know that this was the "house of God." Later, after Jacob's wife Rachel died, he also put a pillar over her tomb (v. 20). Though the NET calls the pillar a "marker" (v. 20), it's the same Hebrew word used in verse 14. Thus, the NIV and ESV translate it "pillar." No doubt, it was a memorial of Rachel, but it also was a place of honor for God. (1) Jacob worshiped when he got to Bethel, as he built an altar. (2) He worshiped after God spoke to him, as he built a pillar and consecrated it. (3) Then he worshiped again, as he built another pillar right over Rachel's grave. Even, potentially, Jacob's greatest trial could not stop him from worship.

Similarly, if we are going to experience revival and sustain it, we also must constantly worship God. The opposite of worship could be said to be complaining or being bitter. Bitterness can destroy revival or hinder it from taking place, both in our lives and others. Hebrews 12:15 (ESV) says, "See to it that no one fails to obtain the grace of God; that no 'root of bitterness' springs up and causes trouble, and by it many become defiled." Likewise, 1 Thessalonians 5:18-19 says, "give thanks in all circumstances; for this is the will of God in Christ Jesus for you. Do not quench the Spirit." When we're not giving thanks to God in our various circumstances, but instead complaining, we miss

God's grace and quench his Spirit. We quench the joy, peace, patience, and perseverance, he can give us.

If we are going to experience revival, we must learn to live a life of worship. Like Job, in the midst of trials, we must cry out, "The Lord gives and he takes away, blessed be the name of the Lord" (Job 1:21 paraphrase). Like Jacob, we must build altars and pillars everywhere, even in the midst of threats and tragedies.

Application Question: Why is worship so important for revival?

1. *Worship reminds us of the greatness of God and how everything else, even our trials, are minute in comparison.* This is why Christ taught us to begin our prayers, not with our problems, but with petitions for God's name to be hallowed (Matt 6:9)—to be worshiped. Worship helps remind us that God is greater than our problems and that he is sovereign over them.

2. *Worship silences the competing voices around us—worry, anxiety, criticism, etc.* When we worship, these voices get quieter and the Lord's voice gets louder. We need to hear our Lord's voice at all times, but especially during trials.

3. *Worship builds our faith.* It breeds courage, forgiveness, and peace, as we trust in our Father.

Are you worshiping God despite your circumstances? Worship is an integral step to experiencing revival, individually and corporately.

Application Question: In what ways have you experienced God's peace and strength, as you worshiped in the midst of your circumstances? How is God calling you to grow in public and private worship?

To Experience Revival, We Must Remember Past Times of Special Grace

He built an altar there and named the place El Bethel because there God had revealed himself to him when he was fleeing from his brother... God appeared to Jacob again after he returned from Paddan Aram and blessed him. God said to him, "Your name is Jacob, but your name will no longer be called Jacob; Israel will be your name." So God named him Israel. Then God said to him, "I am the sovereign God. Be fruitful and multiply! A nation—even a company of nations—will

180

descend from you; kings will be among your descendants! The land I gave to Abraham and Isaac I will give to you. To your descendants I will also give this land." Then God went up from the place where he spoke with him. So Jacob set up a sacred stone pillar in the place where God spoke with him. He poured out a drink offering on it, and then he poured oil on it. Jacob named the place where God spoke with him Bethel.
Genesis 35:7, 9-15

It's interesting to consider that at Bethel, God doesn't say many new things to Jacob; he reminds him mostly of old things. When God speaks, he again calls Jacob, "Israel" (v. 10). He repeats promises already given to him—that he would become a nation and the land of Canaan would be given to him (v. 11-12). The only new things seem to be the fact that God uses the name El Shaddai, "Sovereign God" or "God Almighty" and that God mentions that kings will come from him (v. 11). When speaking to Abraham in Genesis 17, God also used the name El Shaddai and mentioned that kings would come through his line. God was re-confirming his covenant with Jacob, while adding a little more information.

When we experience revival, God often does the same with us. Many times, we think that we need new revelation to experience revival or change in our lives. However, this is seldom the case. Often, we just need a fresh revelation of what we already know—who God is, what he has promised us, and who he says we are. We need to remember that God is sovereign—in control of all our circumstances (Eph 1:11), that he is loving (1 John 4:8), and that he works all things for our good (Rom 8:28). To revive us, God often has to take us back to our Bethel experiences—times of renewal when he spoke to us through the Word, prayer, worship, and godly brothers and sisters.

Therefore, to experience revival, we also need to continually return to Bethel. Pastor Bruce Goettsche said it this way:

We need to learn to think differently. If we were as good at remembering the good times in our life as we are replaying the hurts, we would be so much better off. We are prone to nurse a grudge and forget a kindness. We dwell on a failure but dismiss a victory. And as a result, things get distorted. When our spiritual lives begin to feel stale and unfruitful, we need to take a trip back to Bethel,

- remember the day you met Christ and how your life changed because of Him
- recount the circumstances and people that God used to lead you to His grace
- re-read a book that stirred your soul

- compare who you are (by God's grace) with who you used to be
- walk through the church and remember special times you have had in the various rooms
- review some of your favorite passages of scripture
- recall the spiritual teachers and leaders that have impacted you (I like to let my eyes browse over the books on my shelves and think of the way God has used these authors to teach and mold me).

Looking back . . . gaining perspective is only one step in the process but it is a valuable step and an important step.[62]

The first time God met with Jacob at Bethel (Gen 28), he was preparing him for twenty difficult years of working for Laban. When God wrestled with Jacob and originally named him Israel (Gen 32), he was strengthening him to meet Esau. Now, in his second stint at Bethel (Gen 35), God was encouraging Jacob as he faced the threat of the pagans and future traumatic events which happened shortly after, like the death of Rachel.

How is God calling you to return to Bethel? How is God calling you to remind yourself of who God is, what his promises are, and who he says you are?

This is one of the reasons why the ordinances of Baptism and the Lord's Supper are so important. Baptism is a visual reminder of what has happened to us spiritually at salvation. It's one of the Bethel altars, we should always return to. When we went under the water, it pictured our dying to sin in Christ. When we rose out of the water, it pictured our rising with him from the dead to live new lives—righteous lives. Similarly, the practice of the Lord's Supper is a continual reminder of Christ's death and therefore our forgiveness of sins and his future coming. These are just some of the ways we return to Bethel and experience revival in our hearts.

Application Question: What are some significant Bethel experiences that you need to remind yourself of for encouragement, strength, and revival? How do you remind yourself of them? Is there a discipline or practice that you employ?

To Experience Revival, We Must Respond in Faith to Our Trials

(Deborah, Rebekah's nurse, died and was buried under the oak below Bethel; thus it was named Oak of Weeping.) ... They traveled on from Bethel, and when Ephrath was still some distance away, Rachel went into labor—and her labor was hard. When her labor was at its hardest,

the midwife said to her, "Don't be afraid, for you are having another son." With her dying breath, she named him Ben-Oni. But his father called him Benjamin instead... Then Israel traveled on and pitched his tent beyond Migdal Eder. While Israel was living in that land, Reuben had sexual relations with Bilhah, his father's concubine, and Israel heard about it... So Jacob came back to his father Isaac in Mamre, to Kiriath Arba (that is, Hebron), where Abraham and Isaac had stayed. Isaac lived to be 180 years old. Then Isaac breathed his last and joined his ancestors. He died an old man who had lived a full life. His sons Esau and Jacob buried him.
Genesis 35:8, 16-18, 21-22, 27-29

Trials are both a catalyst for revival in our lives and, at the same time, potentially a detriment to revival. God uses trials to help us grow and know him more. But, Satan uses them to draw us away from God. As with Job, Satan uses trials to tempt us to curse God. Similarly, after Jacob's Bethel experience, trials came with the potential of continuing to ignite the flames of revival or extinguish them. Jacob faced many new trials: (1) First, Rebekah's nurse, Deborah, died (v. 8). In Scripture, she was never mentioned by name before this text. When Rebekah left Haran to marry Isaac, Genesis 24:59 says her "female attendant" went with her, which was probably Deborah. She was probably around 150 years old.[63] She had nursed Jacob, and at some point, probably after Rebekah's death, came to live with Jacob and helped care for his children. Obviously, she was dearly loved, as she was buried under a tree, which they named "Oak of Weeping." (2) Then, Jacob experienced the death of Rachel (v. 18), who was his favorite wife. He worked fourteen years to attain her. She died while giving birth to Jacob's twelfth son, Benjamin.

(3) Next, after Rachel died, Jacob experienced betrayal, as his oldest son, Reuben, had sexual relations with Rachel's handmaid, Bilhah (v. 22)—who was also Jacob's concubine. Why did Reuben do this? We can only speculate. Possibly, since Rachel was always Jacob's favored wife, Reuben hoped to remove a potential rival to Jacob's affection for his mother Leah. By sleeping with Bilhah, Jacob would have despised her and may have been more inclined toward Leah, who was always desperate for his affections (Gen 29). Another potential reason was that Reuben was trying to claim his right of firstborn. "Near-Eastern custom held that the possession of the concubines of a man's father or vanquished enemies validated succession."[64] This is why Absalom, the son of David, publicly laid with his father's concubines, after taking the kingdom from him (2 Sam 16:22). Like the prodigal son, Reuben was trying to claim his inheritance then and not later (Luke 15). (4) Finally, Jacob experienced the death of Isaac, his father (v. 29). Both Jacob and Esau buried him after he lived to 180 years old. All of these negative experiences were opportunities for revival or threats to it in Jacob's life.

183

How does Jacob respond to these trials? Did he respond in faith or with a lack of faith? It seems that he responded faithfully. We see this in several ways: After Rachel's death, as mentioned, Jacob builds a pillar, which seemed to be a memorial for her but also a way to worship God (v. 20). Also, he renames their child Benjamin—"son of my right hand"—instead of keeping the name Benoni—"son of my sorrows" (v. 18). Jacob refused to see his son in a negative light. He saw Benjamin as his strength, which the right hand represented. Also, there are further hints that Jacob responded in faith. The fact that the narrator uses the name "Israel" right after Rachel's death in verse 18 and also after Reuben's betrayal in verse 22, seems to imply that Jacob was living according to his new name—"God commands"—in the midst of these tragedies. Though he doesn't seem to judge Reuben immediately, at his death, he does eventually remove the right of the firstborn from him and gives it to Joseph's sons (Gen 49:3-4). First Chronicles 5:1 says, "The sons of Reuben, Israel's firstborn—(Now he was the firstborn, but when he defiled his father's bed, his rights as firstborn were given to the sons of Joseph, Israel's son."

Experiencing revival doesn't necessarily remove trials from our lives; as with Jacob, trials tend to follow revivals. Often it is right after a wonderful experience at church or going to a retreat that a major temptation will confront us. This is why youth often experience great highs during a retreat and really low, lows after. Temptations often follow periods of revival. It was right after Christ's baptism and the Holy Spirit falling on him, that he was led into the wilderness to be tempted by the devil. Also, it was right after the Mount of Transfiguration that Christ confronted the demon in the boy and his disciples' failure to cast him out (Matt 17). Though revivals don't guarantee the removal of trials, if properly used, they do provide strength to confront them. After Jacob's revival, he confronted four strong tests. In them, he responded as Israel and not as Jacob. By doing this, he continued to stoke the fires of revival in his life, instead of allowing them to be blown out.

How are you responding to your trials? They represent both opportunities and threats for revival. Are you confronting them with faith or with doubt, with joy or with bitterness, in the Spirit or in the flesh? Are you confronting them as Israel or as Jacob? May the Lord give us grace to confront them as Israel—with faith, joy, and in the power of the Spirit.

Application Question: What are your current trials, which God is aiming to use for your good and Satan for your bad? How is God calling you to respond to them in faith, like Israel, and not in the flesh, like Jacob?

Conclusion

How can we experience revival in our lives and our communities?

1. To Experience Revival, We Must Recognize Our Desperate Need for God
2. To Experience Revival, We Must Hear and Respond to God's Word
3. To Experience Revival, We Must Remove All Spiritual Hindrances
4. To Experience Revival, We Must Practice the Discipline of Worship
5. To Experience Revival, We Must Remember Past Times of Special Grace
6. To Experience Revival, We Must Respond in Faith to Our Trials

Study Group Tips

Leading a small group using the Bible Teacher's Guide can be done in various ways. One format for leading a small group is the "study group" model, where each member prepares and shares in the teaching. This appendix will cover tips for facilitating a weekly study group.

1. Each week the members of the study group will read through a select chapter of the guide, answer the reflection questions (see Appendix 2), and come prepared to share in the group.

2. Prior to each meeting, a different member can be selected to lead the group and share Question 1 of the reflection questions, which is to give a short summary of the chapter read. This section of the gathering could last from five to fifteen minutes. This way, each member can develop their gift of teaching. It also will make them study harder during the week. Or, each week the same person could share the summary.

3. After the summary has been given, the leader for that week will facilitate discussions through the rest of the reflection questions and also ask select review questions from the chapter.

4. After discussion, the group will share prayer requests and pray for one another.

The strength of the study group is the fact that the members will be required to prepare their responses before the meeting, which will allow for easier discussion. In addition, each member will be given the opportunity to teach, which will further equip their ministry skills. The study group model has distinct advantages.

Reflection Questions

Writing is one of the best ways to learn. In class, we take notes and write papers, and all these methods are used to help us learn and retain the material. The same is true with the Word of God. Obviously, all the authors of Scripture were writers. This helped them better learn the Scriptures and also enabled them to more effectively teach it. In studying God's Word with the Bible Teacher's Guide, take time to write so you can similarly grow both in your learning and teaching.

1. How would you summarize the main points of the text/chapter? Write a brief summary.

2. What stood out to you most in the reading? Did any of the contents trigger any memories or experiences? If so, please share them.

3. What follow–up questions did you have about the reading? What parts did you not fully agree with?

4. What applications did you take from the reading, and how do you plan to implement them into your life?

5. Write several commitment statements: As a result of my time studying God's Word, I will . . .

6. What are some practical ways to pray as a result of studying the text? Spend some time ministering to the Lord through prayer.

Walking the Romans Road

How can a person be saved? From what is he saved? How can someone have eternal life? Scripture teaches that after death each person will spend eternity either in heaven or hell. How can a person go to heaven?

Paul said this to Timothy:

> You, however, must continue in the things you have learned and are confident about. You know who taught you and how from infancy you have known the holy writings, which are able to give you wisdom for salvation through faith in Christ Jesus.
> 2 Timothy 3:14-15

One of the reasons God gave us Scripture is to make us wise for salvation. This means that without it nobody can know how to be saved.

Well then, how can a people be saved and what are they being saved from? A common method of sharing the good news of salvation is through the Romans Road. One of the great themes, not only of the Bible, but specifically of the book of Romans is salvation. In Romans, the author, Paul, clearly details the steps we must take in order to be saved.

How can we be saved? What steps must we take?

Step One: We Must Accept that We Are Sinners

Romans 3:23 says, "For all have sinned and fall short of the glory of God." What does it mean to sin? The word sin means "to miss the mark." The mark we missed is looking like God. When God created mankind in the Genesis narrative, he created man in the "image of God" (1:27). The "image of God" means many things, but probably, most importantly it means we were made to be holy just as he is holy. Man was made moral. We were meant to reflect God's holiness in every way: the way we think, the way we talk, and the way we act. And any time we miss the mark in these areas, we commit sin.

Furthermore, we do not only sin when we commit a sinful act such as: lying, stealing, or cheating. Again, we sin anytime we have a wrong heart motive. The greatest commandments in Scripture are to "Love the Lord your God with all your heart and to love your neighbor as yourself" (Matt 22:36-40, paraphrase).

191

Whenever we don't love God supremely and love others as ourselves, we sin and fall short of the glory of God. For this reason, man is always in a state of sinning. Sadly, even if our actions are good, our heart is bad. I have never loved God with my whole heart, mind, and soul and neither has anybody else. Therefore, we have all sinned and fall short of the glory of God (Rom 3:23). We have all missed the mark of God's holiness and we must accept this.

What's the next step?

Step Two: We Must Understand We Are Under the Judgment of God

Why are we under the judgment of God? It is because of our sins. Scripture teaches God is not only a loving God, but he is a just God. And his justice requires judgment for each of our sins. Romans 6:23 says, "For the payoff of sin is death."

A wage is something we earn. Every time we sin, we earn the wage of death. What is death? Death really means separation. In physical death, the body is separated from the spirit, but in spiritual death, man is separated from God. Man currently lives in a state of spiritual death (cf. Eph 2:1-3). We do not love God, obey him, or know him as we should. Therefore, man is in a state of death.

Moreover, one day at our physical death, if we have not been saved, we will spend eternity separated from God in a very real hell. In hell, we will pay the wage for each of our sins. Therefore, in hell people will experience various degrees of punishment (cf. Lk 12:47-48). This places man in a very dangerous predicament—unholy and therefore under the judgment of God.

How should we respond to this? This leads us to our third step.

Step Three: We Must Recognize God Has Invited All to Accept His Free Gift of Salvation

Romans 6:23 does not stop at the wages of sin being death. It says, "For the payoff of sin is death, but the gift of God is eternal life in Christ Jesus our Lord." Because God loved everybody on the earth, he offered the free gift of eternal life, which anyone can receive through Jesus Christ.

Because it is a gift, it cannot be earned. We cannot work for it. Ephesians 2:8-9 says, "For by grace you are saved through faith, and this is not from yourselves, it is the gift of God; it is not from works, so that no one can boast."

Going to church, being baptized, giving to the poor, or doing any other righteous work does not save. Salvation is a gift that must be received from God. It is a gift that has been prepared by his effort alone.

192

How do we receive this free gift?

Step Four: We Must Believe Jesus Christ Died for Our Sins and Rose from the Dead

If we are going to receive this free gift, we must believe in God's Son, Jesus Christ. Because God loved us, cared for us, and didn't want us to be separated from him eternally, he sent his Son to die for our sins. Romans 5:8 says, "But God demonstrates his own love for us, in that while we were still sinners, Christ died for us." Similarly, John 3:16 says, "For this is the way God loved the world: He gave his one and only Son, so that everyone who believes in him will not perish but have eternal life." God so loved us that he gave his only Son for our sins.

Jesus Christ was a real, historical person who lived 2,000 years ago. He was born of a virgin. He lived a perfect life. He was put to death by the Romans and the Jews. And he rose again on the third day. In his death, he took our sins and God's wrath for them and gave us his perfect righteousness so we could be accepted by God. Second Corinthians 5:21 says, "God made the one who did not know sin to be sin for us, so that in him we would become the righteousness of God." God did all this so we could be saved from his wrath.

Christ's death satisfied the just anger of God over our sins. When God saw Jesus on the cross, he saw us and our sins and therefore judged Jesus. And now, when God sees those who are saved, he sees his righteous Son and accepts us. In salvation, we have become the righteousness of God.

If we are going to be saved, if we are going to receive this free gift of salvation, we must believe in Christ's death, burial, and resurrection for our sins (cf. 1 Cor 15:3-5, Rom 10:9-10). Do you believe?

Step Five: We Must Confess Christ as Lord of Our Lives

Romans 10:9-10 says,

> Because if you confess with your mouth that Jesus is Lord and believe in your heart that God raised him from the dead, you will be saved. For with the heart one believes and thus has righteousness and with the mouth one confesses and thus has salvation.

Not only must we believe, but we must confess Christ as Lord of our lives. It is one thing to believe in Christ but another to follow Christ. Simple belief does not save. Christ must be our Lord. James said this: "...Even the demons believe that – and tremble with fear" (James 2:19), but the demons are not saved—Christ is not their Lord.

Another aspect of making Christ Lord is repentance. Repentance really means a change of mind that leads to a change of direction. Before we met Christ, we were living our own life and following our own sinful desires. But when we get saved, our mind and direction change. We start to follow Christ as Lord.

How do we make this commitment to the lordship of Christ so we can be saved? Paul said we must confess with our mouth "Jesus is Lord" as we believe in him. Romans 10:13 says, "For everyone who calls on the name of the Lord will be saved."

If you admit that you are a sinner and understand you are under God's wrath because of them; if you believe Jesus Christ is the Son of God, that he died on the cross for your sins, and rose from the dead for your salvation; if you are ready to turn from your sin and cling to Christ as Lord, you can be saved.

If this is your heart, then you can pray this prayer and commit to following Christ as your Lord.

Dear heavenly Father, I confess I am a sinner and have fallen short of your glory, what you made me for. I believe Jesus Christ died on the cross to pay the penalty for my sins and rose from the dead so I can have eternal life. I am turning away from my sin and accepting you as my Lord and Savior. Come into my life and change me. Thank you for your gift of salvation.

Scripture teaches that if you truly accepted Christ as your Lord, then you are a new creation. Second Corinthians 5:17 says, "So then, if anyone is in Christ, he is a new creation; what is old has passed away – look, what is new has come!" God has forgiven your sins (1 John 1:9), he has given you his Holy Spirit (Rom 8:15), and he is going to disciple you and make you into the image of his Son (cf. Rom 8:29). He will never leave you nor forsake you (Heb 13:5), and he will complete the work he has begun in your life (Phil 1:6). In heaven, angels and saints are rejoicing because of your commitment to Christ (Lk 15:7).

Praise God for his great salvation! May God keep you in his hand, empower you through the Holy Spirit, train you through mature believers, and use you to build his kingdom! "He who calls you is trustworthy, and he will in fact do this" (1 Thess 5:24). God bless you!

Coming Soon

Praise the Lord for your interest in studying and teaching God's Word. If God has blessed you through the BTG series, please partner with us in petitioning God to greatly use this series to encourage and build his Church. Also, please consider leaving an Amazon review and signing up for free book promotions. By doing this, you help spread the "Word." Thanks for your partnership in the gospel from the first day until now (Phil 1:4-5).

Available:
First Peter
Theology Proper
Building Foundations for a Godly Marriage
Colossians
God's Battle Plan for Purity
Nehemiah
Philippians
The Perfections of God
The Armor of God
Ephesians
Abraham
Finding a Godly Mate
1 Timothy
The Beatitudes
Equipping Small Group Leaders
2 Timothy

Coming Soon:
Jacob
The Sermon on the Mount

About the Author

Greg Brown earned his MA in religion and MA in teaching from Trinity International University, an MRE from Liberty University, and a PhD in theology from Louisiana Baptist University. He has served over fourteen years in pastoral ministry and currently serves as Chaplain and Assistant Professor at Handong Global University, pastor at Handong International Congregation, and as a Navy Reserve chaplain.

Greg married his lovely wife, Tara Jayne, in 2006, and they have one daughter, Saiyah Grace. He enjoys going on dates with his wife, playing with his daughter, reading, writing, studying in coffee shops, working out, and following the NBA and UFC. His pursuit in life, simply stated, is "to know God and to be found faithful by Him."

To connect with Greg, please follow at http://www.pgregbrown.com.

Notes

1 Meyer, F.B.. Jacob: Wrestling with God (Kindle Locations 68-73). Kindle Edition.

2 Wiersbe, W. W. (1997). *Be authentic* (p. 13). Colorado Springs, CO: Chariot Victor Pub.

3 Guzik, D. (2013). *Genesis* (Ge 25:19–26). Santa Barbara, CA: David Guzik.

4 Wiersbe, W. W. (1997). *Be authentic* (p. 14). Colorado Springs, CO: Chariot Victor Pub.

5 Hughes, R. K. (2004). *Genesis: beginning and blessing* (p. 337). Wheaton, IL: Crossway Books.

6 Kidner, D. (1967). *Genesis: An Introduction and Commentary* (Vol. 1, p. 162). Downers Grove, IL: InterVarsity Press.

7 Guzik, D. (2013). *Genesis* (Ge 27:1–4). Santa Barbara, CA: David Guzik.

8 Guzik, D. (2013). *Genesis* (Ge 27:39–40). Santa Barbara, CA: David Guzik.

9 Hughes, R. K. (2004). *Genesis: beginning and blessing* (pp. 353–354). Wheaton, IL: Crossway Books.

10 Wiersbe, W. W. (1997). *Be authentic* (pp. 29–30). Colorado Springs, CO: Chariot Victor Pub.

11 Preacher's Outline and Sermon Bible - Commentary - The Preacher's Outline & Sermon Bible – Genesis II.

12 Accessed 3/30/2018 from https://bible.org/seriespage/lesson-53-how-god-begins-us-genesis-281-22

13 Preacher's Outline and Sermon Bible - Commentary - The Preacher's Outline & Sermon Bible – Genesis II.

14 Preacher's Outline and Sermon Bible - Commentary - The Preacher's Outline & Sermon Bible – Genesis II.

15 Wiersbe, W. W. (1997). *Be authentic* (p. 33). Colorado Springs, CO: Chariot Victor Pub.

16 Wiersbe, W. W. (1997). *Be authentic* (p. 34). Colorado Springs, CO: Chariot Victor Pub.

17 Hughes, R. K. (2004). *Genesis: beginning and blessing* (p. 366). Wheaton, IL: Crossway Books.

18 Pink, Arthur W.. Gleanings in Genesis (p. 310). Neeland Media LLC. Kindle Edition.

19 Pink, Arthur W.. Gleanings in Genesis (p. 310). Neeland Media LLC. Kindle Edition.

20 Preacher's Outline and Sermon Bible - Commentary - The Preacher's Outline & Sermon Bible – Genesis II.

21 Preacher's Outline and Sermon Bible - Commentary - The Preacher's Outline & Sermon Bible – Genesis II.

[22] Getz, Gene. Men of Character: Jacob (Kindle Locations 1685-1689). B&H Publishing Group. Kindle Edition.

[23] Hughes, R. K. (2004). *Genesis: beginning and blessing* (pp. 368–369). Wheaton, IL: Crossway Books.

[24] Accessed 4/7/2018 from https://bible.org/seriespage/lesson-54-god-s-boot-camp-genesis-291-30

[25] Guzik, D. (2013). *Genesis* (Ge 29:15–20). Santa Barbara, CA: David Guzik.

[26] Hughes, R. K. (2004). *Genesis: beginning and blessing* (p. 368). Wheaton, IL: Crossway Books.

[27] Meyer, F.B.. Jacob: Wrestling with God (Kindle Locations 762-768). Kindle Edition.

[28] Preacher's Outline and Sermon Bible - Commentary - The Preacher's Outline & Sermon Bible – Genesis II.

[29] Getz, Gene. Men of Character: Jacob (Kindle Locations 1946-1947). B&H Publishing Group. Kindle Edition.

[30] Hughes, R. K. (2004). *Genesis: beginning and blessing* (p. 384). Wheaton, IL: Crossway Books.

[31] Hughes, R. K. (2004). *Genesis: beginning and blessing* (p. 384). Wheaton, IL: Crossway Books.

[32] Matthew Henry's Commentary on the Whole Bible, Genesis 30:37-43, E-sword Bible Software.

[33] Matthew Henry's Commentary on the Whole Bible, Genesis 30:25-36, E-sword Bible Software.

[34] Matthew Henry's Commentary on the Whole Bible, Genesis 30:37-43, E-sword Bible Software.

[35] Boice, J. M. (1998). *Genesis: an expositional commentary* (p. 803). Grand Rapids, MI: Baker Books.

[36] Pink, Arthur W.. Gleanings in Genesis (p. 333). Neeland Media LLC. Kindle Edition.

[37] Preacher's Outline and Sermon Bible - Commentary - The Preacher's Outline & Sermon Bible – Genesis II.

[38] Steven Cole's sermon on Genesis 31, Accessed 4/27/2018, from https://bible.org/seriespage/lesson-57-between-rock-and-hard-place-genesis-3117-55

[39] Hughes, R. K. (2004). *Genesis: beginning and blessing* (p. 395). Wheaton, IL: Crossway Books.

[40] Wiersbe, W. W. (1997). *Be authentic* (pp. 53–54). Colorado Springs, CO: Chariot Victor Pub.

[41] Boice, J. M. (1998). *Genesis: an expositional commentary* (p. 811). Grand Rapids, MI: Baker Books.

[42] Hughes, R. K. (2004). *Genesis: beginning and blessing* (p. 399). Wheaton, IL: Crossway Books.

[43] Henry, Matthew, Matthew Henry's Complete Commentary on the Whole Bible, Genesis 32. Accessed 5/4/18 from https://www.biblestudytools.com/commentaries/matthew-henry-complete/genesis/32.html

[44] Wiersbe, W. W. (1997). *Be authentic* (p. 58). Colorado Springs, CO: Chariot Victor Pub.

[45] Wiersbe, W. W. (1997). *Be authentic* (p. 58). Colorado Springs, CO: Chariot Victor Pub.

[46] Meyer, F.B.. Jacob: Wrestling with God (Kindle Locations 1082-1084). Kindle Edition.
[47] Boice, J. M. (1998). *Genesis: an expositional commentary* (pp. 819–820). Grand Rapids, MI: Baker Books.
[48] Accessed 5/9/2018 from https://www.biblestudytools.com/dictionary/peniel/
[49] Boice, J. M. (1998). *Genesis: an expositional commentary* (p. 824). Grand Rapids, MI: Baker Books.
[50] Pink, Arthur W.. Gleanings in Genesis (p. 360). Neeland Media LLC. Kindle Edition.
[51] Preacher's Outline and Sermon Bible - Commentary - The Preacher's Outline & Sermon Bible – Genesis II.
[52] Preacher's Outline and Sermon Bible - Commentary - The Preacher's Outline & Sermon Bible – Genesis II.
[53] Hughes, R. K. (2004). *Genesis: beginning and blessing* (p. 405). Wheaton, IL: Crossway Books.
[54] Wiersbe, W. W. (1997). *Be authentic* (p. 62). Colorado Springs, CO: Chariot Victor Pub.
[55] Bruce Goettsche's sermon from Genesis 34, "When God Is Absent," accessed 5/25/2018 from http://www.unionchurch.com/archive/101099.html
[56] Guzik, D. (2013). *Genesis* (Ge 35:1). Santa Barbara, CA: David Guzik.
[57] Guzik, D. (2013). *Genesis* (Ge 34:1–4). Santa Barbara, CA: David Guzik.
[58] Accessed 5/25/2018 from https://www.rainn.org/statistics/victims-sexual-violence
[59] Accessed 5/25/2018 from https://www.huffingtonpost.com/brian-earp/1-in-4-women-how-the-late_b_8191448.html
[60] Boice, J. M. (1998). *Genesis: an expositional commentary* (p. 836). Grand Rapids, MI: Baker Books.
[61] Getz, Gene. Men of Character: Jacob (Kindle Locations 3604-3607). B&H Publishing Group. Kindle Edition.
[62] Pastor Bruce Goettsche's sermon on Genesis 35, accessed June 1, 2018, from http://www.unionchurch.com/archive/101799.html
[63] Boice, J. M. (1998). *Genesis: an expositional commentary* (pp. 839–840). Grand Rapids, MI: Baker Books.
[64] Hughes, R. K. (2004). *Genesis: beginning and blessing* (pp. 424–425). Wheaton, IL: Crossway Books.

Made in the USA
San Bernardino, CA
06 December 2019